Secrets of Victory

Secrets of Victory

The Office of Censorship and the American Press and Radio in World War II

Michael S. Sweeney

THE UNIVERSITY OF NORTH CAROLINA PRESS

Chapel Hill & London

© 2001

The University of North Carolina Press

All rights reserved

Manufactured in the United States of America

Designed by Richard Hendel

Set in Carter Cone Galliard and Champion types
by Tseng Information Systems, Inc.

The paper in this book meets the guidelines for
permanence and durability of the Committee on
Production Guidelines for Book Longevity of the
Council on Library Resources.

Library of Congress
Cataloging-in-Publication Data

Sweeney, Michael S.

Secrets of victory : the Office of Censorship and
the American press and radio in World War II /
Michael S. Sweeney.

    p. cm.

Includes bibliographical references and index.

ISBN 0-8078-2598-0 (cloth : alk. paper) —
ISBN 0-8078-4914-6 (pbk. : alk. paper)

1. World War, 1939–1945 — Censorship — United
States.   2. United States. Office of Censorship —
History.   I. Title.

D799.U6 S834 2001

940.53 — dc21   00-044721

05   04   03   02   01   5   4   3   2   1

In memory of
Donnis F. Sweeney,
1921–1999

Contents

ILLUSTRATIONS

Acknowledgments

Many people—family, friends, and even casual acquaintances and students—have helped make this book possible. My thanks go to Patrick Washburn, who helped guide the original research; my parents, Don and Betty Sweeney, for their support; Rick and Elise Sweeney for the base camp near Washington, D.C.; Utah State University, which helped finance part of the research through a grant for new faculty; Utah State graduate student Jill Richards, who helped make sense of the mountain of files on Drew Pearson; Penny Byrne, Janel Andersen, and Jessica Wishnie, who critiqued early versions of the manuscript; the history class at Tell City, Indiana, High School; the helpful staffs at the State Historical Society of Wisconsin, the National Archives, Franklin D. Roosevelt Library, and the libraries at Yale and Catholic Universities; Jim Parker of Double Delta, who helped research many of the photographs; Professors Joseph Bernt (for the honesty), Robert Cole (for the support) and Edward C. Pease (for everything); Kathy Bradshaw; the student reporters and editors of *The Post* at Ohio University; and the editors at the University of North Carolina Press. And, of course, thanks to my wife, Carolyn, and my son, David, for the gift of time.

Secrets of Victory

Introduction

A young Frenchman who came from a royalist family but hoped to shape his country along more democratic lines spent nine months observing life in the United States in 1831 and 1832. His original intention was to focus on the prison system, but as he traveled and talked and observed the young republic, his mind wandered much further. He sought the reasons for the vitality and deficiencies of America's public sphere, and among his interests was an issue he considered crucial to the future of France: the balance between liberty and equality. When Alexis de Tocqueville returned home and wrote his insightful *Democracy in America,* he described Jacksonian democracy in terms that still ring true. He noted that although political liberty occasionally gives citizens great pleasure, equality "every day confers a number of small enjoyments on every man." As much as democratic communities crave and cherish freedom, he said, they harbor an equally ardent passion for sharing life's conditions. These communities "call for equality in freedom; and if they cannot obtain that, they still call for equality in slavery. They will endure poverty, servitude, barbarism, but they will not endure aristocracy."[1]

If Tocqueville had been able to observe the mature republic a little more than a century later, he would have seen his words still fitting America like a well tailored suit. The nation's citizen army and navy, under the direction of a citizen government, fought World War II with dual motivations. Foremost, expressed in government-approved Hollywood films, armed forces training lectures and movies, and publicity from the White House and the Office of War Information, was the belief in the need to halt fascism and preserve democracy. But underneath was an equally powerful reason that ordinary Americans chose to put themselves at risk. Once they were in combat, they were not fighting for their country and its ideals as much as they were fighting for a team. They felt strong bonds of comradeship, and it was hard to let down the rest of the team's members. Each person was expected to shoulder a portion of the load, and as long as soldiers and sailors were willing to recognize such a sharing of responsibility, they were willing to make the necessary sacrifices of war.[2]

On the home front, Americans made sacrifices, too—willingly, as long as the burdens appeared to be shared. Most ordinary Americans accepted rationing as necessary. Homemakers adjusted to cutbacks in the availability of sugar, meat, and butter in order to do their part for the war. Unfair advantages in obtaining scarce items were met with howls of outrage by the have-nots, especially during mid-1942, when thousands of drivers fraudulently obtained rationing cards entitling them to extra gasoline. Those who willingly had sacrificed their automotive freedom protested that others had placed their own selfishness above the needs of the country, prompting renewed federal efforts to foster cooperation and restore the feeling of equality.[3]

And in the news media that covered the war both overseas and domestically, journalists also were willing to cooperate and do their part. The public did not see journalists (and journalists did not see themselves) as being *against* the team. Journalists were *part of* the team. Some, such as roving correspondent Ernie Pyle, repeatedly visited combat zones even though they did not have to do so, and they paid with their lives. Others, such as *Wisconsin State Journal* publisher Don Anderson, were too old to fight or cover the war in person but nevertheless felt compelled to volunteer for war-related duty. In Anderson's case, he monitored the newspapers of his home state for compliance with the domestic censorship code and tried to educate the rule breakers to work harder to comply.[4] In the case of Associated Press (AP) executive editor Byron Price, wartime service called him to abandon the business he loved and direct the nation's censorship system.

Voluntary domestic censorship was one of the shared sacrifices of war for American journalists. On one hand, World War II was perhaps the most newsworthy event of the century, offering opportunities for lucrative and significant "scoops." On the other hand, no nation can fight a modern war by refusing to exercise some control of information. Journalists who wrote or broadcast stories about wartime secrets would, in effect, be handing the enemy a weapon. To prevent the disclosure of sensitive information during wartime requires a restraint that is distasteful to democracies; but if successful, such censorship can become what one memoir of World War II describes as a "weapon of silence." The dynamic question of the war for American journalists was whether they would agree to restrain themselves or report some of the biggest stories of their careers.

This question embodies the same tension between liberty and equality that Tocqueville documented more than a century earlier. Under the rules of voluntary, domestic censorship in the United States during World War II (as opposed to the army's and navy's mandatory censorship in the combat zones), each journalist had the freedom to report an especially sensitive news story, resulting in a short-term gain at the expense of others who suppressed the story or were ignorant of it. However, to violate the voluntary censorship code would have conflicted not only with the needs of the military and government—which ostensibly were fighting in defense of liberties such as free press and free speech—but also with the value of equality. Journalists claimed the rights of the First Amendment, and they demanded that censorship give no one an advantage in exercising those rights. At least, they demanded that their competitors enjoy no advantage over them. If they must sacrifice, they reasoned, all must sacrifice to be members of the team.

"It is an amazing fact to me to see the press and radio asking for rather than standing solidly against such a thing as censorship," presidential press secretary Stephen T. Early said on the last day of December 1941.[5] Even the *Chicago Tribune,* the metropolitan paper that most objected to the politics of the man in the White House, was willing to submit to the censorship system the president had helped establish. "We recognized that you had to have a censorship code," said *Tribune* reporter Walter Trohan.[6] It is curious today to realize the degree to which American journalists abided by the voluntary rules of censorship. No print journalist, and only one radio journalist, ever deliberately violated the World War II voluntary censorship code after having been made aware of it and understanding its intent. Thousands of violations did occur, but they were ones of omission rather than commission. Journalists who had not received a copy of the censorship code, or had not read it, or had not understood it, violated it in many ways, from revealing the departure of troop units to giving the location and nature of stateside war industries. What did not occur was a wholesale sabotage of censorship for personal or corporate gain. Journalists who possessed military secrets, kept them. Liberal crusading columnist Drew Pearson knew about the development of the atomic bomb many months before the bomb was tested in New Mexico and dropped on Japan, but he never revealed that fact.

The same is true for William L. Laurence of the *New York Times,* who signed on with the Manhattan Project to chronicle the bomb's development but did not publicize it until after the bomb was dropped on Hiroshima. Journalists also agreed to comply with censorship prohibitions on everything from publicizing President Franklin Roosevelt's many trips to Hyde Park, to the 1942–43 broadcast regulations that so severely limited weather news that baseball announcers were not supposed to say a game had been halted by rain.

This book aims to explain why the Office of Censorship, which administered voluntary censorship inside the United States and mandatory censorship of information crossing the nation's borders, had so many successes and so few failures. It examines the censorship of American newspapers, magazines, and radio, focusing on personalities from the highest government offices to the smallest weekly journals and rural radio stations. This book is the first to examine World War II censorship in America by thoroughly analyzing the records of the Office of Censorship's Press and Broadcasting Divisions at the National Archives, in addition to the censorship director's personal papers and many other primary sources. The only other histories of the Office of Censorship are fragmentary or anecdotal, or they treat censorship of the press and radio as a small piece of a much larger picture of information control.

It is unfortunate that this book must rely so heavily on written sources. Death has claimed all who staffed the Press and Broadcasting Divisions, as well as Byron Price and his assistant, Theodore F. Koop. Fortunately, the written record is rich and full. The Office of Censorship kept records of every telephone, mail, and telegraph inquiry it received between mid-January 1942 and August 1945, claiming a substantial portion of the 539 cubic feet of space occupied by World War II censorship records at the National Archives. Yet, it is difficult to assess the full impact of censorship. It remains impossible to describe the unrecorded impact of the many censorship decisions reached independently in the early 1940s by the nation's 2,700 daily newspapers; 11,000 weekly newspapers; 7,000 magazines; 5,000 trade, scientific, and business journals; 14,000 commercial and industrial house organs; and 9,000 miscellaneous publications from newsletters to fraternal lodge bulletins.[7] The historian happily can discover much of what the news media censors said and did, and what was said and done to them. Almost without exception, journalists, military leaders, and government officials considered domestic censorship to have been wisely administered.

President Harry S. Truman awarded Price the Medal for Merit on January 15, 1946, congratulating him for "distinctive and complete success" in his administration of censorship and his simultaneous defense of freedom of the press.[8] After voluntary censorship expired in August 1945, Stephen T. Early told Price he should receive an award for "best performance of service to Government and Country in time of war."[9] That sentiment was echoed by the American Civil Liberties Union, which declared in 1945 that wartime censorship "has raised almost no issues in the United States."[10] And James F. Byrnes, who was in charge of war mobilization, inscribed a book that he gave to the chief censor, "To Byron Price, who did what I thought impossible—censored the press and made them like it."[11]

Byrnes exaggerated, of course. No journalist likes being censored. What the press and radio appreciated about the voluntary censorship program was that it was better than the alternatives. Complete lack of censorship would have helped the enemy. Complete government control would have been intolerable in a nation that had been born during a revolution in which the press played an active role and that had cemented freedom of expression in the First Amendment. At the very least, the absolute control of media would have led to public distrust of the news, as well as the recklessness of a democracy attempting to wage war without the advantage of an open and robust discussion of its options. In between these extremes lay a more acceptable path. American censorship rules in World War II had no built-in legal penalties for journalists who violated the censorship code. If a newspaper or magazine broke the rules, the censor could do little more than publicize the offense and subject the offender to ridicule and competitors' wrath. Fines and prison time could be assessed only if the code violation were so egregious as to cause demonstrable damage to the war effort. With one exception, involving the *Chicago Tribune*'s reporting of the battle of Midway in 1942, the government never considered any journalist's code violation severe enough to warrant prosecution under the Espionage Act. Army and navy officers cringed at violations they considered dangerous, but journalists tried to stay within the boundaries of the censorship guidelines they received from the Office of Censorship. They knew that to do otherwise could damage the nation's security, lead to compulsory censorship, or both. Even more compelling, being identified as a code violator could hurt a newspaper's circulation or the size of a radio audience, posing a threat to profits and perhaps the paper's or station's survival.

Price had faith in most journalists. A former reporter and wire service administrator, he knew hundreds of them. One key to his wartime success was his belief that journalists were as supportive of the war as other Americans, and that his role would be to help them censor themselves. As he sought their cooperation, he followed his rule "that you could get more out of people by asking them to do something than by ordering them" and that press and radio censors must be courteous.[12] Price decreed that censors would suggest, not order, although sometimes the suggestions were pointed when journalists threatened to violate the code.

On the wall of Price's office in the Federal Trade Commission Building at Seventh and Pennsylvania Avenues in Washington, D.C., was a framed quotation. The author was British publicist Owen Tweedy, and Price considered his words as something of a "God Bless Our Home" motto. Not only did he place the quotation in his own office, he ordered copies displayed at the dozen censorship stations that read mail entering and leaving the country and monitored cross-border telephone and cable traffic. The motto listed among the virtues of a good censor "the Voice of a Dove"—the soft attempt at persuasion, rather than the noisy threat.[13] That was Price's way. A censor should speak softly, or even better, not have to speak at all. At the end of the war, Price was happy to put a quick and quiet end to his role as censor and leave the Fourth Estate as he found it.

Of all of the federal offices created during World War II, none had a corporate life so closely paralleling the period of American combat as the Office of Censorship. It was born within days of the attack on Pearl Harbor, and it expired when Japan announced it no longer would fight. Thus, censorship existed no longer, and no shorter, than was necessary. This was appropriate for Price's administration. Strangely, it seems so many decades later, the conduct of American censorship during World War II is symbolic of the need for the news media to be as free as they can, for as long as they can.

Squarely in the Lap of
the Director of Censorship
The Origins and Scope of
World War II Censorship

Four months after the bombing of Pearl Harbor, as a formality, Byron Price requested a ruling from the Justice Department on whether as director of the Office of Censorship he could censor or close America's radiotelegraph companies. He unexpectedly received an invitation to almost absolute power.[1]

Attorney General Francis Biddle agreed that Price not only had jurisdiction over the tiny transmitters that sent instructions to ships on the Great Lakes and oil field roughnecks in the Southwestern desert, but he also could control the nation's 900 commercial radio stations. Price had not sought an opinion about his authority over commercial radio. Nevertheless, Biddle had opened the door to a takeover of everything from the NBC, Blue, CBS, and Mutual networks to the mom-and-pop independent stations that spun records and broadcast cattle and hog prices. He had offered Price the power to kill or alter any program. All Price had to do to be dictator of radio was accept responsibility for his actions.

Could Price afford to decline the offer? He did not know. American broadcasting stations, which sprang up two years after the end of World War I, had never been tested during wartime. There was no way to predict how radio stations would perform if broadcasters followed the course Price had advocated, censoring themselves with a minimum of government interference. An error in his judgment might be disastrous. A radio station might slip, accidentally giving secret military information to the Axis powers. Or a German- or Italian-language announcer might try to sabotage the Allied war effort by sending news about troop departures or secret weapons across the ocean, at the speed of light, to the homeland—to the enemy. Or perhaps a spy might grab a microphone at an announcer's booth and broadcast a coded message. If any such scenario occurred and American lives were lost, Price knew, according to Biddle's written opinion, who would get the blame. It would be the censor who had refused to take control.[2]

Price's nature was to think and act deliberately even though he had a hot temper. As director of the Office of Censorship since its creation in December 1941, Price had deflected attempts by government and military officials to cut into his powers. He had nudged stubborn newspaper publishers and radio commentators into compliance with the censorship guidelines his staff had developed. He privately had chastised the rule breakers and admonished them to be more vigilant, but he had not browbeaten them. "Least said, soonest mended," he often said.[3] He considered censorship so distasteful that it should be practiced only by those who were, by nature, "unspeakably profane" about it.[4] Yet, Price considered his work crucial to winning the war. He hid whatever conflicting emotions he felt behind blue-gray eyes and baby-fat cheeks. He might twist or peel or continually relight one of his custom-made black cigars, and when pressed too far might explode in profanity; still, he would never rush into action without weighing the consequences.

Assistant Solicitor General Oscar S. Cox had drafted a response to Price's initial inquiry about radiotelegraphy and sent it to Biddle along with a note stating that Price had been apprised of its contents and that the opinion might "create a howl from the radio people."[5] When Biddle endorsed the opinion and formally sent it to Price on May 18, the censorship director carefully plotted a course of action. First, he would call for a meeting of the Censorship Policy Board, which advised him, and inform the members of Biddle's opinion. He would lay out the problems of wartime radio and present the pros and cons of government seizure of domestic stations. Only then, he decided, would he reveal his opinion and call for a vote of support.

Price often had spoken about the problems of voluntary censorship in radio broadcasts to the public, in closed-circuit talks to editors and broadcasters, and in interviews with newspaper and magazine reporters. He had even preached what he called "the gospel" of voluntary censorship in a 1942 textbook explaining the war to high school students. That message was a simplified version of the same argument he always used. How, he had asked, could sensitive military information be kept from the enemy once it was published or broadcast in the United States? Even if the nation built a high wall along its borders, patrolled its skies for planes and carrier pigeons, and carefully monitored its gates, vital information still could leave the country undetected in a traveler's memory. Printed materials could be smuggled out in diplomatic pouches. And finally, there was radio. Walls were no defense against its invisible energy.[6]

As he prepared a memo for the board, Price probably recalled his first Sunday in office. Price and his wife, Priscilla, had dined in Virginia at the home of Lowell Mellett, an old friend who had worked with Price in newsrooms and relaxed with him at Washington's annual Gridiron Show. Mellett, who had been one of President Franklin Roosevelt's initial candidates for the top censor's job, told Price after dinner that radio's power was too great to be left unchecked. The federal government must seize control, he said. Perhaps Price had heard Mellett make the same argument in March 1941 at an off-the-record question-and-answer session before the National Press Club, when Mellett told reporters that in the event of war, "There will be definite control over radio."[7] No reporters spoke out at that time, but at the private dinner Price made his objections known. Control of radio would create a huge bureaucracy, be difficult to administer, tend to linger after the war, and hamper the voluntary censorship of the print media, he said. Price knew, however, that many people in Roosevelt's administration agreed with Mellett. Another group of Washington officials favored continuing the private ownership and operation of radio but establishing some form of compulsory censorship that had legal penalties for violations. A third group, headed by Price but largely silent, wanted to give radio a chance to prove itself early in 1942. If a voluntary system failed, tougher censorship rules could be imposed later, they reasoned.[8] But if it worked, radio would emerge from the war as independent and lively as it had entered it. That was Price's goal, he once told a radio audience. War might not be worth winning if the First Amendment had to be sacrificed.[9]

When the Office of Censorship released its guidelines for domestic censorship on January 15, 1942—a seven-page, church-bulletin-sized pamphlet for radio stations and a five-page version for newspapers and magazines—many broadcasters were surprised that they had escaped direct federal control. They had believed that the New Dealers who expanded the government in the 1930s would invoke the Communications Act of 1934, under which the president could seize radio in an emergency.[10] "Many of us thought the government would take over all the stations and all of us station managers would become majors in the Army," one small-town station operator said.[11] Broadcasters also were relieved that one code had been devised for all stations. Some had expected one set of guidelines for stations in the interior of the country and another for stations near the borders, on the assumption that cross-border broadcasts posed a greater threat to security. The Office of Censorship had vetoed that idea partly out of competitive concerns. It would be unfair if stations operating under the more liberal code could attract listeners from nearby stations that operated under the more conservative version.[12] In addition, having one code for all would contribute to a feeling of wartime unity. Enforcement of the code on all stations, large and small, would promote the perception of fairness and equality and thus make any station that sought exception appear to be selfish or opposed to national solidarity.

Radio stations were not the only broadcasters, however. The Office of Censorship policed six other forms of radio: backyard "ham" broadcasts; wireless commercial communication across the oceans; international radiotelephone; a small number of network and government-sponsored shortwave broadcasts aimed at a global audience; a collection of government and private point-to-point message services used by airlines, taxis, and police cars; and the tiny radiotelegraph services that competed with companies using telegraph wires. Price decided to suppress ham radio for the rest of the war, and he used a variety of controls and requests to keep the next four categories on the air but subject to censors' scrutiny. The final category presented a problem. Radiotelegraphy, a business, involved the property rights of its owners. Some companies were operating nationally at a profit. Smaller companies worked regionally. Naval officers and the Defense Communications Board, which oversaw radio's role in the wartime emergency, had alerted Price early in 1942 to the dangers of leaving uncensored the point-to-point radiotelegraph broadcasts that were intended not for a mass audience, but rather for a single listener.[13] They were concerned that spies near the borders and coastlines could eavesdrop or use the radiotelegraph transmitters to send messages. Price believed that the most effective way to prevent such espionage was to halt all private radiotelegraphy.[14] However, he hesitated to close the companies during the war, depriving them of income, without verifying his authority to do so. Therefore, he asked Biddle to rule on the legality of seizing control.

Price had considered his request a minor one. But Biddle's opinion answered a question Price had not asked and put the issue of censoring every broadcasting station, in Price's words, "squarely in the lap of the Director of Censorship."[15]

The attorney general's opinion said that Congress, in passing the First War Powers Act in December 1941, clearly had intended to grant the power to censor radio communications "which could not practically and with certainty be confined to the continental limits of the United States." Interpreting the act, along with Executive Order 8985, which established the Office of Censorship, the opinion said that "practical and effective" control must include all communications "which in fact can be received outside the United States, even though the purpose of the sender was solely to convey a message to other persons within this country." Applying this logic to broadcasting, the opinion drew upon a 1932 Supreme Court decision in which Chief Justice Charles Evans Hughes said, "No state lines divide the radio waves." Furthermore, the attorney general's opinion continued, "It is equally true that no national boundaries divide the radio waves. The power of censorship over all international communication granted by Congress is illusory unless it is of a breadth commensurate with technological necessities. It must be assumed that Congress intended the President, and thus in turn the Director of Censorship, to exercise control over domestic broadcasting as is necessary to the practical and effective censorship of international radio communication."[16]

Price noted in his memoir that Biddle made no direct statement, pro or con, on whether the Office of Censorship could seize control of stations that aimed their broadcasts at many listeners instead of specific ones through radiotelegraphy. However, Price had no doubt that he would be blamed if a military tragedy resulted from too much caution. The path of least resistance was obvious, he recalled: "pass through the door" opened by the Justice Department and put all of radio under government control.[17]

Because his decision was so momentous, he felt he had to convene the Censorship Policy Board. It consisted of the nation's vice president; the secretaries of war, navy, and treasury; the attorney general; the postmaster general; and the directors of two government information agencies, the Office of Facts and Figures and the Office of Government Reports.[18]

Price sent each member a memo stating Biddle's opinion as well as his own arguments for and against a government takeover. The memo's argument for absolute, mandatory censorship was brief but pointed. Such control would allow the government to stop worrying about

FBI director J. Edgar Hoover, left, Office of Censorship director Byron Price, center, and Attorney General Francis Biddle conferring in 1942. Hoover directed American censorship immediately after American entry into World War II, before turning operations over to Price, who declined Biddle's invitation to assume complete control of radio. State Historical Society of Wisconsin, Negative WHi(X3)51975.

enemy reception of domestic broadcasts, end all subversive radio commentary, and ease the problem of monitoring the 200 American radio stations that carried programs in German, Italian, or twenty-nine other foreign languages. The memo's listing of possible objections was much longer and more complicated. First, Price said that complete control would require nearly 3,000 highly trained censors, roughly one for each eight-hour shift at each of the nation's radio stations. Second, keeping information from the enemy would mean not giving it to Americans as well, and the limited value of such censorship might not offset the damage of having a poorly informed public. Third, compulsory censorship would probably cause resentment among broadcasters, who had been cooperating with the voluntary codes, and such ill will in a vital national industry would be unwise. Fourth, newspapers might interpret the takeover of radio as an attack on free expression as well as an indication of lack of faith in mass media as a whole. Finally, the public might suspect that the government had instituted compulsory censorship to hide its military blunders; people might become fearful or distrustful.[19] In short, Price believed that the benefits of total censorship were outweighed by the disadvantages.

The board met at 4 P.M. on May 19 in the office of its chairman, Postmaster General Frank C. Walker.[20] Price had invited a guest. Federal Communications Commission (FCC) chairman James Lawrence Fly, director of the agency that licensed domestic radio stations, had wanted to be on the board but apparently had been snubbed because he was disliked and distrusted by Roosevelt's inner circle.[21] Fly had a reputation as an activist who believed that the FCC should do more than issue permits and occasionally punish misbehavior. Many thought Fly favored more direct government control of radio.[22] In his defense, however, Fly had told the American Civil Liberties Union in a speech early in 1941 that citizens would be robbed of their birthright if free discussion were banned from the radio dial.[23] Price wanted him at the meeting because the group's eventual decision—whatever it was—would require Fly's cooperation. However, Price did not know Fly's opinion on the issue.

Price opened the meeting by explaining that his memo to the board members was meant as background for what he said next: He opposed mandatory radio censorship not only for the reasons listed, but also because "if this sort of control once were established, the stations never would be returned to private hands. . . . Compulsory censorship would only prove a first step to government monopoly."[24] In an interview three decades later, Price said ironclad censorship would have led to postwar American broadcasting being "completely under the thumb of the government [and] used for propaganda purposes."[25]

Some board members appeared startled by Price's conclusions, and Price wondered privately if they had given the matter much thought. The representatives of the War and Navy Departments said little. Surprisingly, the director of the Office of Government Reports supported Price's call for voluntary censorship of radio. Mellett, who headed that information-monitoring office, apparently did not tell the board that he had voiced the opposite conclusion in December. Mellett had a few reservations, however. He thought any radio station being used to send messages to the enemy should be subjected to compulsory censorship. Nevertheless, he said radio should be as free as the press. Fly also agreed with Price. The supposedly repressive radio chairman stoutly defended the freedom to broadcast during the national crisis. In addition, he said, it was not a good time to harass the industry, which was caught between the rising cost of war news coverage and the short-term decline of advertising revenue linked to the shift from a consumer to a wartime economy, rationing, and the loss of advertiser-sponsored programs that ran afoul of censorship codes.[26]

Given the agreement of Price and Fly, the two people central to any broadcasting censorship plan, the board easily endorsed private owners' control of radio. Fly and Price also were in agreement on ending radio-telegraphy. The following week, Fly, as chairman of the Defense Communications Board, announced the wartime closure of radiotelegraph circuits, effective June 30.[27]

The Censorship Policy Board made one more decision: to censor itself. According to the notes that Walker's secretary made of the meeting, Price asked if Biddle's opinion should be made public along with a statement that the Office of Censorship would not use the power it had been offered. Fly objected that broadcasters would find such action "definitely upsetting."[28] That settled matters. Price typed in the notebook journal he kept throughout the war that the members "agreed . . . that the whole matter should be kept confidential, and that nothing should be published about the Attorney General's opinion because of the widespread apprehension it would create." In pencil, Price inserted four words, "for the time being," indicating a willingness to change his mind if pressed to do so. His notes referred to the opinion as a "club in the closet." He believed that although broadcasters might never learn how close they had come to being servants of the state, they knew that their performance was being watched by a keenly interested government.[29]

No news about Biddle's ruling apparently leaked during the war, although a few dark hints appeared. Theodore F. Koop, an assistant to Price who headed the Press Division of the Office of Censorship in 1945 before embarking on a career with CBS, revealed a year after the war's end that "persons high in the administration . . . earnestly advocated that radio stations should be controlled" and were in a position to press their case with the president.[30] Price believed that his secret was secure. At the time he was working on his memoir in the 1960s, he must have thought Biddle's ruling had been swallowed by an archive and forgotten. A copy of the ruling was declassified by the National Archives in 1971 as part of a history of the Office of Censorship produced internally after the war, but the records are so massive that it is no small wonder that one document in them could remain obscure.[31] Copies of the opinion also are on file at the Franklin D. Roosevelt Library in Hyde Park, New York, and Price gave his notes about the opinion to the State Historical Society of Wisconsin in 1976, five years before his death. The revelation of Price's refusal to seize control of American radio, although he had legal authority to do so, has reposed quietly in each archive.

It is surprising that historians have overlooked such a momentous decision, involving an action not taken, like a road not traveled, and leading to one construction of the future instead of another. And yet, historians have been neglectful of the Office of Censorship and the voluntary censorship of domestic news media supervised by its Press and Broadcasting Divisions. This is poetic justice. Not only does it seem appropriate that historians should be relatively silent about the most bureaucratic machinery of censorship in the nation's history, but the omission of much of the Office of Censorship's work from many standard histories of World War II is also in keeping with the personal philosophy of the censorship director. Price did not want to call attention to his office or to his work. His reasons for keeping a low profile were not so much that his brand of censorship could not tolerate the sunshine—he was proud of his organization and his methods—but rather that he believed he had a formula for success and did not want others to ruin it. As a journalist, he hated censorship, but he was convinced that if America had to be subjected to it during World War II, it had to be the right kind.

THE EXCESSES OF GEORGE CREEL

Price had learned from the excesses of World War I. His soft-pedaled approach to censorship contrasted with the more visible forms of information management practiced during that war by the Committee on Public Information. Its director, Colorado journalist George Creel, had started his censorship operations from scratch in 1917. Organizing and staffing a news and censorship committee was "like asking the Babylonians to build a threshing machine, for there was no chart to go by," Creel said in his autobiography.[32] Yet, the lack of a blueprint had allowed Creel to shape the committee much as he saw fit, and he gave it a powerful voice. Although the committee's directors included the secretaries of war, navy, and state, the agency informally assumed the name of its fourth, and most visible, leader. The "Creel Committee" acted not only as leader of voluntary censorship but also as government publicist and propagandist.

The government needed to build public enthusiasm in 1917. Many Americans had been indifferent about the European war they suddenly were called upon to fight in 1917, and for eight million, Germany was their land of origin. In the six weeks after the United States declared war, only 73,000 men enlisted in the American armed forces. Creel responded to the need by mobilizing movie actors and directors, artists, and speakers known as "four-minute men"—because of the duration of their talks—to drum up support for the war. He also encouraged newspapers and magazines to print news that would help the Allies but not the enemy. He organized the Division of News, which distributed 6,000 press releases during the year and a half of American participation in the war.[33] Historians James R. Mock and Cedric Larson describe the effect of Creel's information management on a typical farm family in the Midwest: "Every item of war news they saw—in the country weekly, in magazines, or in the city daily picked up occasionally in the general store—was not merely officially approved information but precisely the same kind that millions of their fellow citizens were getting at the same moment. Every war story had been censored somewhere along the line— at the source, in transit, or in the newspaper offices in accordance with 'voluntary' rules established by the CPI."[34]

The Division of News advised journalists about information that should not be published, interpreted government requests for secrecy, and referred tough questions to the War and Navy Departments.[35] Writing three decades later, Creel said Washington correspondents worked hard to comply with civilian censorship requests but that "chaos" reigned outside the capital. Accounts differ on how often Creel's voluntary censorship code was violated deliberately between its promulgation on May 28, 1917, and the end of censorship on November 14, 1918. Mock said 99 percent of the press observed the rules of voluntary censorship, and in an article written after World War II, Creel placed the number of deliberate violations at "two or three."[36] Another time, Creel indicated that the total was far higher, lamenting "many bold and open breaches" of censorship due to editors' addiction to exclusive stories. He named the Associated Press as being among the violators. It ignored one of Creel's occasional bulletins that supplemented the censorship code. Creel's memorandum had asked the press to print nothing about a series of troop transports until the last four groups had reached France safely. According to Creel, the AP announced the arrival of the first while the other three were still in transit. Not surprisingly, the AP's largest competitor, United Press, sent Creel a telegram protesting the violation.[37]

Beyond the bureaucracy of information management, the passions of World War I curbed the press and other forms of speech with a series of laws, some of which remained in effect at the beginning of the next war. The first law, the Espionage Act of 1917, had broad applications to all forms of expression. It established fines of up to $10,000 and prison terms of up to twenty years for anyone convicted of willfully making or conveying "false reports or false statements with intent to interfere with the operation or success of the military or naval forces of the United States," willfully causing, or attempting to cause, "insubordination, disloyalty, mutiny, or refusal of duty" in the army or navy, or willfully obstructing recruitment and enlistment.[38] It added that any publication violating the act would be declared unmailable. The government could use this provision to punish newspapers beyond the simple withholding of one issue from mail delivery. Newspapers and magazines were entitled to a low-cost, second-class mailing permit, according to the Mail Classification Act of 1879. However, in order to qualify, periodicals had to be issued at stated intervals at least four times a year. The postmaster general could revoke the second-class permit of any periodical that failed to meet the requirement, and there was no judicial review of the decision because he was deemed to be the expert on the subject—just as an inspector has the last word on the safety of a public building. If the postmaster general decided to withhold just one issue of a publication, he could declare that regular distribution had been interrupted and suspend the publication's special permit. The second-class rate was by far the cheapest, and publishers and government officials knew that its loss would prove disastrous to offending publications.[39] By mid-1918, Postmaster General Albert S. Burleson used the 1879 law against about seventy-five newspapers, including forty-five socialist ones. Not all had their second-class permits suspended; many agreed voluntarily to stop commenting on the war.[40]

A second law, the Trading with the Enemy Act of 1917, allowed the president to censor any communications "by mail, cable, radio, or other means of transmission" between the United States and any foreign country. The law formalized censorship and singled out foreign-language newspapers and magazines. It required translations of foreign-language articles "respecting the government of the United States . . . or the state or conduct of the war" to be filed with the local postmaster on or before the date the publication was offered for mailing. It declared that any non-English publication that failed to conform to the law would be declared unmailable; however, publications that did file such translations could apply for a permit allowing distribution.[41] Enforcement was carried out with zeal. The elderly editor of the *Herold,* a German-language paper in Eau Claire, Wisconsin, published an editorial critical of the army's smallpox vaccination program. He did not file a translation and was indicted under the Espionage Act and Trading with the Enemy Act. Despite evidence of senility, the editor was convicted and sentenced to a year at the federal prison at Leavenworth, Kansas, where he died.[42]

A third law, an expansion of the Espionage Act known as the Sedition Act of 1918, created the strongest restrictions in the history of the First Amendment by punishing even casual and impulsively disloyal speech.[43] About 2,000 people were arrested under provisions of the Espionage and Sedition Acts, and nearly 1,000 were convicted.[44] The Sedition Act was repealed in 1921, but the postmaster general's right to revoke second-class permits was endorsed that same year and could be used effectively after the outbreak of hostilities.[45] The original Espionage Act remained on the books, its provisions inactive until brought to life by a declaration of war.

These laws could only be enforced after the fact of publication or broadcast. It was evident at the end of World War I that such federal laws by themselves were inadequate to plan and coordinate wartime censorship; long-range planning, including the creation of a civilian and military bureaucracy, was needed.[46] Before the Creel Committee was dissolved in 1919, it laid the groundwork for censorship for the next war. The committee recommended that the director of censorship be a civilian and have two military assistants: an army officer in charge of mail, telephone, and telegraph censorship, and a naval officer in charge of cable and radio censorship. The committee also recommended that the Post Office, State Department, and War Trade Board have liaison officers on duty at the censorship director's office, to improve coordination of censorship decisions and avoid inconsistencies. In 1921, the secretaries of the War and

Navy Departments submitted a jointly written censorship plan, in accordance with these recommendations, to the postmaster general, the secretary of state, and the secretary of commerce. The recommendations were based on the principle that the army and navy needed enough censorship to ensure the safety of military and naval operations. The secretaries of state and commerce agreed to the plan, which varied from the Committee on Public Information's recommendation by giving most of the responsibility for mail censorship to the Post Office Department. However, the postmaster general dissented. He offered an alternative—a censorship board similar to the one formed in World War I, which he would lead. Neither plan was adopted. More proposals were drafted through out the 1920s and 1930s, but despite the growing tensions in Europe and the Far East, none got beyond the planning stages.[47]

CENSORSHIP BEFORE AMERICA'S ENTRY INTO WORLD WAR II

When Germany invaded Poland on September 1, 1939, and Britain and France declared war, the United States officially decided not to choose sides. However, American censorship and other forms of influence on mass communication proceeded on four fronts: the tendency of majority voices to overwhelm minority views, especially when financial interests were at stake in the marketplace of ideas; the voluntary censorship by sympathetic journalists acting on their own in support of Germany's enemies; the voluntary censorship by journalists responding to requests from government officials; and plans for an official censorship system if it should become necessary.

Roosevelt's popularity with reporters and with the American public contributed to the shaping of a majority view of news and public opinion in the late 1930s and early 1940s. The president was skilled at promoting his political agenda in the mass media as well as diverting unwanted attention. Not only did Roosevelt have two press conferences a week, totaling nearly 1,000 during his tenure, he also abandoned the existing rule that required questions to be submitted in writing in advance. In the relaxed, clubby atmosphere of his press conferences, which encouraged journalists to believe that they had a close relationship with the president, Roosevelt personally influenced the presentation of many major news stories about his administration. Supplementing the news from the Oval Office was the creation of a federal public relations machine that was producing 1,000 press releases a month by the end of Roosevelt's first year in office. Washington journalists, most of whom supported the

president's political agenda (unlike their more skeptical or hostile publishers and editors), were made to feel important. Some, however, also
began to feel as if the Roosevelt administration was controlling the press
by creating a reliance on handouts. One reporter said that although routine contacts between journalists and the president's administration were
the best in history, never before "had the door been shut so tightly against
information" other than what was written in the handouts or otherwise
officially approved. The president's most notable success in controlling
the news kept most of the nation ignorant of the extent of the polio-
induced paralysis of his legs. A wire service reporter recalled that White
House reporters were engaged in "a friendly conspiracy which was based
on basic principles of American sportsmanship—not taking advantage
of a man's physical infirmities." Press Secretary Stephen T. Early and the
Secret Service had an unwritten rule that photographers could not take
pictures of Roosevelt in his wheelchair or on crutches. Instead of protesting the rule, the supportive Washington press corps willingly con-
formed to it in a sort of gentleman's agreement. Photographers who did
not know the rule had their lenses blocked or cameras knocked to the
ground by fellow journalists if they tried to shoot a forbidden picture.
When Roosevelt fell full-length down a ramp at the speaker's platform at
the 1936 Democratic National Convention in Philadelphia, not a single
cartoon or picture was published about it.[48]

By acquiescing to the government's publicity program and avoiding
an obvious physical deficiency, many journalists were well-heeled in a
form of self-censorship long before America's entry into World War II.
The news media's economic concerns sometimes made censorship less
subtle, and the most basic concern was survival. The Federal Communications Commission could revoke or refuse to renew the license of any
radio station, a fact not lost on broadcasters as they reported on the war
in Europe. The New York Times quoted one broadcaster as saying in June
1940, "Every word is being carefully sieved these days." Some stations
banned news analyses from Axis countries even though the federal government had no regulation against them.[49] In July 1940, the FCC ordered
all 100,000 broadcasters under its jurisdiction to provide proof of citizenship, such as affidavits and fingerprints, as opposed to the previously
acceptable sworn statements. The FCC also increased its monitoring of
radio broadcasts, and the American Legion voted to ask the FCC to bar
subversive groups, including communists, from access to the airwaves.
Broadcasters got the message. They policed themselves and cooperated

with army and navy requests to avoid many defense topics.[50] Beyond mere survival, however, the print press and radio, both privately owned, were driven by the need to earn profits and believed they could ill afford news and commentary that might antagonize their advertisers or the audiences who supported them. Mutual Broadcasting System news commentator Arthur Hale was censored by Transradio Press Service and by his sponsor, Richfield Oil Company, when he attempted to inject his moderately isolationist and anti–New Deal opinions into his scripts in mid-1941.[51] Radio commentators could even lose their sponsorship or be kicked off the air if their commentary led to friction with sponsoring advertisers.[52]

Another form of censorship involved journalists' own initiative in limiting what they wrote or broadcast about the nation's defenses in order to prevent Germany from exploiting such information. In early October 1939, Elisha Hanson, general counsel for the American Newspaper Publishers Association, told journalists at a New Jersey convention that no paper should publish information on the movements of troops, ships, or planes that might endanger American lives in a national emergency. An editorial in *Collier's* magazine that month agreed that censorship of troop movements and plans of attack would be necessary if America entered the war.[53] In addition to calls for future restrictions, some reporters actively censored themselves. The director of Canada's public information office, G. H. Lash, was surprised to find military secrets in the *New York Herald Tribune* newsroom in December 1939, about the time the Canadian First Division sailed for Europe. A *Tribune* editor pulled from his desk an unpublished story that included the date of the division's departure from Halifax, the number of troops and ships, and various other secret details. The editor told Lash that he had been keeping the story for several days, awaiting a time he could print it safely. He added that the large papers in Boston and New York "had entered into a mutual agreement not to print anything which they thought might endanger the lives of Canadians."[54]

Some journalists who had balked at supporting the Roosevelt administration during the 1930s began to cooperate with the president's news management in the spring of 1940. The march of Nazi armies through Denmark, Norway, and the Low Countries had changed their minds; after that, some publishers who had opposed the New Deal, including the *Los Angeles Times*'s Harry Chandler, pursued ways to help prepare the nation's defenses. Chandler sought a meeting of government and newspaper representatives to discuss a press campaign to build interest in European affairs, but the idea fell through when Roosevelt's advisers thought it might be misconstrued as a move toward press control.[55] Two other highly respected newspapers took stronger steps. In May 1940, publisher Barry Bingham of the *Louisville Courier-Journal* told Lowell Mellett, who monitored the news media for Roosevelt, that the *Courier-Journal* was trying to stop other newspapers from comparing the emergency powers enacted in Britain and France with the totalitarian abuses of the Nazis. Bingham said he had told a dozen publishers that the two were not alike, and comparing them misled the public. Even the *New York Times* swung from ignoring the White House's lectures in December 1940 about "the role and responsibility of the press" to self-imposed suppression of a story exposing low morale and deplorable conditions in military training camps in September 1941.[56]

The administration's open efforts to persuade journalists to censor themselves began only eight hours after news of the German invasion of Poland reached Washington. Roosevelt called a press conference at 10:40 A.M. on September 1, 1939. Many of the reporters who packed the Executive Office were groggy, having been up since 3 A.M. writing and broadcasting the news that had arrived from Europe. The president had little news about the invasion, but he urged the press corps to be careful in reporting anything it uncovered. "I hope particularly that there won't be unsubstantiated rumors put out, whether they originate here or elsewhere, without checking," he said.[57] He hoped that reporters would turn to his administration for confirmation of stories and refuse to publish rumors. Since most government officials are reluctant to speak on the record about secrets or events that cast the government in an unfavorable light, Roosevelt's request served to limit information that the administration disliked.

Roosevelt wooed the public in a fireside chat two days later, telling a national radio audience, "You are, I believe, the most enlightened and the best informed people in all the world at this moment. You are subjected to no censorship of news, and I want to add that your Government has no information which it withholds or which it has any thought of withholding from you. At the same time . . . it is of the highest importance that the press and the radio use the utmost caution to discriminate between actual verified fact on the one hand, and mere rumor on the other."[58]

In the next few months, army and navy officials made a series of requests for voluntary censorship of defense news, some of them general and some concerning specific topics. News sources dried up at the War and Navy Departments. All the while, the president, his press secretary, and members of his cabinet insisted that there would be no control of publications in wartime. The *New York Times* reported on June 14, 1940, that the War Department had ordered its top administrators and officers not to talk to reporters unless the department's press section, staffed by officers, gave its approval. Similar restrictions also were under way at the Navy Department. Questioned by reporters, Early said that no news denied by the White House should be published. The White House was aided in its attempts to control news by recent expansions of the federal laws of security classification of sensitive information. A law passed unanimously by Congress in 1938 had forbade unauthorized photographs, sketches, or maps of bases, and gave the president the authority to define military and naval information that he believed needed security protection. Roosevelt had cited the law in issuing Executive Order 8381 on March 22, 1940, which asserted presidential control of the classification system of "all official military or naval books, pamphlets, documents, reports, maps, charts, plans, designs, models, drawings, photographs, contracts or specifications," and explicitly gave him discretion to expand the classification to other "articles or equipment" as needed.[59]

Secretary of the Navy Frank Knox took the most dramatic step in the campaign to get the press to adopt censorship voluntarily. He prepared 5,000 copies of a not-for-publication letter to newspapers, magazines, radio stations, and photographic agencies on December 31, 1940, asking for restrictions on naval news. Too much information was reaching the Axis powers about the U.S. Navy's preparations for national defense, the letter said. As the publisher of the *Chicago Daily News* and a Republican whom Roosevelt chose partly out of a desire for bipartisan support, Knox called upon his fellow journalists to avoid publicity about ship and aircraft movements, secret weapons and their development, new ships and planes, and onshore naval construction projects. He promised that the navy would release as much information as it considered "consonant with public interest and with the effectiveness of the Navy's preparations."[60]

Knox asked for Treasury Secretary Henry Morganthau's opinion of the letter. Morganthau passed the letter to three of his assistants for comment. The opinion of Assistant Secretary Herbert Gaston, who often represented the Treasury in interdepartmental meetings, was short and to the point. Knox's letter was "unwise," Gaston said on January 13, because it taxed reporters' goodwill. Too many appeals for voluntary censorship would "weaken [the government's] authority when a real emergency occurs."[61] His analysis was too late; Knox's secret letter already had been mailed. Soon it became public. *Uncensored*, a mimeographed weekly publication in New York City, printed the letter that month. *Time* magazine, considering that the leak had freed it to comment on Knox's list of prohibited information, noted the letter encompassed nearly everything newsworthy about the navy. The magazine said Knox was particularly upset about a story that had appeared in October 1940 in the *Congressional Record*. Representative Carl Vinson of Georgia had placed in the *Record* a table of naval construction projects, including seventeen battleships, twelve carriers, and fifty-four cruisers, all of which a spy could learn for the $1.50 a month it cost to subscribe.[62]

Although reporters harbored some reservations, Knox secured the endorsement of the American Newspaper Publishers Association, the American Society of Newspaper Editors, and nine other newspaper groups. All agreed to seek and accept news about sensitive naval matters only through the navy's press office because they believed they had an obligation to national defense.[63] Knox announced that the nation's press almost unanimously accepted his requests and curtailed coverage of the navy. However, he said, "Nothing is further from my mind" than peacetime censorship. "The Navy has nothing to hide from the American people."[64]

But the navy, in fact, wanted much to be kept secret. So did the army. Less than two weeks after Knox's declaration that the navy was not covering up information, Roosevelt admonished Washington journalists for their reporting on the closed-door testimony of General George C. Marshall to the Senate Military Affairs Committee. The panel's members had leaked details to reporters, who publicized Marshall's comparisons of American planes with those of the Axis. At a press conference on February 21, 1941, Roosevelt was asked to comment on Marshall's statement to the committee that the United States was strengthening its forces in Hawaii.

Who quoted him? the president asked. Members of Congress, a reporter replied.

Roosevelt shot back, "In what kind of meeting?"

"In a secret meeting," the reporter said.

Roosevelt said he thought that "ethically, morally, [and] patriotically" Marshall's testimony ought to have stayed confidential. Yet, while he considered the story to have damaged America's defense, he did not blame reporters for ferreting it out. "It is perfectly all right for the reporter to take the story to his office, because that is part of a reporter's business . . . but the printing of the story or putting it on wires by press associations or newspaper offices in Washington presents another very different, very difficult problem," Roosevelt said. When reporters pressed him to define a national defense secret, he replied that the definition was up to the army, navy, and president. Reporters tried to pin him down, but Roosevelt sidestepped a pointed question about the press's constitutionally guaranteed freedom. The president closed the conference by agreeing with a reporter's comment that papers should find their own way to suppress sensitive defense stories.[65]

In March 1941, Knox issued a letter containing a second request for press secrecy. He asked that nothing be published or broadcast about British ships being outfitted or repaired in U.S. ports under the Lend-Lease program, which aided Britain's defense without technically committing America to war.[66] The political issue of helping one belligerent while remaining neutral was a sensitive one, and it even was possible that news stories could provide valuable information to German spies. The first test of Knox's request came on April 6, when the HMS *Malaya* limped into New York Harbor after being torpedoed in the North Atlantic. Thousands of New Yorkers—and any foreign agents who might be in the city, including those at the German consulate at Battery Place—could look out their windows and see the battleship with a hole in its side. Worse, the ship's identity was easy to verify. British sailors attended Broadway shows in their uniforms, complete with caps bearing the word "Malaya" in big letters.[67]

Two New York newspapers defied Knox's request. The *Daily News*, owned by Joseph Patterson, a cousin of the publisher of the anti-Roosevelt *Chicago Tribune*, printed an aerial photograph showing a collision mat covering a twenty-six-foot break in the ship's portside armor plate.[68] The *New York Herald Tribune*, which advocated aid to Britain but chafed at Knox's order, reported the presence of the ship but published an old photograph.[69] Knox protested that the papers had given military information to the Germans, but the *Daily News* and *Washington Times-Herald*, owned by Patterson's sister, published a joint statement defending their decision to print the news.[70] The *Malaya* story did result in one concrete change: the U.S. Navy "emphatically" urged Britain to hide all distinguishing marks and silence all crew members when its ships docked at American ports.[71]

The army also tightened its news operation. Undersecretary of War Robert P. Patterson announced on April 10, 1941, that all news stories about army operations outside the United States would be subject to "censorship at the source," meaning the army expected reporters to clear such stories before filing them. Eleven days later, the army reduced the flow of information to reporters by ordering its officers not to give out news of the arrival, departure, or presence of U.S. troops outside the forty-eight states.[72] Roosevelt tried to calm fears of official censorship by sending a letter to the American Society of Newspaper Editors on April 16. Suppression of opinion and censorship of news "are among the mortal weapons that dictatorships direct against their own peoples and direct against the world," he wrote. "As far as I am concerned there will be no Government control of news unless it be of vital military information."[73]

Further requests for voluntary censorship in 1941 included an army ban on photographs of new equipment, especially in airplanes;[74] the president's suggestion that reporters ask themselves whether publicity about Allied factories would provide valuable information to Axis military intelligence;[75] and an extension of the requested ban on shipping news to movements of mail boats and merchant vessels.[76] Knox told reporters at a news conference on June 11, one week after he halted press releases about navy contracts, that he expected all reporters to follow one rule: "If you can't confirm it, don't print it." Without using the word "censorship," he added that his office would be the sole judge of what should be confirmed about the navy.[77] It soon became evident that the navy would not clear much information about the danger to American ships helping the British move war supplies from East Coast ports. Knox had little to say when Senator Burton K. Wheeler of Montana revealed in July that American troops would embark for Iceland. When sixty reporters attended a Knox press conference after Roosevelt ordered the navy to guard sea lanes serving American defense outposts, the secretary ducked questions about the navy's authority to fire its guns. Instead, he read the presidential order aloud three times.[78]

In September 1941, Knox tried to clarify his requests on naval news after the *Bainbridge Review,* a weekly paper published near Seattle, reported early that month on the British battleship *Warspite* undergoing repairs in the Bremerton Navy Yard. Brashly, the paper wrote a headline, "Review Violates a National Censorship," and sent a copy to the Navy Department's Public Relations Office in Washington, D.C. According to *Time,* the paper reasoned that the United States was not at war, and there was no secret in Bremerton to keep because the entire town knew the British had arrived. The editors of the paper were independent-minded enough to ignore peacetime requests for cooperation that originated in the federal government and to protest publicly what they considered to be unnecessary and overly intrusive attempts at censorship. In addition, the *Review* was less prone to hysteria about combat in the Pacific than most newspapers because it served a large and loyal Japanese American community on Bainbridge Island, which included many of the editors' friends. In a second incident in September, *Time* said sailors at the Sand Point Naval Air Station at Seattle fired four warning shots at a reporter and a photographer who had strayed too close to a hangar to get pictures of Russian aviators in training. On the next day, the publisher of the *Seattle Post-Intelligencer*—John Boettiger, who happened to be Roosevelt's son-in-law—accused Knox of stupidity and attempting to alienate the press.[79] Within a week, Knox adjusted his restrictions on news of British ships by agreeing to distribute press releases that would give no information about ship damage or combat but would identify ships in port seven days after their arrival.[80]

The government had accomplished little throughout the 1930s on a comprehensive plan for censorship after a declaration of war. The army and navy drafted several censorship proposals similar to the one designed by the Joint Army-Navy Board in 1921, but none was formally submitted to the president. Discussions began again as early as 1935 but were not carried out in earnest until early 1940. In April of that year, an interdepartmental board, including military, State Department, and FBI officials, debated the form censorship should take in the event of American entry into the war. By June 10, a joint board approved and sent to Roosevelt a $50 million "Basic Plan for Public Relations Administration" that would have authorized complete censorship of all mass media, including motion pictures and radio broadcasts, as well as international communications. The plan languished. Lowell Mellett recalled years later that the president feared political repercussions if it were discovered, and Mellett asked Early to bury it. According to historian Richard W. Steele, the

Joint Army-Navy Public Relations Committee, puzzled by the silence that the plan received, resubmitted it on February 1, 1941. Roosevelt flatly rejected it and chastised the board for its political naïveté.[81]

The president instead ordered work to begin on a plan for the censorship of international communications only. A board of three army officers and three navy officers submitted such a plan, which won Roosevelt's approval on June 4, 1941.[82] The board's report called for the drafting of legislation that would permit the creation of a censorship office by executive order, and the beginning of army and navy training of personnel for censorship of international messages. The report did not address domestic censorship of the mass media other than an initial "requirement" that journalists cooperate voluntarily.[83] The army and navy moved quickly after receiving Roosevelt's support. On June 19, 1941, the War Department expanded its G-2 intelligence division by creating an office to prepare for censorship of international mail, international land-based telegraph, and communications carried by travelers crossing U.S. borders. Named as the head of the Censorship Branch, as the office became known, was W. Preston Corderman, an army major whom Secretary of War Henry Stimson also designated to be the acting chief postal and wire censor in case of war. Corderman set up a school in the Old Dominion Building in Clarendon, Virginia, where he and infantry captain Gilbert S. Jacobus, who had studied British postal censorship in Bermuda, taught 187 officers and 43 civilians the art of censoring land-based communications. Classes began on August 15, 1941, and ended on September 20. Corderman also drew up a plan for mail censorship that identified prospective postal censorship sites and estimated that 10,000 to 12,000 people would be needed to read the mail entering and leaving the country.[84] In the navy, Commander (and later, Captain) Herbert K. Fenn began plans for cable censorship shortly after Roosevelt had declared a national emergency in September 1939. He picked five officers to help him train censors for control of cable communications outside the United States, and they trained more than 300 reserve officers through December 7, 1941.[85]

In February 1941, *Collier's* magazine examined the possibility of peacetime censorship of the news media to stop what Roosevelt considered "irresponsible" disclosures on military preparedness. Author Walter Davenport noted that the State, Navy, and War Departments wanted immediate censorship of the news. He said the government aimed to use censorship and propaganda to get the country excited about the war

W. Preston Corderman, right, and Byron Price, left. Corderman trained postal censors in the summer of 1941 and then directed the Postal Division of the Office of Censorship. Price had authority to censor communications leaving the United States as he saw fit. State Historical Society of Wisconsin, Negative WHi(X3)51976.

in Europe, and predicted that Mellett, director of the Office of Government Reports, would be named censorship director. Journalists should prepare their own censorship plan, Davenport suggested, because otherwise one would be imposed upon them.[86] Mellett sent letters to *Collier's* and prominent newspaper publishers repudiating Davenport's "preposterous dreams," but he did not ask for a published correction.[87]

Davenport may not have been the greatest prognosticator—in June he touted the defenses of "impregnable Pearl Harbor"[88]—but he touched a nerve in his identification of Mellett as the likely censor. Mellett had become a key White House adviser in the previous months, reporting on the attitudes of the public and the press toward Roosevelt's policies, and distributing press releases in response. His background as former editor of the *Washington Daily News* and *Collier's,* along with his job in press relations, made him a logical candidate to be chief censor. But he was disliked. White House reporters considered him too aloof, too scholarly, and too much of a New Deal cheerleader to rule objectively on censorship questions.[89] A congressional committee examining the Office of Government Reports' proposed budget on February 26 took the opportunity to question Mellett closely, seeking evidence that he planned to turn his office into a censorship agency. The committee voted along party lines to keep his office operating, but only after he assured its members that the Roosevelt administration had "absolutely no plans" to censor the news media in peace or war.[90]

Nevertheless, in the summer and fall of 1941, Roosevelt attempted to consolidate his administration's various plans for the censorship of the news media. His publicized statements on the need to avoid a compulsory domestic censorship of news were in conflict with the army's and navy's concerns that too much information about America's defenses was leaking to the Axis powers. After the president had approved the joint board's report on June 4, army and navy officers had drafted a censorship bill that emphasized military administration. Attorney General Biddle had given an unfavorable opinion of the bill to the War and Navy Departments, arguing for the superiority of civilian-run censorship. When the draft of the army-navy bill was discussed at a cabinet meeting on November 7, Roosevelt appointed an ad hoc committee to study the issue and report to him. The group was comprised of Walker, the postmaster general, who served as chairman; Archibald MacLeish, the director of the Office of Facts and Figures, a government publicity agency; Biddle; and representatives of the Treasury, Navy, and War Departments.[91]

The group quickly polarized over the central issue of ultimate authority. At the committee's first meeting, representatives of the War and Navy Departments argued for a news media censorship organization staffed by officers and filled with employees drawn from the reserves. The navy, the nation's first line of defense against overseas powers and therefore the more immediately vulnerable of the two armed forces, also pressed for "full censorship" as soon as possible. The Justice Department, under Biddle's civil libertarian leadership, and the Treasury Department opposed the army-navy proposal as being too strict. Morganthau had told Knox on October 30 that any censorship organization ought to be staffed and controlled chiefly by civilians. In addition, Biddle believed that Congress was not ready to pass a compulsory censorship bill during peacetime.[92] Biddle wrote in his private diary, in a cramped, telegraphic style, that he suggested to Roosevelt, "no bill now, ultimate control in civilian, preferably newspaper man."[93]

The ad hoc committee considered three possibilities in November: complete news media censorship after a declaration of war, complete news media censorship without delay, or an immediate form of censorship that inspected information in the media but did not delete anything objectionable. "The first possibility does not meet the present need, but the subordinates of all the Departments considering the matter agree that it is desirable," Treasury Department lawyer Edward Foley wrote in a memorandum to Morganthau. He said the second possibility, immediate and complete censorship, "is considered desirable, but it is alleged by Justice that it is not politically feasible at the present time." That left the third choice, which the Justice Department wrote into a draft of a bill that would let the president adopt any system of censorship he desired and later make changes without consulting Congress.[94] It would give Roosevelt considerable room to shape prewar or wartime censorship in response to rapidly changing foreign events.

WARTIME CENSORSHIP BEGINS

The Japanese attack on Pearl Harbor on December 7 transformed censorship from a proposal to a pressing necessity. Hawaii was placed under martial law, and within the week the islands' press and radio were subjected to licensing and censorship. The damage to the Pacific Fleet was considered so devastating that military censorship quickly silenced communications out of Hawaii to protect morale and prevent the Japanese from learning the full extent of the destruction. The Office of Naval Intelligence cut off a United Press reporter's radiotelephone call from Honolulu to San Francisco shortly after the Japanese planes that bombed Pearl Harbor had begun returning to their aircraft carriers.[95] The army initiated its own censorship the next day, when Stimson ordered officers to listen in and, if necessary, cut off communications carried by international telephone and telegraph wires. Telephone and telegraph companies immediately began setting up the necessary equipment to route calls through the army censors' offices.[96] Radio stations in California, Oregon, Washington, and Idaho cooperated with the requests of the FCC and the army's Eighth Air Interceptor Command and went off the air at 5 P.M. on Monday, December 8, out of fears that their signals could act as homing beacons for enemy planes. They were permitted to air one-minute news flashes every fifteen minutes until midnight, when they shut down until 9:30 A.M. Tuesday and then were permitted five-minute newscasts every half hour. Normal broadcast routines resumed on Friday.[97]

Roosevelt set the tone for the news coverage of the war in which America suddenly found itself. He told reporters at a press conference on December 9 that he placed two conditions on news stories about the war: they must be accurate, and not help the enemy. The journalists asked for instructions on how they could be sure their stories would pass both tests. The president suggested that accuracy should be verified at the highest levels—"We can't leave that determination in the hands of a third assistant . . . captain or major in the Army"—and that the army and navy would decide what gave aid and comfort to the enemy.[98] In a fireside chat that week to a nationwide radio audience, Roosevelt asked listeners to question the truth of any news story that lacked an identified, official source. He then addressed the nation's journalists directly: "If you feel that your Government is not disclosing enough of the truth, you have every right to say so. But—in the absence of all the facts, as revealed by official sources—you have no right in the ethics of patriotism to deal out unconfirmed reports in such a way as to make people believe that they are the gospel truth."[99]

While urging the news media and the public to beware of rumors, Roosevelt also had begun preparing to keep sensitive facts from the enemy. At a cabinet meeting that Roosevelt called at 8:30 P.M. on December 7, Biddle suggested that FBI director J. Edgar Hoover be given temporary control of censorship.[100] Roosevelt agreed and gave Hoover oral instructions to keep reporters from revealing any military secrets. He then sent memos notifying his cabinet of the temporary appointment.[101]

Hoover called a meeting on December 8 of officials from the State, War, Navy, Justice, and Post Office Departments, as well as the Office of Facts and Figures and the FCC. When the group met, Hoover divided it to attack two separate problems—one to shape censorship policy, and the other to act as a "clearing pool" to receive information and make immediate decisions about its release. The first group, which Hoover called the Policy and Principles Committee, was headed by MacLeish and included Hoover.[102] In its first meeting, the policy committee discussed problems that should be addressed by censorship. On December 9, Hoover sent Roosevelt a list of subjects, compiled by the committee, that he said should be banned altogether from international communications, including news of Allied shipping, troop movements, munitions production, and economic matters that would benefit the enemy.[103] The committee also recommended federal background investigations of all radio station employees who were "Axis aliens." It endorsed German- and Italian-language broadcasts as an asset to national defense but said they should be monitored by the FCC. The committee also urged an end to Japanese-language programs on the radio, without noting for the record why the language of one enemy posed a greater threat than the language of two others. The three American radio stations that carried Japanese-language broadcasts dropped them voluntarily in the weeks after December 7, and the Japanese language remained off the air for the remainder of the war.[104] The FBI and the Radio Intelligence Division of the FCC began monitoring the airwaves for transmissions from enemy agents. According to historian David Kahn, federal agents found only one "bona-fide Axis station" in the United States during the entire war: The German embassy in Washington, D.C., tried to contact Berlin on December 19, 1941. FCC personnel in radio trucks near the embassy detected the shortwave broadcast and jammed it.[105] However, a history of German espionage based on captured Nazi intelligence documents details other clandestine radio broadcasts that aired after America entered World War II, including a German double agent's apparently undetected shortwave transmissions from Rochester, New York.[106]

The second group formed by Hoover, called the Technical Committee and headed by FBI assistant director Hugh H. Clegg, met frequently after the Japanese attack. Its first major decision was to suggest to Hoover, on December 10, that mail to and from foreign countries be censored at once. Hoover issued the order on the next day, placing responsibility for postal censorship in the War Department. Meanwhile, military censors began arriving at posts that had been designated by the earlier army-navy plans. The first mail censorship office opened in New York City at 2:29 P.M. on December 12. Offices in eight other cities opened on the next day, and federal agents began spot-checking communications carried across the Mexican border one day after that.[107]

Hoover's committee formed a plan for nationwide censorship of press and radio. According to Ralph de Toledano, a Hoover biographer, the FBI director wanted to end his association with censorship to free his organization to catch spies and subversives.[108] When the committee sent Roosevelt its recommendation, it called for the creation of an agency under a civilian administrator who would be shielded from the control of the army, navy, and other government offices.[109]

Washington journalists speculated on whom Roosevelt would select for the monumental task of overseeing all existing censorship as well as extending some form of control to domestic press and radio. Four names were mentioned most often. Mellett still was considered a possibility. So was MacLeish, but he had the same strike against him as

Mellett. His record of publicizing the Roosevelt administration's activities had reporters wondering if he would focus on the public's information requirements rather than the president's political agenda. Also mentioned in the gossip mill were Jonathan Daniels, a newspaperman and contributor to *Fortune* magazine whom Roosevelt had suggested as his choice in a private talk with Biddle in November, and Ulric Bell, who covered Washington for the *Louisville Courier-Journal* and whom Mellett and Harold Ickes, secretary of the interior, had championed in May 1941 as a likely candidate to run a government propaganda office during a national emergency.[110]

In a move that surprised the Washington press corps, the job went to Price, whom Biddle and Walker had recommended to the president at a cabinet meeting on December 12.[111] Mellett, who later became the government's liaison to the motion picture industry, seemed to express sour grapes in a letter to Early shortly after Price's appointment. He said that "Byron, with all his admiration and respect for the President, does not share the President's whole political philosophy," but this did not alter Early's high opinion of Roosevelt's choice.[112] In a letter to Kent Cooper, general manager of the Associated Press, Early called Price "ideal" for the job.[113]

Price got a hint of his nomination when the phone rang in his New York City apartment at 10:30 P.M. on December 12, shortly after he had returned home with his wife from seeing a movie. An Associated Press editor read him the text of a telegram that had arrived at the news desk during the dinner hour. In it, Walker asked Price to meet him and Biddle the next day in Washington. Price had heard rumors that week that he would be asked about his availability for government service, so the summons was not unexpected. He was inclined to agree to whatever was asked, having been a soldier in World War I and knowing the importance of duty in wartime. In meetings with Price on the afternoon of December 13, Walker, Mellett, Early, and Biddle confirmed that Roosevelt wanted Price to direct the nation's censorship during the war. Price recorded in his memoir that before he made a decision, he wanted the answers to three questions: Who would be his boss? How much would he be insulated from outside interference in censorship decisions? Did Roosevelt expect voluntary censorship to continue? The responses were heartening. The chief censor was to have broad powers, unchecked by anyone except the president, who did not want a compulsory system of press and radio censorship. Given these assurances, Price asked for a week to get his affairs in order before beginning his new job.[114]

Price sat in his Associated Press office in New York and typed an announcement while reindeer imported for the Christmas season stomped in the snow of Rockefeller Plaza below his window. When he finished, he sent the statement via airmail, special delivery to Early in Washington. Early placed it in Roosevelt's hands just before the start of his press conference at 4:10 P.M. on December 16.[115] The president glanced at the words, announced off the record that Price was the author, and then read aloud:

All Americans abhor censorship, just as they abhor war. But the experience of this and of all other Nations has demonstrated that some degree of censorship is essential in wartime, and we are at war.

The important thing now is that such forms of censorship as are necessary shall be administered effectively and in harmony with the best interests of our free institutions.

It is necessary to the national security that military information which might be of aid to the enemy be scrupulously withheld at the source.

It is necessary that a watch be set upon our borders, so that no such information may reach the enemy, inadvertently or otherwise, through the medium of the mails, radio, or cable transmission, or by any other means.

It is necessary that prohibitions against the domestic publication of some types of information, contained in long-existing statutes, be rigidly enforced.

Finally, the Government has called upon a patriotic press and radio to abstain voluntarily from the dissemination of detailed information of certain kinds, such as reports of the movements of vessels and troops. The response has indicated a universal desire to cooperate.

In order that all of these parallel and requisite undertakings may be coordinated and carried forward in accordance with a single uniform policy, I have appointed Byron Price, Executive News Editor of the Associated Press, to be Director of Censorship, responsible directly to the President. He has been granted a leave of absence by the Associated Press and will take over the post assigned him within the coming week, or sooner.[116]

When Roosevelt came to Price's title, he mumbled. A reporter asked him to repeat. In a loud voice, Roosevelt said, "Director of Censorship!"[117]

The choice was applauded, as was the candor with which Roosevelt described Price's duties. *Business Week* said Roosevelt "could not have picked a better man."[118] *The Quill* agreed, saying Price enjoyed the confidence of both government officials and journalists.[119] And privately, former president Herbert Hoover told Price, "You could censor me any time and I would know you were right."[120] A rare negative note was sounded in the liberal New York newspaper *PM,* which said Price was unfamiliar to young journalists and as an AP executive had been reluctant to bargain with newspaper unions.[121]

Price's appointment became official on December 19, one day after Congress approved the First War Powers Act, which authorized the president to censor international mail, cable, radio, and other means of cross-border communication.[122] Under the new law, Roosevelt issued Executive Order No. 8985 establishing the Office of Censorship. The order gave Price the power to censor international communications "in his absolute discretion," issue censorship rules, and set up two advisory panels to assist him. The first group, the Censorship Policy Board, served as a sounding board for proposed regulations, such as the takeover of domestic radio. The second, the Censorship Operating Board, was to help Price carry out his task in censoring international communications. Membership was left to Price's discretion, and he filled the roster with representatives from the FBI, State Department, Treasury, army, navy, Post Office Department, and other federal agencies that might be affected by censorship decisions.[123]

Price was sworn in on December 20 in Walker's office by Ugo Carusi, executive assistant to the attorney general. Price told reporters that his first job would be to clear up the "muddle" over voluntary censorship of press and radio.[124] The executive order that established his office had given him no guidelines about the domestic news media, which had been following the various military and government requests as well as their own common sense about national security. Price intended to clarify the issue but did not indicate his specific plans. Since he lacked legal authority to supervise domestic censorship—the War Powers Act addressed only international communications—his reticence was prudent. Price wrote in his wartime notebook that as he took office he realized he stood between two perils. One was the possibility that journalists would revolt against further censorship requests. The other was that other government departments would refuse to cooperate with his new agency and perpetuate the confusing prewar censorship system.[125]

Who was this man facing such serious concerns? Oddly enough for a censor, Price was known for his wit and for playing the role of a baby in the capital's annual Gridiron Show.[126] His unpretentious nature was captured in a newspaper food column when he agreed to pose, hoisting a giant drumstick for a photographer. He recalled for the writer how he had caught and cleaned chickens for the family dinner when he was a boy.[127] His hobbies included poker, which he played badly, and golf, which he played abominably, seldom breaking 100. Other pastimes suggested refinement and patience. He enjoyed growing bearded irises and collecting first editions of books by his favorite authors. He had many works of poetry by E. A. Robinson, fellow Hoosier James Whitcomb Riley, and Walt Whitman, including seven copies of Whitman's *Leaves of Grass*. But Mark Twain was his favorite. Price was a charter member of the Mark Twain Association and had sixty rare editions of Twain's books, many of them autographed. His skill at bridge brought praise from his wife, Priscilla Alden Price, a descendant of the John and Priscilla Aldens of Plymouth Colony.[128]

His family always had expected him to work hard. His father, John Price, and mother, Emaline Barnes, farmed in the northeast corner of Indiana, near the Michigan border. Byron was born March 25, 1891, at home near Topeka, in LaGrange County, and did farm chores before and after school. He had his first experiences in both journalism and censorship while he was a boy. He used leftover bits of slick wrapping paper and a lead pencil to start a newspaper about his family in 1901, but his father eventually stopped him. He edited a monthly periodical at Topeka High School, and attended Wabash College in Crawfordsville, Indiana, paying his way by delivering newspapers. He worked in both the news-editorial and the circulation departments of the *Crawfordsville Journal*, writing stories about Wabash at night and then delivering the papers that contained them to subscribers the next morning. He cooked at the Ben Hur Dairy Lunch, served as janitor for one of the college's buildings, and was secretary to the college president. In his senior year he edited *The Bachelor*, Wabash's twice-weekly newspaper. Shortly after graduating in

1912, he joined the United Press in Chicago for $16 a week. He stayed with the UP for a few months, established a bureau in Omaha, Nebraska, and then leaped to the Atlanta office of the UP's larger competitor, the Associated Press.[129]

Except for two years as an infantry officer in the United States and France during World War I,[130] Price stayed at the wire service for the next twenty-nine years. "Associated Press is a religion with me," Price told the newspaper *PM*. No one could criticize the AP within earshot of Price without eliciting "a flicker of deep hurt," the newspaper said.[131]

Price spent the summer of 1920 in Marion, Ohio, playing nickel-a-point hearts after dark with reporters Raymond Clapper, Samuel W. Bell, and George R. Holmes, along with the publisher of the Marion newspaper, Warren G. Harding, who ran a front-porch campaign as the Republican presidential nominee and was elected in November.[132] He covered the Washington Arms Conference of 1922 and that year became news editor of the AP's capital bureau. Five years later he had risen to the rank of bureau chief, a job that allowed him to write a twice-weekly column, "Politics at Random," and supervise a stable of reporters that included Early and another future Roosevelt aide, William D. Hassett. The prestigious wire service job also gave Price the opportunity to attend eleven national political party conventions as a journalist.[133]

The 1932 Democratic convention gave Price a close look at the political skills of Roosevelt, the New York governor whom the party picked to oppose President Hoover in the fall. Price professed to be apolitical. Still, he admired Roosevelt's skill at establishing rapport with an audience. Price admired his mental agility, his warm style of speaking, and his "almost uncanny" faculty of sensing public sentiment.[134]

Price left Washington in 1937 to become executive news editor of the Associated Press in New York. The job put him in charge of the news produced by the AP and in contact with journalists around the country. His boss, Cooper, gave Price the freedom to try new things. One was Price's announcement that he had terminated all AP rules of writing. His new rule was that as long as stories were accurate, impartial, and free of libel, writers could do nearly anything. "If you can write, write!" Price told the AP's employees.[135]

He was offered a government job early in February 1941, and had he taken it, the experience might have blocked him from becoming director of censorship. Stimson had asked Price to leave the Associated Press and take a post in army public relations during the months when reporters were asked to avoid certain military topics despite the nation's official neutrality. The secretary of war considered Price "a man of high character." In return, Price had special fondness for Stimson, who had helped him weather a storm over an inaccuracy in one of Price's AP stories. Despite their mutual admiration, they could not agree on the scope of Price's duties. Stimson recalled that he wanted someone to be the civilian assistant for publicity under the supervision of an army general, while Price remembered being offered a free hand. After three days of negotiations, Price was told that if he took the job, he would share responsibility for army publicity with a general. "I am afraid I exploded," Price said, recalling his rejection of the offer. "There is no such thing as joint responsibility."[136]

Price favored full responsibility coupled with full authority. Oddly enough, considering Roosevelt's usual preference of dividing authority among subordinates while retaining ultimate control himself, Price had been given both—limited, in theory at least, only by the president's own powers. It is a measure of the man that having received such power, Price chose to let the nation's journalists try to be their own censors.

The Censor Has Written Me
a Very Stern Letter
Establishing Voluntary Censorship

"Kansas City Bombed to Ruins" read the banner headline in the March 2, 1942, edition of the *Kansas City Journal*. "Terror and Death Stalk Throughout Widespread Area. Three Waves of Japanese Bombers Devastate Heart of America." In twenty stories that began beneath the inch-high type, the *Journal* described a surprise attack on the apartment buildings, homes, businesses, factories, warehouses, and public utilities at the center of the nation's breadbasket. Sabotage added to the misery. Enemy agents in boats blew up the intake tower of the municipal water works on the Missouri River. Seconds later, a series of explosions— whether from sabotage or bombs dropped in the air raid, no one could be sure—destroyed the A.S.B., Hannibal, and Milwaukee bridges. The United States Cold Storage building, the largest refrigerated plant west of Chicago, disappeared in a roar. So did the Kansas City Gas Company on Indiana Avenue. Citizens who bought the newspaper knew that it was a fake. They could wander the streets of Kansas City and see nothing but an ordinary, late-winter's day. No bomb craters. No fires. No shrapnel wounds. No loss of pressure in pipes connected to the supposedly ruined water works and blast-vaporized natural gas tank. Besides, news of the destruction began on page 13, not where one would expect to find the news of Armageddon. And, if there still were any doubts, each of the stories ended with the same wake-up call to the city's residents: "It could happen here any day."[1]

Bad taste, perhaps. But that was not what concerned the Office of Censorship, which learned about the *Journal*'s vivid imagination when a reader complained about the stories. John H. Sorrells, assistant director of censorship, wrote the *Journal*'s publisher that "some questions valid to the aims and purposes of this office can be raised about this issue." He did not mention the improbability of Japanese planes striking undetected near the geographic center of the nation. From what base would they stage the raid—Texarkana? Wichita? Aircraft carriers on the Platte River? Instead, he noted that if saboteurs were at large, for the price of a single copy they could learn that Kansas City stored much of the nation's food, produced North American Aviation bombers and Remington arms, and had an unguarded water and gas supply. "No doubt a lot of the above information is common knowledge in your community," Sorrells said in the letter, one of 1,065 sent to publications that violated the voluntary censorship code in 1942. "But this information is pointed up in a way to illustrate the strategic value. . . . In the aggregate, doesn't this constitute a pretty clear blueprint for sabotage?"[2]

He did not ask for a reply, and if publisher Harry Newman bothered to make one, it did not find its way into the fat folders of correspondence between the Office of Censorship's Press Division and the nation's newspapers and magazines. In the end, it did not matter. The *Journal* quietly died on March 31 after eighty-eight years of publication, driven out of business by the dominance of the rival *Kansas City Star,* the mounting costs of production, and an unpaid bill of $216,000 for newsprint.[3] Perhaps it had hoped that sensationalism would prolong its survival and that the paper's fanciful report on Kansas City's demise would ward off its own.

The voluntary censorship code that Sorrells accused the *Journal* of compromising was an imperfect document imperfectly followed. It was issued on January 15, 1942, to give guidance to the nation's newspapers, magazines, and radio stations on how to avoid publishing or broadcasting news that would help the enemy during the war. The code required four substantial revisions and was supplemented by dozens of memoranda on specific issues that had not been foreseen. Journalists often stumbled in trying to follow its suggestions. About 7,000 complaints of possible code violations filled a Press Division file folder of 200 single-spaced pages ending with one by the *Paris (Kentucky) Daily Enterprise* on June 28, 1944.[4] There is no indication why the folder's list stopped in mid-1944, for code violations continued until the end of the war thirteen and a half months later. Despite the many revisions that kept the code in flux, and despite its many violations, an examination of the records of the

Office of Censorship and the private notes of its director, Byron Price, reveals an amazing record of compliance. No print journalist and only one broadcast journalist ever deliberately defied the code, after having been told the reasons for its provisions.

Most surprising, perhaps, is that the Office of Censorship obtained such obedience through a voluntary agreement. The codes asked the nation's journalists to censor themselves and provided guidelines to help them. Civilian censors could cajole, suggest, argue, and threaten but had no authority to punish beyond publicizing the names of violators. They did not need such power. The vast majority of journalists endorsed the codes as well as the administration of them. Price and his assistants get much of the credit for shaping this attitude. Beginning shortly after the first codebooks were issued, they answered questions about the code and offered suggestions in a swift, evenhanded manner that encouraged cooperation. During 1942, the Press Division fielded 7,814 questions from journalists before they published items that might transgress the code, and in each case the inquiring journalist complied with the censors' requests.[5]

Censorship's early months were disorganized and sometimes difficult, which was to be expected for a newly created government agency seeking to administer a nationwide program. However, by the end of 1942, the Office of Censorship had proved itself successful. It had established a pattern of compliance, cemented a respectful relationship with the press, and weathered its first major crises over the possibility of failure. After such a strong beginning, successful censorship continued forward on its own inertia.

America's rush into the war gave Price little time to develop a detailed censorship plan. That proved to be a blessing, he wrote in his unpublished memoir. In the winter of 1941–42, he had to answer questions and solve problems quickly, and he fell back on common sense. In the week before Christmas, he had barely settled into his first headquarters, a borrowed room next door to the postmaster general's office, before the Department of Agriculture phoned with a request for his first ruling as censorship director. Would he give his approval for the release of a crop report? He replied that the caller must have a wrong number, for he was no expert on food policy. Government officials were in the best position to know what news about their departments would benefit the enemy, he said, and they should make their own decisions about releasing it. His first major challenge came soon afterward, and it presaged the difficult task of mediating the views of press and government. On his first day of work, he chatted with President Franklin Roosevelt about the general need for censorship, left the White House, and was startled a short while later when Attorney General Francis Biddle gave him a warning. "The boss is not clear in his mind about all of this," Biddle said. "He seems to think he has some mandatory power to control the press in spite of the fact that I have told him he has none. We may get into difficulties about this."[6] Biddle had reached that conclusion at a cabinet meeting on December 19, after which he noted privately that Roosevelt seemed to believe that Price would censor newspapers before publication. In fact, Biddle wrote, not even the president had that power. His notes did not say whether he had tried to explain that the Espionage Act imposed penalties only after publication, and then only for stories narrowly defined as assisting the enemy or harming America's war effort.[7]

Biddle's warning to Price proved prophetic. Thirty-six hours after their conversation, Price was awakened by his hotel room phone. On the other end of the line was presidential press secretary Stephen T. Early, who said British prime minister Winston Churchill was about to arrive in Washington to confer with Roosevelt. Earlier that night, radio station WOL in Washington, D.C., had hinted that Churchill would meet with Roosevelt within twenty-four hours, but the information apparently was not picked up by other news media.[8] However, the president had learned that the *New York Times* was preparing a story about Churchill's scheduled arrival and wanted Price "to order the *Times* to print nothing," Early said. Price asked for clarification. Did Roosevelt really use the word "order," he asked? Early chuckled and replied, "That's what he said." Price called the *Times,* which indeed had the details of Churchill's trip to the Unites States on the battleship *Duke of York.* The editors told him they had no plans for immediate publication because of the possible security risk. He then took the precaution of phoning the Associated Press, the United Press, and the International News Service to ask them to look for any leak of the Churchill story. Nearly every newspaper in the country subscribed to a wire service, and therefore one of the three ought to know if the story was published somewhere. All agreed to help. Although many reporters had heard rumors about Churchill's trip, Early had asked them not to speculate, and the story was not published until after the White House issued a press release at 7 P.M. on December 22.[9]

Price's decisions involving the Agriculture Department and the *Times* contained the seeds of two key elements of the administration of voluntary domestic censorship. First was his willingness to let government and military officials decide for themselves what information under their jurisdiction might benefit the enemy, whether it concerned foodstuffs or a foreign dignitary's visit. Out of this trust grew a censorship doctrine called "appropriate authority," allowing government and military officials to release any information in their areas of expertise without interference from the Office of Censorship. Price's endorsement of authority simplified his work, for without it he would have had to create a broad bureaucracy of censors to act as second-guessers. It also reflected his trust in official sources, just as his confidential talk with the *Times* and the wire services reflected his trust in journalists.

Censorship had to produce confidence, both in the government and in the news media, in order to be effective. The office's internal history, produced in the fall of 1945, said, "We had always on the one hand the possibility that some powerful government department would lose faith in the virility of our program and would initiate a broad-gauge censorship crusade on its own account in a zealous effort to fill the gap. We had always on the other hand the possibility that some individual newspaper or magazine, or group, would lose faith in our honest intentions and our reasonableness and would decline to have any part in the experiment." Price's trust-based approach to his first two issues as director began a pattern for the administration of voluntary censorship of press and radio. As he began working on regulations for domestic censorship, he kept the importance of trust in mind. He wanted a system in which no government agency would have a right to make unreasonable requests, and publications would be willing to follow any requests that could be defended as reasonable.[10]

During his first two weeks in office, Price sought advice on censorship from the army, navy, FBI, Weather Bureau, War Production Board, Maritime Commission, and other government agencies.[11] On December 23, he convened the first meeting of the Censorship Policy Board in the office of its chairman, Postmaster General Frank C. Walker. The board's powers were merely advisory and not well defined under the executive order that founded the Office of Censorship. Walker told Price, "I don't know what the Policy Board is for, but you can be sure that it never will meet unless you ask it to."[12] The board discussed censorship in broad terms and gave Price a free hand in shaping its organization. Roosevelt also kept his distance from Price's decision making. Although the president asked Early on January 26 to schedule a chat with Price, more pressing business evidently intervened and efforts to arrange a private meeting were dropped after four months.[13]

Price split the Office of Censorship into six divisions: Postal, Cable, Press, Broadcasting, Reports, and Administration.

As a result of the army's and navy's prewar training, the Postal and Cable Divisions already were operating, albeit understaffed. Postal censorship, run by W. Preston Corderman and a small staff of army officers, examined printed matter entering and leaving the country.[14] The Cable Division, led by Herbert K. Fenn and staffed by naval reserve officers, censored cables, telegrams, radiograms, and telephone calls across the borders. Price had the option of taking over these operations and placing civilians in charge, but he decided it was wiser to retain Corderman's and Fenn's trained staffs, which soon became supplemented with civilian recruits. The two divisions' army and navy employees formally were transferred to the Office of Censorship on March 15, 1942.[15]

The Reports Division collected and distributed military information of benefit to the Allies that had been intercepted by the cable and postal stations or shared by the British and Canadian censors. The Administration Division oversaw personnel and budgets.[16] An additional, secret, division of censorship soon began supplementing the work of the other branches. Hiding behind a name chosen intentionally to be bland and nondescript, the Technical Operations Division searched for clues to the identity of spies. Led by Colonel Harold R. Shaw, the division supervised the efforts of postal and cable censors to unearth hidden messages in ordinary-looking communications.[17]

The Press and Broadcasting Divisions were by far the smallest. Each had a staff of sixteen at the end of 1942, compared with more than 3,000 workers in the Cable Division and more than 10,000 in the Postal Division.[18] Despite the small size of the radio and press staffs, Price gave them most of his attention during his first weeks in office because while voluntary censorship of press and radio had been discussed before the war, it had never been organized.

Complicating Price's task was the lack of clear instructions from the president as well as confusion among federal agencies on the Office of Censorship's role. Several public relations officers in government departments sent Price drafts of proposals announcing that his office would take control of their publicity apparatus. But Price had decided after his first weekend in office not to combine publicity and censorship. He returned the proposals with a note that he would not censor the government. He did not want the responsibility. Also, he feared that it would prove difficult to separate publicity from propaganda, which he believed had compromised George Creel's work in World War I. Censorship's reputation and effectiveness "should not be jeopardized or weakened by involvement with propaganda," an administrative report on the Office of Censorship said after the war.[19]

Price had concerns about fairness in mind when he chose his assistant to run the Press Division. He picked the executive editor of Scripps-Howard Newspapers, a nationwide chain that owned the United Press news service. Since the UP's main rival was Price's Associated Press, the choice balanced the office's leadership.

Sorrells, a forty-five-year-old native of Pine Bluff, Arkansas, had spent his entire career in newspaper work. After playing football at Washington and Lee University and serving in World War I, Sorrells returned to Pine Bluff, where he became the city's newspaper editor. He worked at papers in Oklahoma, Ohio, Tennessee, and Texas before becoming president and publisher of the *Memphis Commercial Appeal* in 1936. He was filling those jobs and the executive editor's position at Scripps-Howard, which he had assumed in 1930, when Price asked him to join the Office of Censorship. His extensive professional background in all aspects of newspaper production helped him understand the concerns of publications operating under the code, but no less important in winning cooperation was his personality—part metropolitan suave and part country boy, suggested by the polka-dot bow tie he wore for a formal portrait. He put generals and admirals at ease.[20]

Price had little knowledge of radio and wanted help in picking a broadcasting aide who commanded respect. He turned over the problem to the directors of five of the nation's radio trade associations, including the National Independent Broadcasters, a group of non-network stations led by interim president George B. Storer. The associations were meeting on December 22 and 23, 1941, at the Mayflower Hotel in Washington to consider the industry's wartime problems. They accepted Price's invitation to visit his temporary office to hear his pitch for voluntary censorship. He then asked them to deliberate until they had a candidate.[21]

They emerged with a unanimous endorsement for Storer's brother-in-law, a man whom Price had never met. Price did not hesitate to offer the job to J. Harold Ryan, who accepted over the phone from his home in Toledo. Like Price, Ryan had an excellent memory, played a crackerjack game of bridge, and collected first-edition books. The fifty-six-year-old Phi Beta Kappa graduate of Yale University was general manager and cofounder of the Toledo-based Fort Industries, which owned five radio stations. Fort, in turn, was owned by Storer. The two men had started their company in 1928 as a cut-rate gasoline service. Storer had the idea to open filling stations at railroad sidings, where gasoline could be delivered cheaply in tank cars and sold at a discount. Storer and Ryan bought radio airtime to promote the venture, which proved so successful that Storer purchased station WTAL. From there, Fort Industries blossomed and eventually became Storer Broadcasting.[22]

Price, Sorrells, and Ryan were joined by Theodore F. Koop, director of the *National Geographic* news service and onetime news editor on Price's Associated Press staff in Washington. On Christmas Day, Price invited him to join his staff, and he became Price's special assistant four days later. Koop began by answering a stack of mail, including many public requests for strict censorship.[23]

CREATION OF THE RADIO AND PRINT CODEBOOKS

Price, Sorrells, and Ryan drew up codebooks for voluntary censorship. The codebooks' principles had come from Roosevelt's executive order, which said that censorship must be an instrument of war, be administered effectively, and be in harmony "with the best interests of our free institutions."[24] Meeting the requirement of effectiveness was difficult because the law that established the Office of Censorship said nothing about domestic control of press and radio. The lack was apparently not an oversight, Sorrells told a curious editor. "Since it is a voluntary censorship, it probably was not necessary to include it in the executive order," he said.[25] Price, Sorrells, and Ryan focused on the need for national security as a guideline for shaping the code. They reviewed Creel's original code from World War I, and then edited and updated it after consultation with government and military officials, thus giving the code a gloss of approval from the White House and armed services.[26]

Creation of the codes was guided by the censorship office's desire to be as comprehensive as possible, tempered by the need for haste. Newspapers and radio stations needed guidance before America's combat role escalated. Sometime in January 1942, Price looked across a desk and told Sorrells, "We can't let this go on forever; let's go to press." Sorrells replied "Right," and put on his hat to carry the press and broadcasting codebooks to the Government Printing Office.[27] Publication was delayed briefly until Sorrells and Price promised to get legal authority in writing for their voluntary domestic censorship plan. Twelve days after the publication date, Roosevelt made good on that pledge. He sent Price a letter on January 27 that closed a loophole in the First War Powers Act and Executive Order 8985 by specifying the Office of Censorship's duty "to coordinate the efforts of the domestic press and radio in voluntarily withholding from publication military and other information which should not be released in the interest of the effective prosecution of the war."[28]

On January 15, the day 50,000 copies of the codebooks were published, Sorrells's first assistant joined the Press Division staff. When Nathaniel R. Howard, a Columbus, Ohio, native who had been granted a leave from his job as editor of the *Cleveland News*, arrived at the Office of Censorship's new headquarters at the Federal Trade Commission Building, Price explained his plans for voluntary censorship based on common-sense rules. Howard leaned against a door frame until Price had finished speaking. He then joked that before the war was finished, "the only ones who will be against us will be the newspaper and radio people, the Military and the rest of the government, and the general public."[29]

The *Code of Wartime Practices for American Broadcasters* was two pages longer than the five-page *Code of Wartime Practices for the American Press*. The extra pages addressed issues unique to the swiftness with which radio signals disseminated information. Radio stations were asked not to broadcast current weather conditions or unauthorized forecasts, either of which might help enemy naval officers in planning attacks on ships and coastal installations. In addition, the radio code urged an end to unscripted programs in which the public had access to microphones, because of the risk that the citizens unfamiliar with the code would violate it accidentally, or that spies and saboteurs would broadcast secret messages.[30]

The codebooks' introduction asked journalists to use common sense and follow a rule of thumb. They should ask themselves, "Is this information I would like to have if I were the enemy?" and act accordingly. The press code then described eight categories of news to avoid: troops, ships, planes, fortifications, production, weather, photographs and maps, and a "general" category that included instructions on casualty lists and the travels of the president.

First on the list, and perhaps the most sensitive topic, was the clause on troops. It included the location, movements, and composition of army, navy, and marine units inside and outside the United States but did not apply to troops in training camps.

Second, the ships clause applied the same injunction to all movements of U.S. naval and merchant ships, and to enemy ships in or near American waters. The regulations extended to ships under construction and their launch dates.

Third, the clause on planes applied to news about the disposition, movements, and strength of army and navy aircraft.

Fourth, the fortifications clause included the location of forts, bomb shelters, antiaircraft guns, and other defenses.

Fifth, the production clause asked for a ban on specific information about war contracts, including the type of production, schedules, and dates of delivery, plus estimated supplies of strategic materials, and other factory information that would aid saboteurs.

Sixth, the weather clause asked newspapers to avoid forecasts other than those officially issued by the U.S. Weather Bureau. Routine forecasts printed by any single paper were to be limited to the state of publication and not more than four adjoining states, if those states were within a radius of 150 miles of the publication site. News of current conditions was limited to one state.

Seventh, the code asked for restrictions on pictures and maps that revealed sensitive information covered by the code.

Finally, a general roundup included requests for no news about the location of national archives and art treasures; the movements of the commander in chief; the transportation of munitions of war; and enemy propaganda reprinted without careful attribution. It raised no objection to publication of casualty information from a newspaper's "local field," which it did not define, but urged that exact information about military units and locations be omitted from such stories.[31]

The code placed the burden of censorship on journalists themselves. Two clauses were inserted to give them guidance. One encouraged journalists to contact the Office of Censorship if they had questions about the code or wished to challenge any "unreasonable" restrictions on their reporting the news. As censorship director, Price could instruct the press and radio to ignore officials' domestic censorship requests that ran counter to the code, except for those that came from the president.[32] The other clause, set in italics, said journalists could publish any story officially released by an appropriate authority, regardless of whether it violated the code. The clause had a huge impact. Journalists who wanted to publish or broadcast information that might hurt the Allied war effort had to find an official source to release it, and this restriction helped combat the spread of unattributed wartime rumors and helped reduce recklessness. Conversely, sources had to agree to take responsibility for the news they released, which promoted caution and restraint—or, in a worst-case scenario that Price hoped to avoid, might silence justified criticism of military inefficiency or decision making. A reporter for the *Buffalo Evening News* quickly noted that the members of Congress, whose speeches on the floor of the House and Senate were constitutionally protected, were "531 holes in the code," but Price said few lawmakers abused the code once they were held accountable for the information they released.[33] Speaker of the House Sam Rayburn authorized a code violation in April 1942 when he responded to war mobilization critics at the *Dallas Morning News* by revealing that the nation was producing 3,300 airplanes a month. *Time* magazine said reporters had known the figure but had refrained from publishing it until Rayburn released it.[34]

The codes lacked a requirement that only truthful information be broadcast or published. Accuracy often is difficult to assess, especially in news analysis, and demanding it would have been suicidal for a voluntary censorship system built on cooperation. The Office of Censorship sometimes told journalists that official sources had expressed doubts about a story's veracity, but if the story did not violate the code it offered no objection. The code also made no mention of published or broadcast opinions. When confronted with depressing news and caustic editorials, the censors followed Price's instructions that in a democracy the people are best able to judge what to believe and how to react to it.[35]

Price recalled after the war that Roosevelt hoped his critics in the press would be punished, although the president never suggested that he favored amending the code to silence opinions. However, Price said the president did not discourage his assistants who wanted to find a way to punish the *Chicago Tribune,* one of the papers most critical of the Roosevelt administration. While Price was out of town on April 16, 1942, Archibald MacLeish of the Office of Facts and Figures suggested to Sorrells that a clause on criticism be inserted into the code or placed in a congressional bill. Sorrells responded that nothing would be more likely to destroy voluntary censorship than abridging an American's right to express an opinion. He said that any proposed law would fail after a fight that would make the 1937 Supreme Court reorganization conflict, in which Roosevelt tried to pack the court with his supporters, "look like a pink tea party." When Price returned, Sorrells told him that MacLeish wanted to discuss the matter with him personally, but he never did so. Restrictions on opinions stayed out of the code.[36]

Price also decided that because the purpose of censorship was to deny information to the enemy, he would permit domestic publication or broadcast of nearly any story that originated overseas and thus was available to the Axis powers. Early in the war, he said that the Office of Censorship should not create rigid rules defining which newspapers could print a story and which could not. In response to an army request in mid-1942 that news of defense production contracts be authorized for publication only in the contractor's city, Price said, "You could no more publish a story in Minneapolis and expect it to be kept out of publication in St. Paul than you could have a foot of water in one corner of a room and expect the opposite corner to be dry."[37] He preferred a more general rule that allowed newspapers to print information about defense work that was readily apparent to their readers but asked them to avoid specifics that might help saboteurs.[38]

The codebooks did not affect military censorship in the combat zones. Journalists could not travel on a navy ship or visit territory under army control unless they were accredited, and to get accreditation they had to sign an agreement to submit all of their stories to army or navy censorship. The Office of Censorship joined the navy, army, and State Department in issuing a May 29, 1942, memorandum that said each correspondent in a war zone was subject to the censorship rules of the theater commander. Army and navy censorship in the combat zones varied according to the commander's personality. In the Pacific, the image-conscious General Douglas MacArthur threatened to expel reporters who did not get permission to conduct interviews, but in Europe and North Africa, General Dwight D. Eisenhower gave journalists far more freedom, treating them as quasi staff officers.[39] The censorship memo merely affirmed a policy that Price had followed since taking office. In January, for example, he had objected to the *New York Daily News*'s attempt to print details of the damage to the fleet at Pearl Harbor. After reporter John O'Donnell and publisher Joseph Patterson had examined the wreckage in Hawaii that month, O'Donnell submitted several stories to the Press Division. Price looked at them and asked O'Donnell if he recalled signing a commitment to submit his dispatches to the army or navy. He was not sure, so Price inquired and verified that the reporter had signed the standard forms. Meanwhile, Patterson was constantly press-

ing O'Donnell to get his story released. To explain the binding commitment, Price wrote a letter for O'Donnell to give to Patterson. "The authority of the Office of Censorship does not extend to dispatches from
combat zones," he said. "Under the law and the regulations, the Army
and Navy do their own censoring both of news and other dispatches
in those zones." In signing his accreditation forms, O'Donnell had "assumed an obligation to the War Department which I do not see how
you can honestly escape."[40] O'Donnell submitted his articles to military
censors, who deleted nearly all of the news that had been previously unpublished.

At a January 1942 news conference after publication of the codebooks,
Price said that "ninety-nine and ninety-nine hundredths percent" of the
nation's newspapers and radio stations approved of voluntary censorship. If the rest opposed it, "we will just have to cope with the situation
as it arises," he said. The code did not specify actions that would be taken
against violators, and Price seemed reluctant to explore that subject with
reporters. "We are not crossing that bridge until we come to it—if we do
come to it," he said. "There are bound to be slips and inadvertencies. No
one can avoid these. But as for defiance of the code, I doubt if we will
come to that."[41]

He was more forthcoming when pressed for clarification in a radio
interview three days later. In a roundtable discussion sponsored by the
University of Chicago, Price said he assumed that the Justice Department, "which is supposed to do the enforcing," would carry out the Espionage Act if it ever became necessary to do so. "We are not telling the
newspapers what to print or the radio stations what to broadcast. We
originate no news," he said.[42]

The *New York Times* called the code "sensible" and said that if properly
observed it would keep military secrets from the enemy while not in-
fringing upon the freedom of the press. The paper argued, however, that
common sense required identical rules for press and radio because border
censorship could not keep published secrets from leaving the country,
just as borders could not contain radio waves. It did not specify whether
the radio code should be eased or the press code strengthened.[43] *Editor &
Publisher* said the rules would not impose hardships if everyone obeyed
them, and that all journalists were disposed toward cooperating with
the government.[44] That contention seemed to be borne out two weeks
later when the magazine reported that the Virginia Press Association had

endorsed the code and expressed its willingness "to invoke further self-censorship restrictions that may become necessary in the interests of the nation's safety."[45] CBS hailed the radio code as "reasonable and intelligent." NBC said it would have a "salutary effect" on small stations that had overlooked the importance of common-sense censorship.[46]

"MISSIONARIES" AND JUDGMENTS

Price and Sorrells invited representatives from five newspaper associations to counsel the Press Division and to help instruct newspapers, magazines, and other publications about compliance with the code. The group called itself the Editorial Advisory Board, and its initial members were Cranston Williams, general manager of the American Newspaper Publishers Association; W. L. Daley, Washington representative of the National Editorial Association; John W. Potter, acting president of the Inland Press Association; Charles P. Manship Sr., president of the Southern Newspaper Publishers Association; and Dwight Marvin, president of the American Society of Newspaper Editors (ASNE).[47] The board met on February 26, 1942, and its first action was to urge Price to ask the press to downplay stories about prisoner-of-war broadcasts from Japan, which he did the next day. The members also decided to use their newspaper associations to informally ask editors to beware of the danger of coded messages being placed in classified ads. The board grew to have as many as thirteen members during the war and met seven times to give the Press Division advice on censorship problems.[48] Between meetings, Williams helped the Press Division by distributing censorship bulletins to the nation's daily newspapers through the newsletter of the American Newspaper Publishers Association.[49]

Price asked the board to consider the wisdom of opening regional censorship offices. The California Newspaper Publishers Association, meeting on April 30, 1942, urged the creation of a San Francisco branch, and the *Hartford (Connecticut) Times* endorsed having regional offices throughout the country. However, the board rejected the idea on May 14. The Washington office could be reached at any hour by telephone or telegraph and thus was readily accessible. In addition, there were concerns that expanding the bureaucracy might lead to different branches rendering different decisions. Besides, the advisory board already had endorsed its own alternative for disseminating censorship information throughout the country. On February 26, it had asked the Press Division to teach a class on the censorship code to a group of editors and publishers, who would act informally as liaisons to small papers in their regions.[50]

The first class met on April 14 and 15, 1942, in Washington. Its members, whom the nation's publishers' and editors' associations had helped select, received a colorful nickname when Price thanked them for volunteering. "I look on you as 'missionaries,' with the mission of helping to get this thing straightened out as best you can in your communities," he said. The members totaled forty—two from Minnesota, Michigan, Illinois, and one from most other states.[51]

On the first day of class, Chairman Donald Nelson of the War Production Board, General Alexander D. Surles of the War Department's public relations office, and two navy public relations officers, Admiral Arthur J. Hepburn and Lieutenant Commander Paul Smith, gave off-the-record briefings on the need for censorship.[52] The missionary from Louisiana, managing editor George W. Healy Jr. of the *New Orleans Times-Picayune*, wrote in his autobiography that the group saw films of the damage at Pearl Harbor.[53] Missionaries also heard Sorrells, Price, Howard, and Ryan talk informally about the voluntary code, which Price called the heart of wartime censorship. "We are not naive enough to suppose we could ever have a 100 per cent effective border censorship. . . . The only effective way to keep information from the enemy is to keep it from circulation at home," he said. In particular he urged greater vigilance in enforcing the code's production clause, which he said had been violated too often by newspapers quoting boastful contractors and chamber of commerce officials.[54]

When the missionaries returned home, they helped spread censorship information in many ways. Healy recalled that his territory was several states in the Deep South, although he did not specify them. He visited and wrote hundreds of editors and broadcasters who had questions about the codebooks. "When provisions of the code were explained, no editor of my acquaintance questioned a single clause," he said.[55] Tom Keene, the missionary who published *The Truth* in Elkhart, Indiana, performed a special service for the Office of Censorship in the fall of 1942. The aircraft carrier *Wasp* sank on September 15 in the Southwest Pacific, after Japanese torpedoes hit amidships and touched off the magazine. The navy wanted to keep secret the ship's sinking, believing that the attackers might not have remained long enough to verify the kill. The sinking still had not been announced by October, when sailors who

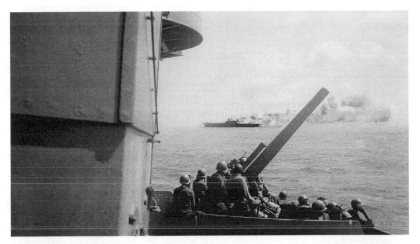

USS Wasp, *background. The sinking of the aircraft carrier* Wasp *was considered a naval secret in late 1942. A censorship "missionary," an unofficial liaison who promoted "the gospel" of voluntary censorship, in Indiana helped smother a news story published in a weekly paper that had interviewed survivors of the sinking.* National Archives.

survived the disaster returned to the States. Two of them, Estel McKim and Chester Hall of Clark Township, Indiana, gave an interview to their hometown paper, the *Tell City News,* describing the *Wasp*'s destruction and their rescue. On October 30, the paper printed the story under a banner headline about the "ill-fated Wasp." [56] The Office of Censorship called on Keene to try to prevent other papers from reprinting the story and having it spread eventually to radio. Keene in turn explained the problem to editors in nearby towns. At least four daily newspapers knew about the *Wasp* story in the Tell City paper before being contacted by Keene or phoning the Office of Censorship directly to inquire about it. None reprinted it.[57]

One of the most practical missionaries in encouraging code compliance was Charles M. Meredith, the publisher of the *Quakertown (Pennsylvania) Free Press.* In the summer of 1943, Meredith sent galley proofs of stories supporting voluntary censorship to all of the papers in Pennsylvania. Editors could easily drop them into their pages to explain to their readers why some of the wartime news stories seemed incomplete. One of Meredith's stories, headlined "One Simple Fact Was All That Was Needed," told of a sailor who refused to disclose naval secrets while he was home on leave.[58]

The Office of Censorship asked the missionaries in the summer of

1942 to bring small, weekly newspapers into compliance with the code.[59] Rural papers were the most common violators for three reasons. First, small weeklies were less well organized than metropolitan papers, which usually belonged to national associations such as the ones represented on Price's Editorial Advisory Board. Thus, small papers had fewer contacts with nationally prominent journalists who were knowledgeable about the code. Second, like the larger papers, weekly publications were inundated with mail from agencies in Washington, but the small papers did not have a staff large enough to digest the material. As a result, they may not have read, or thoroughly read, the codebooks.[60] Third, some small-town editors distrusted anything that smacked of federal bureaucracy. One missionary, whom Price identified only as "Bill," reported that one stubborn, small-town editor chose to ignore the Office of Censorship's registered letters because she hated President Roosevelt. The missionary, possibly William M. McBride of the *Herald News* in Passaic, New Jersey, eventually reached a compromise with her. She told him, "You tell those bastards down in Washington that I'll do what they want me to, but I won't answer their damn letters."[61]

Many of the missionaries took on the Office of Censorship's request as a crusade. Don Anderson, publisher of the *Wisconsin State Journal* in Madison, sent a note to 350 of the state's rural editors explaining the need to adhere to the code, describing his volunteer status as a "missionary," and offering to field censorship questions from his peers or to pass them along to Washington if necessary.[62] He also regularly read many of the state's small weekly papers and quietly pointed out violations. His low-key approach resulted in swift corrective action by the offending publications, with few hard feelings. The publisher of the *Vernon County Censor*, for example, cheerfully agreed to change the way he identified military units in combat zones, and offered—in the best of Wisconsin peacemaking traditions—to drive to Madison to drink a beer with Anderson and discuss the issue that had set them at odds. When Anderson pointed out a similar code violation to the publisher of another rural paper, who apparently had never read the code, he recalled that she initially was "frightened by the enormity of the offense, but I patted her on the shoulder over the telephone the best I could and explained that if she followed the code, she would have no trouble."[63]

The radio industry did not have a missionary group. The Broadcasting Division staff thought it might be difficult for missionaries from independent stations to approach network affiliates, and vice versa.[64] In

Wisconsin State Journal *publisher Don Anderson. Anderson served for more than three years as a "missionary." He regularly scanned many of his state's 350 rural newspapers for compliance with the* Code of Wartime Practices *and offered reassurance and friendly advice to violators.* State Historical Society of Wisconsin, Negative WHi(x3)51974.

addition, the small number of stations compared with the thousands of publications allowed for closer contact with the Office of Censorship and reduced the need for go-betweens. Ryan and two of his assistants, Robert K. Richards and Eugene Carr, often spoke at conventions and sometimes with individual broadcasters to explain the radio code and seek support. In February and March 1942, Richards gave talks on voluntary radio censorship at regional meetings of the National Association of Broadcasters in the South, Southwest, and Midwest. In a marathon of driving and talking, Carr traveled 40,000 miles between October 18, 1942, and August 11, 1943, and met 1,954 broadcasters.[65] The low point of his travels occurred during the autumn of 1942, when a broadcaster in a small Texas town revealed that he thought the censorship codebooks were confidential and had kept them locked in his desk. He asked Carr's permission to call a staff meeting and read the code to his employees.[66]

Introduction of the code hit magazines the hardest. While the day-to-day print cycle of newspapers allowed them to adjust their reporting and editing literally overnight, the longer publication routine for weekly and monthly magazines found some in the middle of production when the codebook arrived in the mail. At the *Saturday Evening Post,* the editors and reporter Richard L. Neuberger read the code and visited the censorship headquarters to ask about a story scheduled for release in the February 14, 1942, issue, which already had been put on the presses. Neuberger had spent six weeks in reporting and writing "Wilderness Defense," an examination of military preparedness in the Pacific Northwest. It included extensive information that previously had appeared in newspapers and War Department press releases. Its color and black-and-white photographs had been taken under army supervision. Yet, Sorrells asked the magazine to stop the presses and delete all but seven paragraphs on the grounds that "the enemy has not yet assembled such a well-organized picture of the situation."[67] In retrospect, Sorrells's decision seems excessive; but, under the fears of the time that the attack on Pearl Harbor might lead to an assault on the West Coast, he considered it prudent to err on the side of caution. The editors agreed to substitute another story at the last minute.

Because the responsibility for censorship rested on individual journalists, each exercising judgment, it is not surprising that shortly after the *Post* censored itself after conferring with the Press Division, one of its competitors published an uncensored version of a similar story that it had researched independently and had decided did not violate the code.

Although the story in *Collier's* assessed coastal defenses in general terms and mentioned the new censorship code, it identified the Aleutian island of Attu as the northernmost military outpost and said "hundreds of millions of dollars' worth of Jap-repellents" were hidden along U.S. Highway 101. Nevertheless, it gave no information that would help target Japanese torpedoes, naval guns, or air strikes.[68]

Possible violations of the code came to the attention of the Office of Censorship through complaints by citizens, journalists, and government agencies and the military, as well as the office's own monitoring of newspapers, magazines, and broadcasts. By the end of 1942, the Press Division was reading 112 newspapers daily, as well as newspaper and magazine stories, books, almanacs, and corporate reports that were submitted voluntarily before publication. It also was receiving fifty to sixty inquiries a day about the code.[69] For the entire year, the division had spot-checked 29,140 issues of daily and weekly papers, 794 copies of weekly and monthly magazines, 624 trade and industrial magazines, and 3,019 newsletters, house organs, and miscellaneous publications.[70]

Many people reading their papers in 1942 thought they saw evidence of subversion. Among the early letters from readers to the Office of Censorship was one that complained about the *Kansas City Journal* stories detailing the ease with which the city's utilities could be sabotaged. Another letter came from a reader in New Jersey who grew alarmed when Arpad, the cartoon weather-forecasting rooster of the *New York World-Telegram*, "was a little too cryptic" in his announcement of the spring equinox. Arpad's musings that "at 2:11, a brown rabbit ran across Home-lawn St. in Jamaica" and "squirrels sat in Grand Central Pkwy., near Jamaica Estates, and looked pretty sore" apparently seemed too much like a secret message for the reader's peace of mind. Her letter found its way to Sorrells, who passed along her concern to *World-Telegram* city editor B. O. McAnney. The city editor explained, "Please tell our reader Arpad is going to reform . . . [and is not] a spy. We're going to try to get him back to simple language."[71]

The appropriate-authority clause proved to be a continuing problem. Managing editor Fred M. McLennan of the *Buffalo Courier-Express* received a letter from Sorrells shortly after the paper printed on February 15, 1942, that "it is no secret that the Curtiss plant is tooling to convert for the building of the Republic Thunderbolt." In fact, Sorrells said, the army insisted that it was a secret, at least from the Axis, and he asked for McLennan to cite his appropriate authority for the story.[72] When

McLennan wrote back to argue that the story was being discussed openly on the streets of Buffalo, Sorrells, again ruling on the side of caution, replied, "An agent may hear all sorts of talk, or discussion, or even word-of-mouth assurances concerning a given piece of information, but he doesn't know definitely . . . until he sees it in print."[73] McLennan took the lesson to heart. That fall, the *Courier-Express* killed a story about radar at the Office of Censorship's request, but McLennan cried foul when he discovered that the *Buffalo Evening News* printed a similar story without having submitted it first for an opinion. "Your office said 'no' to us and thus the paper that plays the game according to the rules is again the one that suffers," he said. Nathaniel Howard, who had become head of the Press Division on May 1 when Sorrells became assistant director of censorship, tried to calm McLennan by praising his conscientiousness and saying the Office of Censorship would be "taking action immediately" against the *News*—presumably, sending a letter pointing out the code violation and asking for greater vigilance, which was the standard procedure.[74]

Price acknowledged the inexact science of censorship in an address to the ASNE that was broadcast over the Blue Network on April 16. He told the editors that they would never like censorship, and that a voluntary system based on each editor interpreting a codebook would continue to result in a story being published by some papers and spiked by others. Despite these flaws, voluntary censorship would be better than the "chaos" of total newspaper freedom, he said, adding that the success of censorship was up to each journalist.[75]

VIOLATIONS AND THREATS

When a journalist violated the code, his or her editor received a confidential letter from the Office of Censorship pointing out the mistake. Many of the mistakes were attributed to ambitious but inexperienced reporters and society writers eager to publicize the presence of military officials at parties; others could be traced to journalists who had not read or understood the code. According to his rule of equal treatment for all, the Office of Censorship admonished everyone from reporters for small-town weeklies to nationally known columnists—including the president's wife.

"The censor has written me a very stern letter about my remarks on the weather," Eleanor Roosevelt told the readers of her "My Day" newspaper column on August 17, 1942, "and so from now on I shall not tell you whether it rains or whether the sun shines where I happen to be."[76] Actually, Price recorded in his wartime notebook, her code violation was treated with a routine letter from Howard to the editor of the United Features Syndicate, in keeping with the Office of Censorship's policy of dealing with managers, as titular administrators of the code, instead of individual journalists. The editor passed along the letter, which Price said "politely called attention to her habit of discussing the weather and said we hoped she would do as other columnists were doing." The first lady's revelation that she had agreed to silence herself prompted the *Danville (Virginia) Register* to recommend Price for a Distinguished Service Medal.[77]

By announcing her mistake, the first lady became one of the few journalists to be identified publicly as a code violator. In mid-1942, the Office of Censorship came under pressure from editors and publishers to crack down on competitors who were getting scoops by inadvertently violating the code. In nearly six months of the war Price had never named a violator. That changed shortly after the Press Division received dozens of inquiries in May from Washington journalists about the arrival of Soviet foreign minister V. M. Molotov to confer with Roosevelt about the possibility of a second front in Europe. Price's staff answered all callers by invoking the voluntary code and asking for a news blackout. On May 22, Price typed a one-sentence memo that his staff phoned to the offices of Washington newspapers, news bureaus, and columnists. The confidential note said, "The White House will be the sole appropriate authority for any information on movements within a short time of a Russian diplomat."[78]

Jeff Keen of the *Philadelphia Daily News,* who was only vaguely aware of the censorship code, did not see the special note. After speaking with Philadelphians working for Soviet relief efforts, he reported in a June 6 gossip column that Molotov was in the country on "a secret mission of vast importance."[79] Competing papers in Philadelphia and New York, which had known of Molotov's visit but suppressed the news, alerted the Office of Censorship and Early about Keen's column. They asked if "that took the lid off" the story. Early and William Mylander, a press censor on loan from the *Toledo Blade* and *Pittsburgh Post-Gazette,* agreed not only that the story should continue to be censored but that also, in Early's words, "this might be a case to make an example."[80] After Molotov departed with a vague American promise to open a second front against Germany in 1942, Price thanked the American press and radio for withholding information about Molotov's visit but issued a news release identifying the *Daily News* as having violated the code. It was the only time in the Office of Censorship's forty-four-month history that anyone in the Press or Broadcasting Divisions named a violator. On one hand, the decision to do so was curious because the Molotov item was a less serious breach of security than news stories that appeared later about the atomic bomb. On the other hand, it fit Price's management style of "least said, soonest mended." He apparently had been looking for a clear-cut, narrowly focused case to demonstrate the power of public opinion and competitive pressures by identifying a code violator early in the war, in order to warn reporters nationwide of the possible consequences of any recklessness. In selecting a minor case, the Office of Censorship could illustrate the problem without harming the income of a publication or radio station, harm that might have been done if the violation had been both deliberate and significant. He softened the blow in his news release about Molotov by including a statement from the Philadelphia paper's publisher, Lee Ellmaker, that the columnist's violation was unintentional, and by emphasizing the "patriotic self-discipline" of the many journalists who knew of Molotov's visit but did nothing about it. Thus the power to punish, by naming the code breaker, was given the context of unity of national purpose. Headlines on newspaper versions of the Price news release that were collected by the Office of Censorship highlighted this positive spin—"Reporter Integrity," "Price Praises Cooperation of Newspapers," and "Press Thanked for 'Hiding' Molotov."[81]

While the incident may have helped strengthen the working relationship of the Office of Censors and the nation's news media, it set back Keen's career. Although he had twenty-five years' experience, he had made similar code violations earlier in 1942, and Ellmaker suspended him from the staff in mid-June. He still was seeking reinstatement three months later.[82]

After the code had been in operation for six months, Price asked for a report on its impact. His staff found that during April, May, and June, 1,882 stories had been submitted to the Office of Censorship before publication, and according to Price's personal records, the censors' advice was followed in every instance. Submissions came from 497 sources. Atop the list was the Associated Press, with 276 inquiries, followed by the United Press and International News Service.[83] Among individual newspapers, the *Chicago Tribune,* which Price called "the bitterest of the big dailies opposing the Roosevelt policies," had the most submissions with fifty-six. Walter Trohan, Washington correspondent for the *Tribune,* attributed his paper's ranking to the diligence of his managing editor, J. Loy Maloney. Trohan said Maloney asked his reporters to get censorship approval of all stories about the war—not because the anti-Roosevelt paper feared the political consequences of breaking the code, but rather because Maloney was "super-cautious" and "a great pain in the neck" about getting facts correct. In addition, Trohan described himself as "a bit of a devil" in requesting the Press Division's judgment on stories that he knew violated the code. "I knew I couldn't print it," he said. "I just teased them."[84]

Behind the *Tribune* on the list were the *New York Herald Tribune* with forty-five inquiries, the *New York Times* with twenty-six, and the *Washington Times-Herald* with twenty-two. Price probably had expected to have concerns about the *Tribune,* owned by Robert McCormick, and the two papers owned by his cousins, Cissy Patterson's *Washington Times-Herald* and Joseph Patterson's *New York Daily News.* "As a professional newspaperman I despised McCormick's egotism and arrogance," Price wrote in his memoir, and he told *Tribune* reporter Arthur Henning that the paper's anti-Roosevelt editorial policies were prolonging the war.[85] Trohan suggested that part of Price's animosity stemmed from McCormick's membership on the Associated Press board of directors, which would have brought the two men together before the war, when Price was executive editor of the AP. "Maybe Price considered him bossy and difficult," Trohan said.[86] Although the *Tribune* apparently respected Price—it hailed his appointment in December 1941 as suggesting that the government did not intend to abuse censorship[87]—the paper's editorial cartoonist repeatedly hammered the government's news policies in the following few months.

The first possibility of what Price called a "public show down" arose when the Office of Censorship challenged the notoriously strong-willed Cissy Patterson.[88] Early had given Price a clipping of Igor Cassini's "These Charming People" column in Patterson's paper on May 29, 1942, along with a note explaining that he had been asked to send it to the Office of Censorship. Who had asked him, he did not say, but he fashioned the note in a more formal manner than one would expect for a communication between two old friends, and below his name he affixed his title, "secretary to the president." It is likely, then, that Roosevelt or one of his top aides read the column and complained. "I have been asked to . . . say, if this publication does violate censorship rules and regulations, that appropriate action be taken," Early wrote.[89] Attached to the note was a clipping of the column with an ink mark identifying the paragraph that Early felt violated the censorship clause on movements of military forces: "Uncle Sam is planning to open a branch of the War Department in London very soon. Two thousand one hundred U.S. officers will leave, in three shifts of 700 each, from the middle of June to the middle of July, to start their duties at their new desks. Evidently our high command is making all necessary preparations for the great invasion of the continent."[90]

Price wrote a confidential, formal note, informing Early that he had written Patterson and proposed to publish the correspondence unless she explained the code violation with "a satisfactory answer."[91] Although Patterson, a savvy journalist who called herself "a plain old vindictive shanty Irish bitch,"[92] would have made a formidable opponent if she had chosen to challenge censorship, Price pulled no punches in his letter. Quoting the Cassini column, he said, "Unless this news was given out officially for publication, which I understand it was not, the statement quoted is a plain violation of the voluntary censorship regulations which have been accepted generally by the newspaper industry. . . . Will you please advise me whether the *Times Herald* published this information through ignorance of the Code, through carelessness, or because the *Times Herald* has no intention of observing the requests made by the Government?"[93]

Patterson apologized, responding by telegram that her paper had every intention of following the censorship code. She blamed the code violation on an inexperienced city room, in which journalists with little training had replaced twelve staff members who had joined the armed services.[94] In the end, there was no showdown. Price wrote in his notebook that he could not get in a scrap with an opponent who refused to fight back.[95] But, there was more to the Cassini column than Price acknowledged in his private writings. Three days after Price received Patterson's telegram that defused a possible confrontation, *Times-Herald* managing editor Frank C. Waldrop wrote Price to accept the blame for the oversight and to underline his support for the censorship code. An editor spotted the Cassini item before the end of the day's press run and yanked it from the late editions, he said. As a result, more than 100,000 copies appeared without the violation. Furthermore, he had questioned Cassini about the violation and was told, "I printed the item only because it was told to me by responsible officers of the United States Army, in a public place. Since none of these officers warned me not to repeat it, I didn't think it could be a guarded military secret. The story was public knowledge before I printed it." Waldrop appended a note to Price, pointing out that "if traps had been kept shut news could not have escaped."[96]

The year's gravest threats to the voluntary censorship code did not come from the Patterson-McCormick press. Instead, two formidable opponents, *Time* magazine and the *New York Times*, served notice that they were considering deliberately violating the censorship code. Price was more concerned by the threat from the newspaper, which carried more prestige among journalists than *Time*, which he characterized as a "parasite and Pariah." As a former wire service reporter who valued short, clear prose, Price disliked what he called *Time*'s "glib manipulation of words to make harmless facts appear as startling disclosures." And he had doubts about the magazine's publisher, Henry Luce. All other major publishers, including the sensationalizing William Randolph Hearst, had expressed their support of voluntary censorship, but Luce, the creator of *Time*, *Life*, and *Fortune*, had not. He did not know why. Luce's *March of Time* newsreel initially had included footage of a sinking U.S. tanker in a documentary film early in 1942, despite the navy's objections and Price's concerns that it would discourage enlistments. However, after Price threatened to use his powers over international communications to deny the film a lucrative export license, the footage was removed. Luce's magazines had flirted with the code repeatedly but actual violations always were followed by apologies. Price believed that few journalists would support *Time* if it chose to challenge the Office of Censorship. Still, he felt a twinge of guilt when *Time*'s editorial vice president, Eric Hodgins, became the first journalist to warn the office that he might ignore the code. When the Office of Censorship issued the first comprehensive revision of the *Code of Wartime Practices*, on June 15, 1942, it added a clause asking for a ban on news of "premature disclosure of diplomatic negotiations or conversations." Price said the clause was intended to protect news of wartime planning, but critics found the wording too inclusive and accused the office of trying to protect secret diplomacy. Price blamed himself for not recognizing the clause's poorly constructed phrasing. Cranston Williams, a member of his advisory board, told him to ignore the criticism and let the storm blow over.[97]

But Hodgins seized the issue and refused to drop it. He wrote Price on July 1 to take exception to the clause and put the Office of Censorship on notice "that if in this particular we were to encounter a conflict between Code and conscience, we would feel bound to follow our conscience."[98] Censorship was a hot topic at the magazine. In the previous week, it had attacked military and voluntary censorship as excessive, complaining that the government was "fighting World War II without taking its own people into its confidence."[99]

For once, Price was on the defensive. His response to Hodgins acknowledged that the diplomatic clause was "broad and inclusive," but he said the same criticism could be made of the rest of the censorship code if it were badly administered. Anyone who had worked with the Office of Censorship would know that it was not interested in covering up mistakes or stifling criticism, he said. He offered a suggestion: "Instead of undertaking to break down and destroy the Code and substitute a code of your own, perhaps at the expense of bringing about a national diplomatic defeat which would be as costly as a national military defeat, why not give us a ring in any specific case which may arise."[100]

The letter had the intended result. Hodgins backed off. He had merely wanted to go on record as protesting the clause in advance, in the abstract, before any situation arose to test it for real. While pledging not to act arbitrarily in the future, he reiterated his "plain dislike" of the one-sentence diplomatic clause. "I thought you would want me to state that dislike openly rather than conceal it until such time as a first class Incident might arise," he said.[101]

Price said the censors "kept our fingers crossed" to see if *Time* would stay within the code. It did. In fact, the Office of Censorship's judicious handling of its relations with the press converted Hodgins to a vocal supporter by October. "So far as the Office of Censorship is concerned," he stated in a speech in Boston, "as administered by Byron Price and his deputy, John H. Sorrells, I think it is almost beyond reproach in the understanding it displays of the necessity for keeping the American press as unfettered as possible within the limits of true security."[102] In a private letter to Price, Hodgins said his remarks "came from the heart."[103] Price followed up on his contacts with Hodgins by seeing that the diplomatic clause was rephrased in 1943 to apply only to news of military operations.[104]

The *New York Times* posed a greater challenge. Its protest of the censorship code represented a broad-based belief among journalists and the public that the navy had covered up its losses to conceal weakness and error. At the *Times* itself, sentiment had been building since early 1941 that censorship should be clarified and enforced with some form of punishment for transgressors. Initially, publisher Arthur Hays Sulzberger had been cooperative with the navy and the president about voluntary censorship. In early 1941 he had prevented the *Times* from printing a United Press story about the shipment of planes to Hawaii, after he personally had tried to call Roosevelt to ask about it. Advice from the Navy Department settled the question for Sulzberger, but other papers printed the dispatch.[105] He also had directed his staff to observe Frank Knox's request for voluntary censorship over damage to British ships, only to see competitors do the opposite and "scoop" the paper.[106] Journalists at the *Times* complained to each other and to officials in Washington about the problems of voluntary censorship in 1941 and 1942, but without much effect. A typical sentiment was expressed in mid-January 1942 by managing editor Edwin James. In protesting the bungled naval censorship of news about the sinking of American ships off the East Coast, in which the *Times* lost a competitive edge in breaking the stories, he told Washington bureau chief Arthur Krock, "The idea I am trying to put over is that the newspapers deserve a better break than this if they are expected to cooperate willingly and with enthusiasm."[107] Throughout 1942, Sulzberger pushed Price to try to get more details about the Pearl Harbor attack in print. Price failed, at first, to pry more cooperation out of the navy. Meanwhile Sulzberger directed his restless staff to wait for official approval of any story that ran afoul of the censorship code.[108]

Patience wore thin in the fall of 1942. *Times* military reporter Hanson Baldwin, a former naval officer, visited Price on October 8. Four days earlier the *Times* had published his account of combat in the Solomon Islands.[109] He filled Price in with facts he had left out of his story, including revelations that three American cruisers and the *Wasp* had been sunk by the Japanese.

According to Price's memoir, Baldwin, whose reports from the Pacific would win him a Pulitzer Prize, said many navy officers thought inefficient commanders were being unfairly protected from criticism. Baldwin had shared his views with Sulzberger, who had asked the reporter to deliver a message to Price: "If official secrecy became too great, the *Times* might feel that it should lead the way in breaking the Code in the hope, perhaps, that a bold stand would force a change in command."[110]

Public hints of the depth of the *Times*'s dissatisfaction with censorship appeared in the same issue as Baldwin's report from the Solomons. The lead editorial on October 4 urged the president to give more facts and fewer lectures about the war. Although it focused on Roosevelt's just completed, two-week tour of military bases and defense plants, after which he had criticized wartime pessimists, the editorial's broad appeal for less censorship may have reflected Baldwin's and Sulzberger's concerns. It asked Roosevelt to discipline the members of his administration who were trying to sell the war to the public "as though it were hair tonic." The editorial added that sometimes information might be worth little to the enemy, but its release might have far greater value in stimulating American citizens toward support for the war.[111]

Four days after Baldwin's visit, the navy announced the sinking of three cruisers, the *Quincy,* the *Astoria,* and the *Vincennes,* but said nothing of the other losses in the Solomons. Sulzberger visited Price, who reported that he and Office of War Information (OWI) director Elmer Davis were planning to talk on October 14 with Admiral Ernest King, chief of naval operations. They hoped to persuade the navy to release more information, he said, but in the meantime he asked Sulzberger to warn the Office of Censorship if the *Times* decided to break the code deliberately. Sulzberger replied that he would not violate the code without consulting Price first.[112]

The crusty King, whom his daughter had called "the most even tempered man in the navy" because "he is always in a rage," disliked naval publicity because he saw it as a security threat. Washington journalists joked that if he had his way, King would issue one press release about the war: It would appear at war's end and say who won.[113] At the meeting, King sparred with Davis about the government's information policy but finally admitted that Roosevelt recently had asked him to give out more facts about the navy. Historians have noted the president's skill at reading the public mood, so perhaps he had foreseen the crisis, or had learned independently of the *Times*'s unease and had spoken with King in hopes of assuaging it. OWI historian Allan M. Winkler suggested that Roosevelt's concern partly was political; he and Knox wanted to silence rumors that losses were being covered up to affect the congressional elections.[114] In any event, King said he would comply with the request. He said that whenever possible, he planned to balance news of losses with news of replacements, but the *Wasp*'s demise would have to stay secret temporarily because he had evidence that Japan was uncertain of its fate. When Price spoke, he underscored the need for more candor by the navy. He said the censorship code faced direct defiance because of naval secrecy, and that the navy would not want the code to fail. The three men parted on good terms, and the navy's new information policy apparently prevented any rebellion. Price heard no more from the *Times* about breaking the code, although Krock and James continued to grumble privately for the rest of the war.[115]

There was more to the *Times*'s change of heart than Price admitted. On October 28, Price and Davis appeared at a public forum on war news and censorship sponsored by the *New York Times* and broadcast by radio station WMCA. Krock interviewed both men and passed along questions from the audience. The *Times*'s account of their remarks did not say how or why the nation's chief censor and war publicist had been chosen for the forum at New York Times Hall. The story said Knox was preparing a detailed report on the damage at Pearl Harbor. Price emphasized the need for censorship and publicity to work in harmony, telling Krock that "unless ample war news is given out by the government, our voluntary undertaking with the press and radio will collapse." The *Times*'s editorial page followed up by praising the remarks of both men.[116]

Two years earlier, in December 1940, Biddle had written in his diary that Sulzberger was "honest & conscientious.... I think he could be educated, and that we neglect educational opportunities."[117] It is possible that when the government and military learned of Sulzberger's concerns in October 1942, someone highly placed in the Roosevelt administration saw an opportunity to try to "educate" the publisher. Perhaps Price and Davis asked the *Times* to let them go on record in favor of greater openness. Or perhaps Sulzberger had issued invitations out of his own concerns about censorship. The evidence is difficult to assess, particularly because the *Times*'s archives do not contain any records about Sulzberger's threat to violate the code at the time. In any event, the size and prominence of the paper's account of their speeches, which began atop the front page and filled three columns inside, indicated its extreme interest in the topic.

The Office of Censorship considered its day-to-day interactions with the nation's journalists at the heart of its operation. Price's staff believed that editors' and broadcasters' routine restraint, based on their reading of the *Codes of Wartime Practices,* saved "countless" American lives by keeping information from the enemy.[118] An objective assessment of the codebooks' contribution to the war is impossible because the number of ships that were not sunk or factories that were not sabotaged, thanks to control of the news, cannot be measured. However, the record of compliance with the code, which became cemented into journalists' routine by mid-October 1942, suggests the establishment of trust. Or, to use a word Price would have preferred, faith. Krock meant his comment to be derogatory when he observed that voluntary self-censorship by the press in World War II "came to have the force of an imposed one."[119] And he was justified in questioning whether any difference existed between journalists who censored themselves according to a list of "requests," backed by the unmentioned laws of espionage, and journalists who followed some form of compulsory regulations. The products of the two forms of censorship no doubt would have looked much alike. But they would have differed in the degree of enthusiasm with which they were followed. Krock was rare among World War II reporters in his publicly aired, extreme distaste for voluntary censorship; scores of notes of support arrived at the Office of Censorship when it issued its first code revision in June 1942, and none suggested changing the code.[120]

The Office of Censorship's desire for the code to succeed through faith and trust is manifest in the religious imagery its staff adopted. As early as May 20, 1942, Howard asked editors to assist in "spreading the gospel of voluntary censorship."[121] Liaisons who learned the details of the censorship code were "missionaries," while codebooks sometimes were called "Bibles" in Office of Censorship memos. In addition, Price's staff gave him the nickname "Bishop."[122] Such faith has no power independent of the willingness of its followers to abide by it. Likewise, the church commands no armies yet has a powerful influence on the faithful. Whether journalists would have given equal support to compulsory censorship cannot be known. However, journalists and civilian censors greeted with anger and dismay most efforts by the government and military to gain control over the news.

A Miscellany of Volunteer Firemen
Censorship and the Army, the Navy, and
the White House

Associated Press teletype machines in newsrooms around the
nation clattered to life on December 11, 1942, with an unusual story of
sedition charges against an officer at Fort Lewis, Washington, accused of
attempting to "vilify President Roosevelt" and set up a right-wing subversive cell in the army. The wire service had picked up the story from the
Seattle Post-Intelligencer, which had published a report on that day about
the young, unidentified army officer's arrest. "It is understood," the tele-
types tapped out, "that the officer mailed seditious literature to members
of the one-time America First Committee and to William Dudley Pelley's Silver Shirts."[1] Those two groups had advocated keeping America
out of war, with the former boasting the Nazi-admiring aviator Charles
Lindbergh as its most popular speaker and the latter espousing a vicious
hatred of Jews and blacks before its founder, Pelley, succumbed to congressional and legal pressure and disbanded it in 1941.[2]

The account of a sedition investigation against an army officer was
startling, but even more newsworthy in the eyes of the nation's editors
was the confidential note that the AP had added at the top. It said that
army authorities at Fort Lewis had approved the story for publication
under the condition that its headline was only one column wide.[3] Many
of the nation's newspapers saw the request as an affront to journalistic
independence and integrity. *Editor & Publisher* reflected their tone in an
angry editorial: "It is indeed an anomaly that the story of the detection
of an American officer doing the devil's work should have been released

under a restriction that sounds terribly reminiscent of the press techniques of Germany, Japan, and Italy."[4]

What the original AP story did not say was that a *Post-Intelligencer* reporter had submitted his account of the arrest to the army's censors in accordance with censorship regulations governing news originating on military bases. The army, concerned that publication might interfere with its continuing investigation at Fort Lewis, agreed to cut a deal with the newspaper. It would stand as appropriate authority for the story if the paper did not display the news in an "alarmist" manner. The *Post-Intelligencer* and General Kenyon A. Joyce of Fort Lewis then agreed that a one-column headline would meet both their needs. The AP learned of the paper's arrangement with Joyce when it picked up the story for national distribution. It interpreted the restriction as applying to all papers nationwide and passed along the headline restriction, even though Joyce had not asked to make it universal.[5]

At the other end of the continent, censorship office director Byron Price began receiving calls from editors wanting to know whether he supported the army's interference with their decisions on displaying the news. He did not have to think hard. The Press Division already had dealt with a similar issue. Cable censors in Tucson, Arizona, had complained to the Washington office when they saw the May 1 and 2, 1942, editions of the *Raton (New Mexico) Daily Range*. The paper's banner headlines on an army plane crash were too big and sensational, they said. Press censor Nathaniel R. Howard replied that the Office of Censorship "has not yet ventured into the field of passing judgments on size and character of headlines."[6] Price reached the same conclusion on the Seattle story. He canceled the AP's headline restriction, which he privately called "foolish," and told editors that they could display the story in whatever manner they chose. "No authority exists to order any restrictions of press headlines or typographical arrangements of any kind," he said. General Ernest DuPuy of the army's public relations office issued a concurring statement.[7]

The episode was one of many during the war in which Price fought military and government efforts to reduce or remove his authority. "Somehow everybody condemns censorship but everybody loves to be in it!" he observed in an interview twenty-five years after the war.[8] That was especially true in 1942 and 1943, when army and navy officers often attempted to interpret the censorship code for editors and broadcasters and enforce compliance, even though domestic censorship by law was voluntary and under civilian authority. Under decisions that Price made early in the war, government and military officials could agree to release information that violated the codes. Journalists, often backed by the Office of Censorship, pressed authorities to release more news about the war and opposed restrictions that they considered abuses of censorship.

Military officials and journalists often reached different conclusions when they assessed the security value of news. "The military mind . . . easily confuses security with secrecy, while the publicist yearns for disclosure even in matters which he is in no position to understand," Price recalled.[9] General Dwight D. Eisenhower recognized that perfect coordination of press and military could never be achieved. In his memoir of World War II, he wrote that military commanders considered secrecy a defensive weapon, while journalists objected to it.[10]

In addition to his tangling with the military, Price jousted with the government. He nullified the White House's attempt to consolidate censorship and publicity functions in his office, and he opposed plans for a punitive secrecy law.

President Franklin Roosevelt usually was Price's ally despite having reservations about an unfettered press. Roosevelt enjoyed good relations with most reporters even though many publishers opposed his New Deal policies.[11] However, the burdens of war strained the relationship between the president and the press. Roosevelt tried to belittle his irritation with humor, but serious undertones to his jibes and jokes testified to the depth of feeling. On January 5, 1942, he performed an elaborate hoax on Attorney General Francis Biddle, whom he summoned to the White House. Biddle found Roosevelt writing a message and talking with presidential aide Harry Hopkins, legal adviser Samuel I. Rosenman, speech writer Robert Sherwood, and private secretary Grace Tully.[12] With a face that Rosenman described as "serious—almost solemn," Roosevelt earnestly began asking Biddle for legal support to curtail "all freedom of discussion and information." When Roosevelt paused to ask Biddle's opinion, the attorney general replied, "I think not, Mr. President," and began a defense of civil liberties. The crowd, participating in the charade, roared because he had believed Roosevelt. Rosenman said Biddle took the joke well but stayed at the White House for most of the afternoon. "Maybe," Rosenman said, "he thought there might be a germ of truth in it after all."[13] At a press conference on December 18, 1942, the president's joking assumed a cruel edge. Roosevelt shocked the White House press corps when he handed radio commentator Earl Godwin an Iron Cross, a German military decoration, and asked him to give it to the absent John O'Donnell of the *New York Daily News*. Two days before, the *Daily News* had published O'Donnell's satirical column on military censorship.[14]

"Roosevelt was not a strong civil libertarian," one of his biographers, James MacGregor Burns, said. "Like Jefferson in earlier days, he was all for civil liberties in general but easily found exceptions in particular."[15] Biddle's war memoir reached a similar conclusion, portraying Roosevelt as oversensitive to press criticism and too eager to take legal action against the war's most vocal critics. In February 1942, the president began sending him memoranda attached to anti-administration news clippings and asking, "What are you doing to stop this?" Biddle responded that it would not be wise to prosecute seditious speech or publications unless they could be shown to be directly connected to the Axis war aims or to have interfered with recruiting. But, he said, Roosevelt was "not much interested in the theory of sedition. . . . He wanted this anti-war talk stopped."[16]

Price could not tell how much of what he called Roosevelt's "pin pricking" of the press was serious and how much was playful. Press Secretary Stephen T. Early told Price that he had tried to get Roosevelt to stop his teasing because it demeaned the presidency. Early once had asked the president to be "Mr. Big" and ignore his critics, but Roosevelt merely responded with a wry face. In his personal contacts, Price got the impression that the president hoped his detractors somehow would be punished.[17]

Twice in early 1942, Price was asked his opinion of proposed bills that would have toughened domestic censorship. He declined to endorse either one. The first came from an unexpected source. Biddle sent him a copy of a sweeping war-secrecy bill that had been drafted by lawyers in the Justice Department. He told Price that he had not seen the bill's final wording until after it had been introduced in the House of Representatives by Judiciary Committee chairman Hatton Sumners of Texas on February 18. The bill, modeled on a British law, sought to prosecute anyone who permitted public access to secret government files. Price accepted Biddle's assurances that his lawyers had intended the bill to simplify the procedure for punishing government workers who showed secret documents to unauthorized persons. Biddle did not intend to apply the bill to voluntary censorship of press and radio, but the broad language left open the possibility that it could be used as a weapon against inquisitive journalists.[18] It proposed maximum fines of $5,000 and prison terms of two years for anyone who, without authority, willfully furnished, communicated, divulged, or published copies or original forms of "any file, instrument, letter, memorandum, book, pamphlet, paper, document, manuscript, map, picture, plan, record, or other writing in the custody of the United States, or of any agency, officer, or employee thereof, declared to be secret or confidential by statute, or declared to be secret or confidential by any rule or regulation of any department or agency of the United States." Price wrote Biddle on February 26 that passage of the bill would not serve the nation's best interest. While the bill's penalties would relieve the Office of Censorship of the responsibility of seeking compliance with the *Code of Wartime Practices*, he said, passage would imply that voluntary censorship had failed. Journalists would consider the bill a rebuke, he warned.[19]

He was right. Harsh criticism of the bill appeared in newspapers and magazines nationwide. *United States News* warned on March 6 that the "Official Secrets Bill" would give the army and navy more freedom from press and presidential oversight and would place every federal department chief atop his own independent censorship system.[20] Arthur Krock of the *New York Times* editorialized that the proposed law was "an invitation to tyranny" and "evil."[21] Price rejoiced privately that the Judiciary Committee never took action on the bill, and it expired when Congress adjourned in December. The uproar over its introduction had proved discouraging to those in government who favored mandatory censorship, he said.[22]

The other proposed bill that passed across Price's desk was produced by the Office of Naval Intelligence. Price's notes did not record the date, but sometime in the spring of 1942 Lieutenant C. G. Burwell gave Price a copy of the navy's plan to outlaw nearly all newspaper references to specific troop units and ships. Like the Justice Department's bill, the navy's plan would have relieved the Office of Censorship of some of its responsibilities in policing the voluntary code, but Price found the bill flawed. He suggested that by listing only two news topics as illegal, the bill would encourage journalists to publish other stories that contained sensitive military secrets but did not fit either outlawed category. Price said he preferred the broader, existing system of informal censorship codes, which could be updated at a moment's notice and expanded to fit any contingency. Burwell then suggested a law empowering the Office of Censorship to enact restrictions with the force of law behind them, instead of asking for compliance with voluntary ones, but Price doubted that such a law would be constitutional. The navy's bill quietly died.[23]

The government and military made other attempts to get a greater measure of control over the press. Roosevelt pressured Biddle at a cabinet meeting on March 20, 1942, to take vigorous action against "subversive sheets," and the entire cabinet endorsed the suggestion.[24] Biddle suggested revoking some second-class mail permits, prosecuting "one or two" possible violations of the Espionage Act, and seeking new antisedition laws. According to historian Patrick S. Washburn, Biddle undoubtedly cringed at his acquiescence to the president's request, but he probably believed his answer would lessen the pressure from the White House. It did not. On April 1, 1942, seven days after Biddle held a press conference to announce that sedition charges soon would be filed in three or four cases, Roosevelt again talked with Biddle and Postmaster General Frank C. Walker about ways to restrain "isolationist" publications.[25]

Biddle called a meeting in his office on April 13 to discuss the problem. He invited Walker, Fred A. Ironside Jr. of the Post Office Department, Archibald MacLeish of the Office of Facts and Figures, and the Office of Censorship's Price and John H. Sorrells. At the meeting, Biddle asked for opinions on shutting down Charles Coughlin's anti-Soviet, anti-British, and anti-Semitic magazine *Social Justice* and other reactionary publications. Biddle said he had talked to several Supreme Court justices and felt that the Court would uphold restrictions on the publications as long as due process was observed. Everyone at the conference supported the plan, and Biddle expressed confidence that mainstream papers would back him, too. The group agreed to act against only those publications that were violating existing laws. According to Price, the group discussed not only *Social Justice,* run by Coughlin, a priest of the Shrine of the Little Flower Church in Royal Oak, Michigan, but also Pelley's *Galilean,* Court Asher's *X-Ray,* and a few "lesser publications," which he did not identify. The group agreed to take five possible actions against seditious publications. First, the Office of Censorship would monitor the publications for violations of the *Code of Wartime Practices,* but because the code did not apply to opinions, its impact would be limited. Second, the postmaster general would decide whether to bar the publications temporarily from the mail. Third, a hearing at the Post Office Department would decide whether to make the mail ban permanent. Fourth, MacLeish would be consulted about the propaganda value of the legal action. Finally, Biddle would decide whether to prosecute under the Espionage Act.[26]

Sorrells left no notes of the meeting, but apparently he had mixed feelings about suppressing *Social Justice*. Only three weeks earlier, he had written a libertarian defense of the First Amendment in response to a citizen in Ohio who had complained about Coughlin's magazine. Suppressing the magazine probably would do more harm than good by driving it underground or increasing interest in what it had to say, Sorrells said. Furthermore, "I don't believe Coughlin or anyone can reason the American people into a belief that our system is wrong, ideologically; they will become convinced that the system is wrong when it fails to work. Democracy will have failed when it becomes necessary to preserve itself by making criticism of the government a crime."[27] Whether Sorrells's letter was heartfelt cannot be known. It is possible that he changed his mind in three weeks, but it is more likely he was a bit disturbed about suppressing publications and decided not to speak up at the meeting.

Many mainstream journalists attacked their extremist cousins. The *Christian Science Monitor* reported on March 10, 1942, that the United States was harboring ninety-five pro-Axis publications, although it identified only seven.[28] CBS broadcaster William Shirer then issued a call to arms over the *Monitor*'s findings in *Atlantic Monthly*. The ninety-five subversive publications were spreading defeatism and treason, Shirer said, and few Americans would object to a government crackdown on "the enemy within the gate."[29] The Post Office Department helped direct attention against some of the administration's favorite targets by providing *Life* magazine with information on seditious publications and speakers that appeared in an eleven-page article, "Voices of Defeat," on April 13. The article mentioned not only fascist magazines but also the *Chicago Tribune*, which *Life* said "is widely quoted and mention of its name is cheered at meetings of pro-Nazi and defeatist groups throughout the country."[30]

Amid rising pressure from the administration and the mainstream press, Biddle took his first steps in a sedition case. On April 14, he wrote a letter to Walker identifying similarities between *Social Justice* and enemy broadcasts monitored by the Federal Communications Commission. He singled out sixteen articles that had appeared in the magazine since December 15, the date of the first issue to be printed after the attack on Pearl Harbor. Among them was an editorial on February 23 in which the magazine asked if the Japanese sneak attack had been planned with insiders' help. He also cited an article three weeks later that said, "We are becoming more and more convinced that the radicals who have seized our Federal Government care not one whit about driving Hitler from the face of the earth."[31] Biddle asked Walker to withhold distribution of the magazine and to consider revoking its second-class mail permit on the grounds that it violated Section 3, Title 1, of the Espionage Act by obstructing the war effort. He said it had helped the nation's enemies by conveying false information. Walker agreed and notified the postmaster at Royal Oak not to distribute the magazine's next issue. According to the Trading with the Enemy Act, it was illegal to transport material declared unmailable, and so Walker's action allowed copies of *Social Justice* to be seized at newsstands.[32]

Walker scheduled a permit revocation hearing for April 29. Coughlin, who appeared deceptively benign with his apple-cheeked oval face, wire-rimmed glasses, and clerical collar, reacted by dragging the fight into the public arena. He protested in *Social Justice* and sent letters to Biddle and the news media stating his eagerness to testify in his magazine's defense.[33] He was denied the chance. Biddle arranged for a Catholic friend, former Federal Deposit Insurance Corporation chairman Leo T. Crowley, to have the Catholic Church silence the priest. Crowley spoke privately with Edward Mooney, archbishop of Detroit, who ordered Coughlin to give up either the priesthood or his platform in the mass media. Coughlin made his choice. His magazine ceased publication with the April 20 issue, and he did not defend its second-class permit, which was revoked as a precaution at a rescheduled hearing on May 4. An indictment, which the administration feared would stir up hatred between Catholics and Jews, was avoided.[34] Newspapers hailed the magazine's demise. A cartoon in the liberal New York daily *PM* portrayed *Social Justice* as a dead rat swept up by the broom of public opinion.[35]

Based on information from the Justice Department, the Post Office Department barred three weekly newspapers from the mail by May 8— the German-language *Philadelphia Herold,* which had reprinted articles from *Social Justice; X-Ray,* of Muncie, Indiana, which had crowed on January 31 that the Japanese victory at Pearl Harbor had "sunk the hopes of Jewry in this country—and the world forever, Amen and Amen"; and Elmer J. Garner's *Publicity,* of Wichita, Kansas, which had called on March 12 for the destruction of the "Mongolian Jew Controlled Roosevelt Dictatorship."[36] By June 8, all three had lost their permits. Two other publications, the *Boise Valley Herald,* of Middleton, Idaho, and the *Militant,* of New York, lost their permits in the next nine months, but the Post Office Department restored them in 1944. Thus, counting *Social Justice,* six publications lost their second-class privileges during the war, but two had them reinstated. In addition, Pelley's *Galilean* had voluntarily suspended publication in March 1942 after being investigated by the Justice Department.[37]

Although the government's crackdown affected only a handful of journalists, leaving, according to Shirer and the *Christian Science Monitor,* nearly ninety seditious publications in operation, Washburn found no evidence that Roosevelt ever complained again to Walker about sedition.[38] The president apparently was satisfied that the most extreme publications had been silenced. Biddle continued to consider the *Tribune* to be as seditious as *Social Justice* but not as anti-Semitic or "rabble-rousing." Several times during the war he was tempted to bring legal action against the *Tribune,* but he did so only once, after the battle of Midway.[39]

CENSORSHIP AND THE NAVY

Problems began after *Chicago Tribune* reporter Stanley Johnston witnessed the battle of the Coral Sea on May 7 and 8, 1942, aboard the aircraft carrier *Lexington.* The ship was hit by Japanese dive-bombers and torpedoes, caught fire, and sank eight hours later. Johnston was rescued, taken to New Caledonia, and put aboard the naval transport *Barnett,* bound for San Diego.[40] While killing the long hours of the journey across the Pacific, Johnston, whom *Tribune* coworker Walter Trohan described as "persuasive and very charming,"[41] struck up a friendship with a naval officer. The unidentified officer apparently shared with the reporter the most sensitive of secrets, a dispatch detailing the makeup of a Japanese task force en route to Midway Island. The information had been based on the navy's breaking of the Japanese fleet's operational code.[42] Johnston carried a copy of the dispatch with him from San Diego to the *Tribune* newsroom in Chicago. Later, when the Associated Press flashed word of a naval victory on June 3 through June 6 near Midway, he realized he had a scoop that rivaled his first-person account of the sinking of the *Lexington.*[43]

"Navy Had Word of Jap Plan to Strike at Sea," the *Tribune's* front-page headline said on June 7. Johnston's story, which carried no byline and deceptively had been given a Washington dateline, said the strength of the Japanese attack force at Midway "was well known in American circles several days before the battle began." It named the enemy ships in the pivotal Pacific battle and identified their tonnage and some of their armaments.[44] Although the story did not say that the United States had broken the Japanese code, any intelligent enemy agent would infer that fact. It also was apparent that Johnston had seen the secret naval dispatch because he had copied its uniquely identifiable spelling of the Japanese ships.

In Washington, the navy reacted with shock and anger to the story, which had been picked up by the *Washington Times-Herald.* "I came down to the Navy Department . . . and my goodness, the place was shaking," staff officer Arthur H. McCollum recalled.[45] Roosevelt's initial reaction was to consider a Marine occupation of the Tribune Tower in downtown Chicago, and possibly charges of treason against *Tribune* publisher Colonel Robert McCormick.[46] More moderate opinions prevailed. Aside from the eventual preparation of a criminal case against the *Tribune,* Roosevelt proposed that all correspondents except members of the three major wire services be excluded from army and navy "expeditions." Secretary of War Henry Stimson considered the proposal too drastic and talked with Secretary of the Navy Frank Knox about either replacing all civilian combat correspondents with navy and army public relations officers, or gradually reducing the size of the accredited press corps to weed out all but "reliable" reporters.[47] As the buzz in Washington died down, however, all of these proposals were abandoned in favor of the status quo.

According to Trohan, Johnston's account of the Midway battle was the only major war story that the *Tribune* did not submit to the Office of Censorship. If managing editor J. Loy Maloney had submitted the story, Trohan said, the censors would have passed it, for the first edition of the *Code of Wartime Practices* said nothing about the movement of enemy ships in enemy waters—an oversight that was corrected in the codebooks' revision.[48] Maloney had read Johnston's story over the phone to his paper's Washington bureau chief, Arthur Henning, and asked if it conflicted with the code. Henning, who knew the code well, said it violated no censorship restrictions, and he did not inform the Press Division about it.[49]

Knox, at Roosevelt's request, asked Biddle to prosecute the *Tribune* on suspicion of violating the Espionage Act by willfully publishing secret naval information during wartime. In his memoir, Biddle said he told Knox, whose *Chicago Daily News* was a rival to the *Tribune,* that the crux of the issue was whether the Midway story had damaged national security. After consulting with the navy's top admirals, Knox gave his assurance that the navy would provide enough evidence for a conviction. On this promise, Biddle arranged for William D. Mitchell, who had been President Herbert Hoover's attorney general, to prosecute.[50] Many observers in the government considered the legal action a perfect opportunity to punish the newspaper and its publisher, McCormick, for their years of criticism of the Roosevelt administration.[51]

On June 19, Biddle forwarded to Price a letter he had received from Mitchell suggesting that the censorship code be tightened. Price noted that Mitchell evidently wanted a direct link between the code and the Espionage Act, even though the former attorney general realized the voluntary code had no legal authority. Price's reply to Biddle said any attempt to formally connect the code and the Espionage Act would create "involuntary censorship" and render obsolete the original code. He held up the distribution of the first revised edition of the censorship codebooks until he could talk with Biddle. When they met on June 23, Price said he could not see how the *Tribune* story could be any concern of the Office of Censorship. The story had never been submitted for review and was not covered by the code. It should have been submitted to naval censorship because Johnston had gathered his information in the Pacific combat zone, Price said, but the navy had neglected to get Johnston's signature on an accreditation agreement and therefore could not challenge him for evasion of naval regulations. Biddle appeared satisfied with the explanation and urged Price to release the updated codebooks. He did so but agreed to Biddle's suggestion that he send a memorandum to the nation's editors and broadcasters to clarify the combat zone rule. Accordingly, on July 10, Price issued a note to editors and broadcasters reminding them that the army and navy controlled combat zone censorship.[52]

Meanwhile, Biddle proceeded with his investigation. He told Price that he was reluctant to try a case that he might lose because it would turn McCormick into a "martyr" persecuted by the government. Nevertheless, Biddle announced on August 7 that "upon the recommendation of the Navy Department," he had ordered a grand jury in Chicago to investigate the publication of "confidential information concerning the Battle of Midway." He asked the panel to investigate a possible violation of the Espionage Act.[53]

When the grand jury met to consider charges, the navy suddenly reneged on its pledge to provide evidence that Johnston's story had revealed a sensitive war secret, because that would lead to the public release of information that the navy still hoped to keep hidden. Without evidence, the grand jury refused to indict the *Tribune*. "I felt like a fool," Biddle admitted twenty years later.[54]

Ironically, some of the published reports of the grand jury's decision alluded to widespread knowledge of the supposed secret. *Newsweek* said the topic "had been bandied about for weeks in Washington clubs, pressrooms and cocktail bars"; *Time* reported that scores of people in Washington knew the nature of the unspoken evidence.[55] On August 31, Representative Elmer J. Holland of Pennsylvania said on the floor of Congress that the public knew the *Tribune* had tipped off Japan that its naval code had been compromised.[56] Assistant Attorney General James Rowe lamented to Biddle, "It seems that everyone in the United States except the grand jury knows the facts."[57] Japan, however, did not learn of the extent of the navy's code-breaking ability. American cryptographers continued to read Japanese radio messages and used the intelligence to shoot down Admiral Isoroku Yamamoto's airplane in the Pacific in April 1943.[58]

Many army and navy officers initially greeted voluntary, civilian censorship with skepticism. They had numerous reasons for doubt early in 1942, when confusion reigned over the appropriate-authority clause. The censorship codes issued on January 15 had given the army and navy the right to act as such authorities in releasing information but did not spell out which officers could speak for the armed forces. The lack of clarity became evident when torpedoes began slamming into ships off the East Coast. A German submarine sank the British tanker *Coimbra* near Long Island on January 14. The three wire services had assembled the bones of the story by the next morning. The United Press had a statement from the police chief of Quogue that the ship had been sunk and officials onshore were awaiting the arrival of survivors. The AP knew that an army bomber had flown over the tanker's last known position and seen an oil slick on the water's surface and that whiskey and food had been dropped to fourteen people in a lifeboat. The International News Service knew that rescue planes and ships were en route to the scene.[59] None released the story that morning. They had just received the *Code of Wartime Practices* and frantically sought an appropriate authority who would agree to supersede the code. When they asked Price to define such authority, he replied that they would have to do that themselves. All three took the story to Paul C. Smith, the head of the navy's public relations press section. The AP was the first to arrive in the race to put the news on the wire. Smith approved the AP's version of the story because it said its source was reliable. But when the other two wire services asked Smith to clear their stories, they said they did not know if their sources were appropriate authorities. Smith, the former general manager of the *San Francisco Chronicle,* kept them from filing their dispatches while he called the Office of Naval Operations, the Bureau of Navigation, and the headquarters of the Third Naval District in New York City seeking confirmation of the sinking. All of the naval officers he contacted said they had no confirmation.[60] Admiral Adolphus Andrews, commandant of the Third District, later explained to *Editor & Publisher* that he did not want to give out information about the sinking until the facts had been verified and until the navy was convinced that the enemy submarine had escaped. In addition, he said he wanted to clear the information that he had with the navy's public relations office in Washington.[61] The delays imposed on the United Press and International News Service helped the AP score a clear scoop. The irony was that the AP's source was a Coast Guard captain for the Port of New York, who only released the details of the torpedoing in exchange for a promise that the wire service would verify the story with the navy.[62] Smith apologized to the nation's editors on January 17 and said news of future sinkings would be released simultaneously to the three wire services at the navy's public relations office in the capital. Smith's statement also asked journalists not to publicize a sinking until it had been cleared for release. "This rule applies even though the incident may be within the view of shore observers, and even if the information has been given by local officials, naval or otherwise," he said.[63]

He said nothing about survivors. This flaw became apparent as the submarine attacks continued and victims began floating or swimming ashore. The Office of Censorship and the navy tried to control breaches of security that might arise from interviews with surviving sailors. Early in February, Smith and Commander R. W. Berry presented Price with a draft statement that aimed to end the confusion and overlap. It said the navy would take charge of survivors and warn them about national security before they were interviewed by the press. The statement also said the navy would expect reporters to print nothing beyond the authorized disclosures. For news of enemy attacks, the Navy Department's press office in Washington would be the only appropriate authority. While Price agreed to the naval officers' rationale, he objected that their statement read too much like an order. He talked the two men into allowing the Office of Censorship to reword the request and issue it under civilian authority. The February 4 memorandum to the nation's journalists was the office's first clarification of the code.[64] In it, the Office of Censorship took part of the blame for the confusion but did not elaborate on its error. Press censor Nathaniel Howard later told the "missionaries" that in his zeal, he had tried to kill a submarine sinking story after it had been on the wire for three hours—an impossible proposition, considering the odds that some papers already had printed the item before receiving an order to kill it.[65]

Defending the policy to Krock, Sorrells said, "It might appear silly to make newspaper reporters cool their heels while a navy officer examines survivors of a sunken ship, but usually there is a good reason for that: i.e., the necessity of obtaining whatever information possible for use in a military way, and the bottling up of this information until such time as action might be taken to use this information in a military way."[66]

It might also appear silly to censor newspaper articles about enemy submarines. U-boat commanders were not in the habit of surfacing, docking in enemy ports, and buying the local paper. However, printed news of German attacks would be hard to keep off the radio, which enemy ships and submarines monitored. The Press Division knew that the chance of a submarine commander receiving useful information in this manner was remote, but it decided not to gamble even at such odds. Identical restrictions on press and radio had the added benefit of seeming fair.[67]

While Sorrells was writing to Krock, voluntary censorship of news of submarine attacks was being tested at the tip of Florida. On the evening of February 21, people in and around Palm Beach heard a series of explosions and saw flames light up the dark Atlantic sky. Survivors arrived on shore before dawn Sunday. Reporters from the *Miami Herald* and the *Palm Beach Post and Times* interviewed them on the beach. The stories did not appear in print until February 24, when the navy agreed to release news of the first of three sinkings. In the interim, the only mention of a submarine attack in the *Post and Times* was a front-page editorial, which said in its entirety, "If it's anything WE can't print, YOU shouldn't be talking about it."[68]

On the day the first stories appeared, the Palm Beach and Miami papers wired the Office of Censorship to protest the three-day delay. John D. Pennekamp, managing editor of the *Herald*, obviously had the facts before the navy's release. His telegram identified the three sunken ships as the tankers *Republic, Cities Service Empire,* and *W. D. Anderson,* even though the navy had not released the names of the last two. "Sink-ings public knowledge along coast since survivors already landed, explo-sions heard ashore, one derelict visible," he wrote. "Countless rumors and gossip doing more damage than facts would. We have adhered rigidly to regulations but feel this instance undermining public confidence in newspapers."[69] Don Morris, editor of the Palm Beach paper, wired that "every bootblack and streetwalker for 100 miles" knew the details. Local naval censors apparently wanted to release the story but were dissuaded by the new policy that releases had to originate in Washington.[70] Howard replied that U-boat commanders have imperfect knowledge of their at-tacks. Prolonging any doubts they might have about the damage that they inflicted might affect their next decision, to stay or depart. The navy also customarily notified next of kin of those killed in the attack be-fore releasing the news to the public, he said.[71] That was all well and good, Morris responded, but while his papers and the AP followed regu-lations and withheld the story, another news service distributed its report nationwide and also broadcast it over a chain of radio stations. "We are still a new and untried bureau," Howard candidly responded. "We make mistakes daily. We need your patience."[72]

The navy continued to announce only those sinkings that it could be sure the enemy knew about, or were apparent because of physical evi-dence such as wreckage. The sinking of the aircraft carrier *Lexington* on May 8 was not revealed until June 12, because the navy was uncertain whether Japan knew the ship had caught fire and sunk after the battle of the Coral Sea. If Japanese intelligence believed the carrier still was steam-ing through the Pacific, it might have altered its battle plans to defend against a ship that no longer existed, thus giving the Americans a tactical advantage.[73]

Delays in identifying ships that had been sunk began to accumulate. On July 19, Admiral Arthur J. Hepburn, director of navy public relations, told Price that 600 American merchant ships had been sunk in the Atlan-tic, but only 400 sinkings had been announced.[74] The slow pace struck many journalists as a cover-up and helped lead to the *New York Times*'s threatened showdown with the Office of Censorship in October 1942.

CENSORSHIP AND THE ARMY

The Office of Censorship's relationship with the army also had a rocky start. Price and his staff stood up to army officers several times when they gave conflicting or ill-advised instructions to journalists. The first showdown with the army occurred on January 20, 1942, when General Alexander D. Surles accused the Associated Press of ignoring War Department instructions to kill a report the AP had distributed on its news wires. The AP had picked up a story from Canada that said about 100 American servicemen had arrived in England after leaving a Canadian port. Surles, chief of army public relations, complained to Price after seeing the story in that day's *Washington Evening Star*. When Price investigated, he discovered that the wire service had notified all subscribers at 2:56 P.M. that the War Department urgently requested that the story not be published. That was two hours after the story had been transmitted over the news wires, and in the interim, papers nationwide, including the *Star*, had printed it in good faith. Price pointed out these facts and added that the War Department had not consulted the Office of Censorship before asking the AP to kill the story. If it had, Price would have approved publication. "This dispatch was released by the Canadian censorship, which certainly is a competent authority," he told Surles. "The fact that it was so released doubtless meant that it was broadcast over Canadian stations and heard in this country and at sea; and that it also was sent to England where, in all probability, it was published in newspapers and broadcast by the BBC." He suggested that the only effect of suppressing it would be to keep Americans ignorant of a story that the rest of the world knew.[75]

Army censorship suffered the same disparities as the navy's in 1942 as the services sought a consistent definition of appropriate authority. Efforts to report on the shelling of California illustrated the inconsistencies. A Japanese naval attack on the mainland occurred on the evening of February 22, 1942. Callers in California dialed Jack Lockhart at the Office of Censorship's late-night news desk to report a submarine firing shells onto the coast near Santa Barbara. The first call came from the AP, at 11:45 P.M., asking who would be the appropriate authority to release news of the attack, which caused no casualties and little damage. Lockhart directed the caller to the navy, but the navy's public relations office refused to accept responsibility. It named the army as appropriate authority because the target of the attack was on land. By 12:05 A.M., CBS radio was carrying the story, apparently without attributing it to an appropriate source; the AP still was waiting for an official to endorse the story, as spelled out in the voluntary code; and the United Press had put the story on its news wire after deciding to quote the Santa Barbara Police

Department as an appropriate authority. The first word that Lockhart received of the army agreeing to release the story came from the International News Service. It obtained permission of the Fourth Army Headquarters at 12:11 A.M., but the permission inexplicably was withdrawn during the next half hour. Finally, the AP called to point out that it had followed the censorship rules to the letter and wound up beaten by the competition. At that point, Lockhart considered the story "out of control" and freed all journalists covering it from code restrictions.[76] The Office of Censorship addressed the confusion on February 25 by confidentially telling journalists they would not need appropriate authority for stories about enemy attacks on the continental United States if they avoided details about military objectives, routes of ships and planes, and defensive responses.[77]

Price had the confusion at Santa Barbara in mind when he drafted a domestic air raid censorship policy after consulting with Surles, Hepburn, and representatives of the Federal Communications Commission, the Office of Civilian Defense, and the Federal Security Agency. His plan called for the army to shut down radio stations in the region threatened by attack, in order to deny the enemy the use of radio signals as a homing beacon. Taking radio off the air meant a greater responsibility for the news wires, which would become the quickest channel of mass communication about the raids. The army, which needed maximum control of information during a raid, would issue communiqués to the news media. Papers would be allowed to print them during the raid, but radio stations were to wait until after the raid to broadcast the news unless the War Department authorized immediate release. Price's plan became part of the revised codebooks for press and radio published on June 15, 1942.[78] The books said that after a raid had begun but before the army had issued any announcement, newspapers and news wire services should limit their stories to the fact that a raid was under way. They were not to estimate the number of planes or bombs but could say antiaircraft guns had begun firing. The codes to be followed by radio and the press after the conclusion of the raid were substantially the same, asking journalists to avoid sensationalism, rumors, and details that would compromise defenses or counterattacks if known by the enemy.[79] The effectiveness of Price's and the army's preparations was never tested; no planes ever bombed the mainland.

Of all of the clauses in the press code, none was trampled so often as the ban on identification of army and navy units going overseas or already stationed there. The revised press code expanded the original request to avoid news of troop movements by specifying that names of sailors should not be linked to ships or bases. In addition, the code said soldiers and sailors should not be linked to combat areas outside the United States unless that information had been released officially.[80] The rationale for the ban was to deny intelligence to the enemy, who conceivably could assemble enough information from leaks to assess the Allies' strength on a particular front. The Office of Censorship reinforced the need for secrecy on military units by distributing news releases in December 1942 and posters in February 1943 for editors to tack up in their newsrooms.[81] Scores of newspapers had asked for help in explaining the ban on military addresses to the parents and friends of servicemen who did not understand the need for silence. In bold, black letters, the poster said that the name and number of a company, regiment, division, ship, or squadron could not be published. "Careless talk costs lives," it concluded.[82]

Hard hit by the ban were the nation's black publications, which took pride in every milestone achieved by black servicemen in the segregated armed forces. Early in 1942, officials of the National Negro Newspaper Association and the *Chicago Defender* pledged to Price that they would cooperate with voluntary censorship, and Price assured them that the black press would play a vital wartime role by offering counsel to black readers "sanely and wisely."[83] Relations between the black press and censorship occasionally were tested during the next two years. The Associated Negro Press, a Chicago-based news service for black newspapers nationwide, and the *Defender,* the nation's second-largest black newspaper behind the *Pittsburgh Courier,* were asked in April 1943 to print virtually nothing about long-awaited combat assignments for the all-black 99th Pursuit Squadron, known as the Tuskegee Airmen. The Office of Censorship responded to their requests for leniency concerning news about the Tuskegee fliers by saying they could publish nothing more than a statement that Representative Frances Bolton of Ohio had placed in the *Congressional Record* announcing the departure of the first squadron of black aviators for overseas assignments. It also forbade any speculation about the squadron's Army Air Corps unit identification.[84] The Associated Negro Press confidentially told its clients that it expected details on the fliers' combat roles to be released when they reached their overseas stations in May 1943. "No paper may publish any information about

Poster issued by the Office of Censorship. Many newspaper editors prominently displayed this poster to explain to relatives of servicemen why they could not publish military addresses, which were considered potentially valuable to the enemy. National Archives.

Poster issued by the Office of War Information. The federal government encouraged ordinary Americans to think about national security with posters such as this.
National Archives.

the departure of the 99th until that time," the agency said in a memorandum.[85] The army released news of the Tuskegee Airmen's kills in the Mediterranean in 1943 and 1944 to an appreciative black press. During the entire war, censors lodged only one major complaint of a code violation by the black press, involving the Associated Negro Press and the *Defender*. The wire service inadvertently released details about the departure of the black 332nd Fighter Group for Europe in January 1944. It asked its client newspapers to spike the story, and all did so except the *Defender*. The paper modified the story in an attempt to make it acceptable for publication, believing it would give black Americans a needed morale boost. However, the Office of Censorship objected that the story still said too much, and it gave the *Defender* a measured reprimand.[86] Overall, black papers violated the censorship code no more than any other types of publications.

PROPAGANDA AND PUBLICITY

The Office of Censorship carried out its duties silently. Unlike the army, navy, and many government agencies, Price kept his office out of the publicity business. The Office of Censorship had only four press conferences during the war, preferring to issue notes, most of them confidentially, to editors and broadcasters. This aversion to publicity was rare in wartime Washington. When the Office of Censorship was established, many government agencies were producing a whirlwind of information for public consumption. The Office of Facts and Figures, under Archibald MacLeish, delivered war reports to journalists throughout the United States. The Office of the Coordinator of Information, led by William J. Donovan, gathered information relating to national security and, through its Foreign Information Service, dispatched propaganda overseas. Outside Donovan's jurisdiction was Latin America, the fiefdom of Nelson Rockefeller's Office of the Coordinator of Inter-American Affairs, which combined propaganda, publicity, and censorship aimed south of the border. The Office of Government Reports monitored the nation's news media and partially duplicated the function of the Office of Facts and Figures by distributing news as well. Many other government agencies also produced their own publicity.

Conflicts among the many agencies jeopardized the entire information system by early 1942. Demands arose for stronger propaganda to be dispatched overseas and more information to be released domestically, but federal officials could not agree on a program. Historian Allan M.

Winkler quotes one observer who characterized the government's information system as chaos: "It all seems to boil down to three bitter complaints: first, that there was too much information; second, that there wasn't enough of it; and third, that in any event it was confusing and inconsistent."[87] In his notebook, Price described the government's system of communicating war news during the first three months of combat as wasteful, contradictory, and counterproductive to effective censorship.[88]

He said the confusion was so widespread that he made an appointment to talk to Stephen T. Early on March 13, 1942. Before going to the White House, he discovered that Samuel Rosenman already had begun work on a plan to consolidate the government's many information offices. Price invited Frank Walker, the head of his Policy Board, to join him at the White House, and they then talked with Early and Rosenman for an hour. Rosenman and Harold D. Smith, director of the Bureau of the Budget, had drafted an executive order to create a war news agency.[89] Walker and Early examined the draft and proposed that the director of the Office of Censorship also lead the new information office and censor government press releases. Price rejected the idea. While it might be possible to combine news policy and censorship, any attempt to combine propaganda and censorship would reproduce the unpopular conditions of the Creel Committee in World War I, he said.[90]

Price took a copy of the draft back to his office, studied it, and decided to write his own version. He sent it to Early on March 18, suggesting that the new agency be called the Office of War Research and Education. It should have the same authority over war news distribution that the censorship director enjoyed over war news restrictions, he said, and it should operate separate divisions for news and propaganda to avoid tainting the "sacred" and "factual" qualities of the army's and the navy's communiqués.[91]

The president preferred to call the new agency the Office of War Information (OWI). He created it by executive order on June 13, 1942. Rejecting advice that Price be put in charge and Sorrells elevated to censorship director, Roosevelt instead followed Rosenman's suggestion and selected Elmer Davis, the broadcast newsman, as director.[92] Under Davis, the OWI combined the Office of Government Reports and the Office of Facts and Figures and absorbed the foreign news–gathering and propaganda functions of the Office of the Coordinator of Information. Conspicuous by its absence in the executive order was any mention of censorship.[93]

In a joint interview with Price and Davis that appeared in August, the *New York Times*'s Arthur Krock elicited from them a simplified description of their relations with journalists. Davis told him, "We give them stuff we hope they will print," and Price said, "We tell them what they cannot print."[94] In practice, the division was not so cleanly defined. The owi's field offices received many journalists' requests for advice on how to present news of the war, because the name of the agency suggested such a function and because the agency had many branch offices, unlike the Press and Broadcasting Divisions of the Office of Censorship. owi employees sometimes asked journalists to suppress information, a request that should have come from Price's office. In addition to quarreling about censoring the domestic press, the owi and Office of Censorship clashed over the authority to shape messages for foreign-language audiences, both in the United States and overseas. The owi considered the censors' interpretation of their duties to be too broad, wrongly expanding from security matters to the exercise of final authority on matters of international, political, and broadcast policy. The censors, while never having killed an owi press release, narrowly interpreted their authority. In particular, Sorrells and Broadcasting Division director J. Harold Ryan were reluctant to let the owi release information without subjecting it to censorship, while Price and Howard were more willing to compromise. In October 1942, Sorrells suggested that the two agencies spell out their responsibilities in a formal agreement.[95] The resulting five-page, single-spaced owi–Office of Censorship agreement appeared on November 15. In it, the two agencies promised to share information but to keep their functions separate along the lines suggested in the Krock interview. The accord recognized Price's office as the sole authority for censoring all domestic news media, including foreign-language radio, but prevented censors from suggesting news themes and topics that would promote the war effort. The agreement reserved that role for the owi and granted it status as an appropriate authority able to supersede the censorship codes.[96]

Yet, some people outside the Office of Censorship—including owi employees—continued to act as censors. In the spring of 1943, Davis and Early, apparently with Roosevelt's blessing, tried to discourage reporters from covering an international conference on postwar food distribution, raising cries of unnecessary censorship. The trouble began when three members of the American Society of Newspaper Editors (ASNE) talked the society's board of governors into letting them form a Washington committee in late 1942. It was to act as a liaison between the federal government and the association's members, collecting and distributing insiders' information. David Lawrence of *United States News,* Ben McKelway of the *Washington Evening Star,* and Alexander F. Jones of the *Washington Post* called themselves the ASNE's Washington committee, and they issued a bulletin to ASNE members on March 19, 1943, that undercut censorship. It said Early and Davis had informed the Washington committee of plans for an International Conference on Food Problems. The two officials had asked for journalists' cooperation in not reporting on the talks, allowing the delegates to work without interruption. The bulletin, signed by Lawrence and Jones but not McKelway, who was out of town, said: "It is hoped by Mr. Davis and Mr. Early that the handling of this particular conference will not be misinterpreted as any desire to exclude the press from knowing what is happening, but it is a plan decided upon in order to enable the conference to study and discuss the problems involved without having the conference impaired by piece-meal articles or by the premature disclosure of items which could be used in Europe and elsewhere to stir up antagonisms against the United States and its policies in handling the food problem." [97]

Technically, the request to refrain from publicizing the conference was in accord with the *Code of Wartime Practices,* which restricted "premature disclosures of diplomatic negotiations or conversations," [98] but the source of the request bothered many journalists as well as the censorship director. Reporters asked Price whether he had abdicated some of his responsibilities to Davis, Early, and the ASNE. They protested that closing the conference, which was scheduled to begin May 18 at Hot Springs, Virginia, would hide important news. Throughout the controversy, Price kept a low profile. The Office of Censorship's sole response was to tell inquiring reporters that it had never made any requests for limiting coverage of the conference, and to add that Price had not relinquished any of his responsibilities. [99] However, the Office of Censorship quietly signed an agreement with the OWI on April 10 that reaffirmed the two agencies' commitment to avoid overlapping jurisdiction. The accord was prompted not only by the Hot Springs conflict but also by the censors' discovery of an OWI attempt to censor a small New York magazine, *She,* for morale purposes. [100] The offending article explored the feelings of American women toward Jews. Although the writers emphasized that 75 percent of women whom they surveyed disapproved of anti-Semitism, they quoted respondents who characterized Jews as "prone to take advantage of their customers," "ruthless and devoid of . . . compassion," "aloof," and "arrogant."[101] Such candor was at least a political embarrassment and at most a useful weapon for Nazi propagandists. However, such opinions could not be censored under the *Code of Wartime Practices* and could be punished only by the confiscation of copies of the magazine addressed to recipients outside the country.

When reporters ignored the Washington committee bulletin and arrived at Hot Springs early in May, they initially were barred from the delegates' building by guards. However, the Roosevelt administration reversed its policy and allowed reporters access to the delegates' quarters after receiving protests from the Ohio Farm Federation and Moses Koenigsberg, the former president of the International News Service, who had arrived to cover the conference.[102] Perhaps Roosevelt sensed that secrecy had too high a price if it antagonized hundreds of journalists.

Throughout the war, the OWI, the army, and the navy continued to exercise information control within their jurisdiction regarding the release of military information, including the censorship of photographs and news stories that might ignite racial, class, and ethnic troubles Photographs from the combat zone were submitted to compulsory military review, and many deemed too gruesome for public consumption were kept hidden by the War Department's Bureau of Public Relations. America's fortunes of war had suffered early in 1942, yet Roosevelt, Henry Stimson, and other government officials believed that morale could be sustained if images of war released for public consumption re mained upbeat. Consequently, for the first twenty months after the attack at Pearl Harbor, the government did not release for publication any photos of dead American soldiers from the combat zones. Hollywood did its part, too. The OWI's Bureau of Motion Pictures reviewed scripts and often worked to make changes, emphasizing the need for an earnest prosecution of the war. But early war films were rose-tinted. From May to November 1942, only five out of sixty-one feature films that contained war scenes depicted American combat deaths. Davis fought the sanitized view of the war, in both fact and fantasy, as being counterproductive. An OWI memo of 1943 suggested that the whitewashed images of war that appeared in print were creating the danger of Americans thinking that "soldiers fight [and] . . . some of them get hurt and ride smiling in aerial ambulances, but . . . none of them get badly shot or spill any blood."[103] Hollywood movies gradually added more physical and emotional pain to their depiction of combat, although the OWI asked producers in 1943 to "minimize the bloody aspects." To keep the home front motivated and to prepare Americans for even greater combat death counts, the military released the first news photographs of dead soldiers for publication in September 1943. The image of corpses in New Guinea appeared in *Life* magazine to readers' generally supportive and understanding reactions, and pictures of dead Americans appeared regularly afterward.[104] Despite the more lenient rules, photographers in the combat zones sometimes refrained from wasting film on scenes they knew would never see publication, and according to novelist and war correspondent John Steinbeck, combat reporters avoided too much of war's awful realities in their dispatches out of the fervently held belief that it was the best thing to do.[105]

Except for an occasional protest when he considered combat zone censorship too severe, Price was content to let the OWI and military agencies shape information within their jurisdictions and suggest themes in movies, advertisements, newsreels, and other media that would promote the desired response from the audience. Concerning actual censorship of the domestic press and radio, however, he fiercely defended his authority. His last major turf battle occurred in the winter of 1943–44. General George Strong, chief of the Military Intelligence Division, phoned Price on Christmas Eve to say he was preparing to seek an end to civilian authority over domestic censorship. Price noted in his memoir that Strong disliked journalists reporting about military affairs in wartime and thought the best way to control them was "a stern command to mind their own business and a swift kick in the rear."[106] In 1943 Strong had become convinced that the press and radio would have to be placed under strong censorship controls. He believed journalists were writing too much about radar, which he considered to be a military secret, and he disliked the rule that an appropriate authority could override the code. What had prompted his concern was the nation's military buildup for the invasion of Europe. Strong, who headed an office established by the Joint Chiefs of Staff to safeguard the secrecy of the 1944 invasion plans, considered all speculation about the date and place of the landings to be a security violation.[107] Strong's office had pressured the army's public relations officers to release less and less information, resulting in both an increase in military secrecy and a more militaristic tone in attempts to dictate details of news coverage to reporters. Price noted the crackdown on December 9, 1943, which was one day before the Office of Censorship planned to announce completion of its third revision of the *Code of Wartime Practices* and two weeks after broadcaster Drew Pearson exposed the three-month cover-up of General George S. Patton's assault of two shell-shocked soldiers in Sicily. Price issued a public statement urging broadcasters and editors to get more news to the public, and not to allow others to censor for them. He warned of a "dangerous psychology of overcensorship" that could be created by "a miscellany of volunteer firemen."[108] At an Office of Censorship press conference introducing the revised *Code of Wartime Practices* on December 10, journalists asked Price to identify the "volunteer firemen" who were overstepping their authority. He grinned and refused, saying his memo spoke for itself and that "anyone whom the cap fits could wear it." Price did not wish to insult the War and Navy Departments by identifying them publicly.[109] However, *Time* said Price's comments were directed at army and navy security officers as well as press agents for domestic war plants.[110] Strong privately asked Price to elaborate about the statement, and Stimson wrote in his diary on December 21 that the general was troubled by censorship regulations, particularly "a recent edict" by Price.[111]

In his yuletide call, Strong read Price excerpts of a letter he was preparing to send to the Joint Chiefs. Price felt relief after the call because the behind-the-scenes sparring between the Office of Censorship and the military was over. An assault on civilian censorship would lead to a decision at the White House that he hoped would clarify the lines of authority. Price passed along Strong's objections to Admiral William D. Leahy, a member of the Joint Chiefs who also was Roosevelt's chief of staff. Leahy considered Price's work "excellent" and preferred Price's voluntary censorship to Strong's military version. He recorded in his memoir that several times during the war he had investigated military complaints about the ineffectiveness of voluntary domestic censorship, only to discover that civilians compromised national security no more often than the military. The Joint Chiefs later discussed the issue and decided to support Price. Leahy noted that not long after being thwarted in his takeover bid, Strong lost his job at military intelligence to General Clayton L. Bissell, who did not share his predecessor's concerns about civilian censorship. Leahy did not indicate whether there was a connection between the two events.[112]

The defeat of Strong's attempt to take over the Office of Censorship left the decisions about censorship in civilian hands at a crucial time of the war. But Price still had one more battle to ensure that his role as censor would not be compromised. In January 1944, Roosevelt asked Price to assume control of an agency combining the OWI and the Office of

Censorship. Price was reluctant to do so for two reasons. First, as a journalist he disliked press agents, considering them akin to salesmen. Second, he considered the OWI to be an administrative mess because of a personality clash between Robert Sherwood, who was in charge of the overseas branch in New York, and his boss, Elmer Davis.[113] Both men were better suited to literary pursuits than administration. Davis told Roosevelt on January 8 that Sherwood's office was ineffective, poorly organized, and compromised by political intrigue. He had ordered Sherwood to discharge three subordinates, but Sherwood refused and declared that Davis himself was incompetent. The two men submitted their dispute to Roosevelt, with Davis threatening to resign unless he received the president's backing.[114] Roosevelt wanted more options and thought he had settled on a solution when he asked his legal adviser, Rosenman, to draft an executive order combining censorship and war information.[115] Meanwhile, Early told George W. Healy Jr., the censorship missionary from New Orleans, that the reorganization would make Price the supervisor of all war information policy and the Press Division's Nathaniel Howard the director of the subagency of censorship.[116]

While Price did not want a job combining censorship and publicity, neither did he want to resign. He stalled for time by requesting amendments to Rosenman's executive order, asking for the same "absolute discretion" that the president had given him at the Office of Censorship. In a memorandum to Roosevelt, Price said it was essential that if he took over the combined OWI–Office of Censorship, he must have the power to fire any employee of either agency. Given his harmonious relationship with his own staff, that request meant he had reservations about some of Davis's staff members. He also asked for control over army and navy publicity. In short, while Price disliked the Creel Committee's combined censorship, publicity, and propaganda functions in World War I, if he took the new job he wanted to avoid the interference that had hurt Creel's effectiveness. He probably knew he was asking for the impossible from Roosevelt in hopes of forestalling the appointment. "My suggestion would be that no attempt be made at the present time to combine Censorship and OWI," he told Roosevelt in the same memo in which he spelled out his conditions.[117]

Rumors of the proposed reorganization leaked, catching Davis by surprise. Davis told Roosevelt he had no intention of resigning; Sherwood feared that a shakeup would hurt the president politically. Roosevelt told

Davis and Sherwood to patch up their differences. The former continued in office and the latter moved to the OWI branch in London.[118]

With the death of the proposal to merge the OWI and the Office of Censorship, and with the defeat of military attempts to assume control over domestic censorship, by the end of January 1944 Price had established clear lines of authority and responsibility. He knew how he wanted to run censorship and defended that vision. He would continue to have differences with the army, the navy, and the White House throughout the war, but none would threaten the foundation of voluntary censorship.

Umpires Have Called the Game
for Reasons I Cannot Speak Of

Radio Censorship

The sky was gray and getting grayer at 9 P.M. on August 28, 1942, when Lee Artoe, a tackle for the Chicago Bears, kicked off to start the annual *Chicago Tribune* charity game at Soldier Field between the defending National Football League champions and the College All-Stars. The college squad ran three plays, gained seven yards and punted, giving Chicago the ball at its thirty-nine yard line. Fullback "Bullet" Bill Osmanski and halfbacks Ray Nolting and Hugh Gallarneau then reeled off fifty-seven yards on eleven carries. Gallarneau capped off the series of plays by taking a quick handoff and slashing four yards into the end zone. The game looked like business as usual for the Bears, who had won two consecutive professional football titles as well as three previous games against the nation's best college players. But this game would be anything but ordinary.[1]

The air on that night was a muggy 71 degrees. Unexpectedly, fog from Lake Michigan began rolling over the stadium. During the second quarter, the white, wet blanket descended from the highest seats and settled on the grass. It lifted a bit at halftime, when 2,500 sailors marched from their seats in the north end zone to midfield and held aloft colored cardboard squares to form a giant American flag, a reminder that the United States had been at war for eight months. But afterward, in the third quarter, fog obliterated everything once more. "From the top tiers, only the blazing lights were visible across the field and the contestants were obscured except for infrequent glimpses of reflected light from silver or white pants of the players," the *Tribune* said.[2]

Sitting in radio station WGN's booth high above the football field, play-by-play announcer Bob Elson could not see well enough to describe the game. Shortly after 11 P.M., Elson told a nationwide audience listening over a Mutual Broadcasting System hookup that he would have to relay information from the public address loudspeakers. At 11:32, he said, "Remember, we have to depend entirely now on field announcers. We are far from the field." Among the listeners that night as the Bears blanked the All-Stars, 21–0, was the staff of the night radio news desk at the Office of Censorship in Washington. Someone jotted down a rough transcript of Elson's commentary, which included the following: 11:41 P.M. — "The All-Stars, I presume, are by now in a huddle. By now they OUGHT to be out of it." 11:43 P.M. — "There's the gun. Well, you could hear that anyway. We know that much." 11:53 P.M. — "This game is being played under the strangest circumstances that I've witnessed in 15 years of being on the sport scene. I've never seen anything like it."[3]

Oddly, Elson never explained why the game was unique. He never used the "F" word—"fog"—or alluded to the weather. Instead of a reprimand for incomplete reporting, however, Elson received a letter of thanks. F. W. Reichelderfer, chief of the U.S. Weather Bureau, wrote, "I wish you would accept our very sincere congratulations upon the most adroit and, at the same time, satisfactory piece of radio reporting." He told the radio censor who had sent him a copy of the WGN transcript that he had read it aloud to four meteorologists and was delighted when they tried to guess the cause of Elson's difficulty. Two said rain, one said snow, and one said a failure of the lights.[4]

Meteorologists and censors approved of radio announcers who said little about the weather during the first twenty-two months of American participation in World War II. Even better, according to the editions of the voluntary censorship code in effect from January 15, 1942, to October 12, 1943, were broadcasters who said nothing at all about rain, snow, fog, wind, air pressure, temperature, or sunshine, unless authorized to do so by the Weather Bureau. Military authorities had asked the Office of Censorship to severely limit weather information on the radio, believing that too much would help the enemy attack ships and coastal installations.

Although the censorship codes for publishers and broadcasters were substantially the same, the radio code included unique sections on weather, live-microphone ad-libs, quiz shows, phonograph-record requests and dedications, "man in the street" programs, and foreign-language broadcasts. All were severely curtailed or knocked off the air during the early war years. The restrictions upset many broadcasters until they devised new programs that served their listeners without running afoul of the code. Little did they know that much stronger controls over radio, including a ban on broadcasts of major-league baseball games, had been discussed and rejected.

Radio, which had been taken over by the navy during World War I,[5] was facing its first domestic broadcasting test during wartime, and not everyone was as confident as censorship director Byron Price that it could walk the narrow line between revealing too much about the nation's defenses and not revealing enough to keep listeners informed and their morale high. On the one hand, the army and navy voiced concerns that radio's freedom posed a security risk. Signals from 901 commercial stations filled the air on the first day of 1942, and only about 510 of them were affiliated with a network. Radio's size, independence, and decentralization made it difficult to monitor, much less control, and the speed with which it might send information to the enemy was frightening. On the other hand, three-quarters of the stations had no more than 1,000 watts of power, too weak to consistently reach Axis ears, causing some small stations to complain that radio's censorship code was unfair.[6]

Within two weeks after America entered the war, the Weather Bureau began asking radio stations to minimize the meteorological information they broadcast. Unrestricted broadcasts would give the German and Japanese navies tactically valuable knowledge of the weather along the American coastlines. Reichelderfer feared that an enemy commander would "shop around" on the radio dial and assemble a weather map by listening to weather broadcasts from several cities. On December 16, he responded to a letter of inquiry from radio stations WRC and WMAL in Washington, D.C., by urging them to limit their weather news to warnings of serious conditions such as hurricanes and floods.[7] He relayed the same message to all of the nation's stations three days later. Only announcements intended to prevent death and serious damage to crops or transportation were advisable, he said, and those statements would be provided by the government. Reichelderfer made his request "for military reasons," and although published reports did not cite his authority, broadcasters knew that the Communications Act of 1934 subjected their stations to government licensing and gave the president the right to control radio during wartime.[8]

Reichelderfer's request came with a price tag. Before the war, many stations had sold airtime to allow advertisers to sponsor the weather news. At WOR in New York, for example, Breyers Ice Cream sponsored the daily forecast.[9] Nevertheless, all stations apparently complied with Reichelderfer's request and dropped their routine weather programs. Radio's most influential professional organization, the National Association of Broadcasters, prepared the way, having asked stations during the week after the attack on Pearl Harbor to cooperate completely with the war effort. After listening to President Franklin Roosevelt include a plea for objective wartime journalism in his December 9 fireside chat, N.A.B. president Neville Miller had wired all American radio stations to urge "unusually careful judgment in selecting news."[10]

Price and his two chief assistants, John Sorrells of the Press Division and J. Harold Ryan of the Broadcasting Division, conferred in early January with Reichelderfer and a group of army and navy public relations officers about the wording of a short weather clause to be included in the first press and radio editions of the *Code of Wartime Practices*. On the night of January 11, four days before the codebooks were to be issued, Sorrells learned that some of the meteorologists at the Weather Bureau and another group of army and navy officers had been writing their own weather regulations and planned to distribute them to newspapers. Price tried to reach Reichelderfer by phone but failed. He then called Postmaster General Frank C. Walker, the chairman of the Censorship Policy Board, to argue that no plan for weather news censorship should be issued without Price's approval. Walker called the Commerce Department and halted the work of the freelance censors until Price could examine their proposed code the next day. "It was about 900 words in length, extremely complicated, and entirely mandatory in tone," Price noted. The Office of Censorship's *History* was more succinct: "No editor could understand it, much less follow it."[11]

Price convened a conference on January 13 at the Weather Bureau and noted that a "great deal of gold braid" arrived to represent the armed forces' viewpoint. He said that the proposed document's militaristic tone would antagonize journalists. When a colonel suggested that the army and navy edit the document, Price reminded them that his authority came from the president.[12]

The army, navy, and Weather Bureau agreed to recognize Price's authority, although they no doubt were keenly interested when the Office of Censorship issued its twin codebooks for press and radio on January 15. The weather clause consisted of about 100 words in both books and constituted the only major difference between the suggested treatment of news stories by the two media. The press code allowed newspapers to print temperature tables for as many as twenty cities, news of existing weather conditions, and Weather Bureau weather forecasts, whereas the radio code asked stations to avoid all references to weather except for reports authorized by the Weather Bureau specifically for broadcast, and those would be to warn of storms and other weather emergencies.[13] A few drops of rain at El Paso, high winds at Kansas City, and snow in Detroit might tell submarine commanders which part of the East Coast soon would have rough weather or fog.[14]

REGULATING "AD-LIB PROGRAMS"

The broadcast code also included special entries for entertainment and informal talk shows, which it called "ad-lib programs." They fell into four categories: quiz programs, forums and interviews, commentaries and descriptions, and request programs.

The code defined a "quiz show" as any program in which people were asked questions and gave unscripted answers. These included question-and-answer game shows, man-in-the-street programs, and interviews with travelers arriving at airports and train terminals. The code asked for a halt to all such shows originating outside radio studios, unless the participants were carefully screened and supervised. The censors feared that if unsupervised groups had access to open microphones, an enemy agent in the crowd might try to send a coded message over the airwaves. The quiz-show section concluded, "In all studio-audience type quiz shows, where the audience from which interviewees are to be selected numbers less than 50 people, program conductors are asked to exercise special care. They should devise a method whereby no individual seeking participation can be guaranteed participation." The section on forums and interviews applied to programs in which people were given the chance for extemporaneous comment, including panel discussions and interviews by broadcasters. The code urged caution in seeking comment from audience members, although it did not ask for a ban. The commentaries and descriptions section was intended to prevent journalists from giving attackers valuable information about the success of any raids on the American mainland, and to avoid details about war installations that might help the enemy plan future offensives.[15]

The codebook's section on request programs called for safeguards to ensure that no one could send a coded message by requesting a song on the radio. No requests for specific dedication times should be accepted, the code said. Many stations had been accustomed to playing musical numbers requested over the phone, with the announcer broadcasting the dedications. Censors feared that spies could inform submarine commanders of the hour of departure and other details of naval movements by keying the message to a clever code consisting of names and song titles. For example, "Don't Sit under the Apple Tree," dedicated to Sarah, might tell a U-boat commander of the departure of a troop transport from Boston at midnight.[16] Broadcasters also were cautioned to accept only written notices of lost dogs and lost property. The possible abuses of lost-and-found advertisements struck Price at an unspecified date early in the war as he listened to his radio while eating breakfast at his Washington home. "Mrs. John Jones has just telephoned me that she has lost a dog," Price heard the announcer say. "It is a black bulldog of medium size, having three white spots on its back. It wears a leather collar with seven brass rivets. The tag number is 897362. Repeat 897362. The dog was last seen at 4:34 P.M. yesterday at the corner of Fourteenth Street and Florida Avenue." He had no doubt that Jones and her dog were real, but he knew that a spy could hide secret information in the combination of colors and numbers that made up the spotted bulldog's description. Price "made such a nuisance" about the story, apparently repeating it to broadcasters and warning them of its dangers, that the bulldog became legendary in American radio. The weather and ad-lib provisions represented financial setbacks for radio. According to Price, ending man-in-the-street interviews hurt the broadcasting industry more than any other Office of Censorship decision. The shows were inexpensive and popular, and killing them cost radio stations, Price estimated, "tens of millions of dollars" in advertising during the war.[17] That may have been true in the initial months of the war, but an advertising boom more than made up for the loss. Wartime production brought high profits to manufacturers, many of whom used advertising as a convenient way to avoid taxes on those profits. Treasury secretary Henry Morganthau Jr. ruled in May 1942 that advertising bearing "a reasonable relation to the business activities in which the enterprise is engaged" was tax deductible.[18] He did not define "reasonable," leaving the gate open for companies to advertise as a means to alter their tax bills. Morganthau announced in August 1942 that ads focusing on the sale of war bonds, conservation, or other government objectives related to the war would be considered institutional or goodwill advertising of the manufacturer and thus deductible.

That ruling led to large increases in war-themed advertisements and ad revenue. Money spent on national spot advertising rose from $58.8 million in 1942 to $91.8 million in 1945; in the same period, local advertising expenditures nearly doubled.[19]

In the first week after the censorship code was released, many radio programs were modified or dropped. WJJD in Chicago killed the program "What's Your Opinion," and WIND, also in the Windy City, stopped accepting telegrams for musical requests on "Night Watch." In Nashville, Tennessee, WLAC dropped the interview program "Air Traveler" and moved "Curbstone College," in which pedestrians gave their opinions, indoors into a studio.[20]

The code's issue prompted the cancellation of the Peabody Award–winning "Mail Bag" program on shortwave station WGEO in Schenectady, New York. The station halted the show to avoid the risk of reading a letter from an Axis agent.[21] But that was a comparatively minor sacrifice. On November 1, 1942, the federal government began leasing the nation's fourteen privately owned shortwave transmitters for the duration of the war. The Office of the Coordinator of Inter-American Affairs, which created programs specifically for Latin American audiences, broadcast in shortwave for eight hours each day, while the Office of War Information, which targeted the rest of the world, broadcast for sixteen.[22]

At a news conference on January 19, 1942, Price said that "because of its international aspects," radio must be more severely censored than the print press, but, Price and Ryan emphasized equal treatment for all stations, large and small.[23] A month later, Ryan told broadcasters that the power of a radio station's signal was irrelevant to the code. Freakish atmospheric conditions sometimes sent even weak radio signals halfway around the globe. A merchant vessel radio operator had reported that he had tuned in 287 American radio stations one night off the coast of China in 1934, Ryan said.[24]

Not all broadcasters accepted censorship readily. A committee of the National Association of Broadcasters chaired by John Shepard III, president of the New England–based Yankee Network, appealed in late January 1942 for a continuance of man-in-the-street programs. He asked the censors to police such shows and complained that about $3 million in local advertising contracts would be affected immediately by the code. Ryan answered that the stakes of warfare were too high to allow open microphones in crowds.[25]

The four national networks did not complain about the code. Compliance with the live-microphone provisions was relatively easy for big-budget programs that originated in studios.[26] The *Code of Wartime Practices for American Broadcasters* allowed quiz shows in large theaters where "the danger is not so great."[27] Price told a closed-circuit nationwide hookup of NBC stations on January 21 that the Office of Censorship had no intention of killing the network programs "Information, Please" and "Doctor I.Q." because they were closely supervised.[28]

At small stations that had no network affiliation or that broadcast their own quiz and ad-lib programs, producers found ways to maintain their live-microphone broadcasts with the censors' blessing. A Cincinnati station, WKRC, replaced its man-in-the-street program with "Mike's Luncheon Party," in which several women, who were selected from the many women who wrote in, participated in a lunchtime game show.[29] A Kentucky station moved its man-in-the-street program into a studio and called it "man-off-the-street."[30] However, no ad-lib program could gain approval until the broadcaster described all precautions it was taking to the censors and obtained written permission to proceed.[31]

In its first six weeks of operation, the Broadcasting Division wrote 500 letters to radio stations. Four-fifths of them contained opinions that broadcasters had requested on whether their programs complied with the voluntary censorship code.[32] For the first six months of 1942, the Broadcasting Division's only direct contact with the airwaves was via a receiver at the Federal Trade Commission building that was not powerful enough to pull in every major station. Aside from the limited number of programs that the staff could hear, the division learned about code violations through stories in trade journals, letters from the public, and letters from stations, some of which contained complaints about competitors' transgressions. When Charter Heslep, the former night news editor of NBC in New York, joined the division in June, he recommended that censors monitor the national networks by installing direct lines from the four affiliates in Washington. Listening to the networks would give censors the pulse of radio nationwide. Monitoring of networks began on July 15, 1942, and by August the Broadcasting Division's news desk was listening to an average of more than thirty broadcast programs per day. Through an agreement with the FCC, the division began spot-checking broadcasts from individual radio stations in November 1942. It also began asking stations to submit foreign-language scripts for review, starting with Italian- and German-language programs in September 1942.[33]

Most of the violations uncovered by the Broadcasting Division involved the weather code. The censors were not surprised; they realized that avoiding news about the weather presented unusual challenges, especially in sportscasts. In January 1942, censors and Weather Bureau meteorologists had several discussions on the special problem of sports. If a storm broke during a baseball game between the Yankees and the Red Sox, how could the announcer explain the reason for the game delay to the radio audience? And, if enemy agents had a complete schedule of major-league baseball games, couldn't they form a crude national weather map by listening to the radio or reading a paper and noting which home games had been "postponed"? One possible solution was to ban broadcasts of outdoor sports events for the duration of the war. It was discussed and quickly rejected. The staffs of the Broadcasting Division and the Weather Bureau agreed unanimously that the intangible costs of banning baseball broadcasts outweighed the benefits.[34] When the Thirteenth Naval District in Seattle warned in August 1942 that the Japanese received valuable weather information whenever radio stations gave a baseball roundup, Ryan replied, "The assistance to enemy agents offered by the deductions that there has been rain in a certain city because a baseball game has not been played as scheduled, or has been discontinued during the playing, etc., is very slight indeed, whereas if no mention were to be made of the game so scheduled, either on the air or in the press, the disappointment and deterioration of public morale might be very great indeed."[35] He suggested that the Seattle naval officer who objected to the broadcasts was no baseball fan. In a letter a few months later to FCC chairman James Lawrence Fly, who had raised the same issue but did not suggest a solution, Price said that baseball had to stay on the radio for the good of the country.[36]

The first radio censorship codebook asked sports broadcasters to take special care to avoid "inadvertent references" to the weather.[37] However, it offered no suggestions for dealing with broadcasts in progress when weather affected a game. In a March 20 memorandum to play-by-play announcers in preparation for the 1942 baseball season, Ryan said that if bad weather canceled a game, stations were to announce the cancellation without giving a reason.[38] The weather clause's sportscasting restriction proved difficult to enforce. Weather plays a key role in athletic performance, and sportscasters were accustomed to talking about it without much thought. Furthermore, the ban on weather news extended to everyone who had access to a microphone, including athletes being interviewed who might not know the censorship code. Dozens of such violations were flagged by the censor. Station WCFL in Chicago apologized to Ryan for the remarks of sportscaster Hal Totten, who technically avoided mention of the weather but left no room for doubt about a major-league game on July 3, 1943. According to the field office of the FCC, which monitored the broadcast, Totten said, "The umpires have called the game for reasons I cannot speak of, but whatever has caused the delay is also making the spectators go back for cover, and yes, here come the ground keepers with whatever is used to cover the ground so whatever is causing the delay won't affect the ground too much."[39]

The FCC sent a transcript to the Office of Censorship. Ryan accused Totten of "nibbling" at the code, and WCFL general manager Maynard Marquardt agreed that Totten's remarks were ill-advised. He promised that whenever weather halted a future game, the broadcast would be switched to the studio without comment except a brief announcement that the game had been "called." Marquardt vowed to fire sportscasters who disobeyed the broadcasting codebook's weather regulations.[40]

By the time of Totten's broadcast, the censorship code had been amended to offer broadcasters guidance on how to end a sportscast without calling attention to rain, snow, or other adverse weather conditions. The third edition of the radio code, issued February 1, 1943, suggested that announcers use one of the following phrases: "Game called because of weather," "wet grounds," or "muddy field." The censors had decided the preceding February that broadcast descriptions of ground conditions, such as flooding, and fishing forecasts were permissible if no mention were made of current conditions in the sky.[41]

The ban on weather news had a serious side. Tornadoes that struck near Memphis, Tennessee, on March 16, 1942, killed 125 people in three states. Radio stations WREC and WHBQ broadcast an appeal at 6:57 P.M. for doctors and nurses to report for hospital duty but did not describe the location or nature of the tornado damage. That was in accordance with the broadcast censorship code, which asked radio announcers to avoid all weather news—past, present, and future—unless authorized by the Weather Bureau or Office of Censorship. (Newspapers, on the other hand, were free to print news of current or previous weather conditions as long as the story did not report on more than one state. This press clause was relaxed in June 1942 to allow papers to publish stories about weather conditions in their home states as well as territory in other states within 150 miles of the city of publication.) The *Commercial Appeal*, a

Clifford K. Berryman cartoon. Until October 1943, weather news was severely restricted in the United States because of concerns that it could aid enemy attacks along the coast. The lifting of most of the restrictions shortly before state elections in November, the subject of this political cartoon, cheered radio stations that had sometimes had difficulty complying with the code. Copyright 1943, *Washington Evening Star.* Reprinted with permission of the *Washington Post.*

Memphis newspaper, was on the streets at 9:30 P.M. with details of the tornadoes. Radio stations did not receive Office of Censorship approval to broadcast the complete story until 11 P.M.[42] This led to a curious turnabout in which the slow medium of print had a competitive advantage over the quicker medium of radio.

The code revision published on June 15, 1942, added a clause that clarified what to do in a weather emergency: "Stations should refrain from broadcasting any news relating to the results of weather phenomena such as tornadoes, hurricanes, storms, etc., unless it is specifically authorized for broadcast by the Office of Censorship. . . . Confusion and inequalities of competition can be avoided if stations will consult the Office of Censorship promptly in all such cases, directly or through their news service."[43]

The codebook granted an exception for emergency warnings specifically released for broadcast by the Weather Bureau. To be in compliance with the code, radio stations were expected to wait for approval before warning listeners to take cover from severe storms. The delay might contribute to casualties, but that apparently was viewed as one of the costs of war. In May 1943, the Broadcasting Division set up a teletype near its news desk that let the staff monitor Weather Bureau emergency announcements. Censors then knew what forecasts and warnings had been officially released, and that information helped them answer stations' questions.[44]

Meanwhile, the ban on ad libs, requests, and dedications continued. "Will you please play 'Moonlight Becomes You' at exactly 1:30 Saturday morning?" a Marine wrote in February 1943 to Ed Fitzgerald, an announcer at WOR in New York City. "That's my girl's favorite song and I want to tune it in soft and sweet at exactly that time. Then I'm going to propose to her." Fitzgerald rejected the request, favoring censorship over romance.[45] Even kids' letters to Santa were subjected to censorship, as Fort Worth, Texas, radio station KFJZ asked the Broadcasting Division how to put such letters on the air without violating the code. The censors replied that although they could not believe that spies had found a way to "draft kiddies as espionage agents," they asked KFJZ to alter the letters' phrasing, stagger their broadcast times, and not mention addresses.[46]

In April 1943, Price said he was impressed with radio's compliance with the censorship code. "We have asked much and received much," he told the annual convention of the N.A.B. He also noted that code violations had become rare.[47] The Broadcasting Division monitored more than 11,000 newscasts and commentaries in 1943, passed judgment on 4,600 radio scripts (including 4,400 submitted for postbroadcast examinations), and handled more than 2,500 inquiries from broadcasters. Only 169 code violations were confirmed during the year.[48] (By war's end, the Office of Censorship reported that it had monitored 17,435 broadcasts and found 310 code violations.)[49]

Infractions of the censorship code's weather clause constituted half of all of the print and radio code violations by the time the provision was relaxed at 12:01 A.M. on October 12, 1943.[50] Ryan sent a message to broadcasters saying they could resume reports of current and previous weather conditions as well as official Weather Bureau forecasts but should continue to delete references to barometric pressure and wind direction, which were among the most sensitive of forecasting tools.[51] The Office of Censorship had decided to alter the code after consulting with the Weather Bureau and the Joint Meteorological Committee of the army and navy.[52] As the danger of attacks on the American mainland faded, the benefits of the weather restrictions had become overshadowed by the handicaps on farming, aviation, and shipping.[53] Within a week of the revision, most stations in Washington and New York City put regularly scheduled weather programs back on the air. Stations across the country raced to do the same.[54]

After the defeat of Germany in May 1945, when the *Code of Wartime Practices* was being updated to apply only to an enemy in the Pacific, Price dropped all restrictions on weather news for both radio and publications. He reasoned that the Japanese already knew the weather patterns headed toward the United States; furthermore, by mid-1945 the Japanese navy was in no position to exploit that news to attack the mainland. Gone, too, were the special injunctions against unrestricted quiz shows, ad-libs, and other live-microphone broadcasts. The final censorship code, issued May 15, 1945, merely asked that broadcasters "measure all programs—special events, forums, interviews, and commercial continuity included—against the Code's requests," which focused on military secrets.[55]

The end to special restrictions on interview programs was a relief to the censors, who had continued to monitor such programs throughout 1944 and early 1945. Stations were tempted to resume interviews when they heard competitors' programs, not realizing that the programs probably had been scrutinized and approved by the Office of Censorship. Ryan asked broadcasters in March 1944 to confirm that they were following the code on phone-in requests, quiz shows, and man-in-the-street programs.[56] The Broadcasting Division made a similar request in January 1945 but relaxed the rules for live broadcasts of the celebrations of Germany's surrender.[57]

Radio had begun the war under a more restrictive code of voluntary censorship than American newspapers and magazines. It had ended the war on par with print, mainly because of the egalitarian application of the code and its acceptance by radio journalists despite its quirks. The knowledge of fog in Chicago and tornadoes in Memphis had little value to the Axis navy because such news was vague, distant, and possibly out of date by the time it reached the coasts. However, the willingness of midcontinent stations to submit to such rules bolstered their observance by coastal and border stations, where broadcasts would have been more likely to aid the enemy.

DEFIANCE IN NEW MEXICO

Price never imposed compulsory censorship on an American radio station. He came close to doing so only once, when challenged by a broadcaster objecting to the most restrictive part of the code—the control of foreign-language programs.

Each week during 1943, the 250-watt transmitter of radio station KFUN beamed ninety-two hours of news, music, and entertainment programs into the thin, desert air of northern New Mexico. Listeners who tuned their dials to 1230 kilohertz could hear the station broadcasting Office of War Information bulletins and a fifteen-minute Spanish version of "Uncle Sam Speaks," but the global conflict still must have seemed distant. Although atomic research secretly was under way about eighty miles to the west, at Los Alamos, not much happened in the sleepy town of Las Vegas, which was tucked more than 6,400 feet above sea level in the Sangre de Cristo Mountains. The town supported a steady livestock trade, the annual reunion of Theodore Roosevelt's Rough Riders, and tourism. KFUN's stationery touted Las Vegas as a place to forget one's cares, "the land of vacation for the nation."[58]

The station's general manager, Ernest N. "Ernie" Thwaites, considered himself a "small fry" in the war. He believed that his transmitter, 275 miles from Mexico and three times that distance from the Pacific Ocean, posed no threat to the nation's security. Much of KFUN's audience spoke Spanish, a language that the Office of Censorship classified as foreign, but Thwaites placed his listeners' loyalty beyond question. Spanish technically was not "foreign" to New Mexico. The state's courts and legislature recognized it as an official language. And KFUN, one of forty-four American stations that carried Spanish broadcasts,[59] had an appreciative audience. Eleven hours of Spanish programs accounted for twenty percent of the station's revenue but only twelve percent of its airtime.[60]

In March and April 1943, Edward H. Bronson of the Office of Censorship visited dozens of Southwestern radio stations to determine if they were complying with the voluntary censorship code. The most recent *Code of Wartime Practices for American Broadcasters,* issued February 1, had asked station managers to obtain advance scripts of all foreign-language programs and compare them with live broadcasts for deviations. Foreign-language stations had to provide translators and program monitors to comply with the code.[61] Bronson found many Spanish-language stations that did not have monitors, and one that allowed an engineer to oversee the broadcast even though he did not speak the language. In addition, many broadcasters were ad-libbing or playing records upon request, which violated the code.[62] When Bronson returned to Washington, he told his supervisors, Robert K. Richards and Ryan, that in his opinion the most efficient way to handle foreign-language broadcasts was to end them for the rest of the war.[63]

That was never seriously considered. Price had decided before issuing the first edition of the voluntary code on January 15, 1942, that foreign-language radio stations were a key medium to inform foreign-born Americans about the country's war objectives.[64] Shutting down foreign-language radio would kill a messenger that could not be easily replaced in the neighborhoods of recent immigrants. Nevertheless, in the spring of 1943 the OWI and FCC were urging Price to end foreign-language stations' "irresponsible conduct," he wrote in his notebook.[65]

Price began by scolding foreign-language stations at the National Association of Broadcasters meeting on April 27, 1943, shortly after Bronson's return to Washington. Foreign-language broadcasters in the Southwest probably had done no harm, Price believed, but he could not allow some to continue their laxity on matters of censorship for fear that other stations would drop their vigilance. "One leak . . . was too many," he said. Price privately told the foreign-language broadcasters that their compliance with the code was "the worst in the industry," and unless they improved he could not guarantee that the FCC would not take action against them under its licensing authority. He also suggested that he had the authority to censor foreign-language broadcasts without restraint.[66] He based his argument on the observation that many foreign-language stations were scattered around the nation's rim and subject to his cross-border censorship powers.

The broadcasters listened. By the summer of 1943, the Office of Censorship was satisfied that foreign-language broadcasters had been brought into line. Bronson found no code violations in monitored foreign-language broadcasts in four of the weeks between May 22 and July 17, telling his supervisors at the end of each error-free week that he was hoisting "the white flag of purity and virtue."[67]

Only Thwaites defied requests to produce scripts and monitor Spanish programs. Bronson, Ryan, and Price worked throughout the summer to coax Thwaites to change his mind but had no success. In June, the Broadcasting Division appealed to Harry Burdick, the manager of station KGGM in Albuquerque, who formerly had worked with Thwaites. Burdick visited KFUN but could not persuade Thwaites to follow the code. In a letter, Burdick said the difficulty "appeared to be due to the typical small station operation and limited staff."[68] Thwaites had built and opened the radio station in 1941, lived in an apartment in the same building as the studio, and ran the operations with the help of his wife. Proud of his accomplishments, he became defensive whenever anyone questioned his character. Dennis Mitchell, the KFUN general manager who succeeded Thwaites, described him as notoriously strong-willed, as evidenced by his undertaking a successful, one-man crusade to have the local government pave a road linking Las Vegas and Tucumcari.[69]

On August 11, 1943, the Office of Censorship decided it could wait no longer and told KFUN to observe the code or halt foreign-language broadcasting. Thwaites refused, accusing Price's agency of "hampering, heckling and hamstringing a small station." He said it would be "utterly preposterous" for him to prepare scripts and monitor his broadcasts. To do so might bankrupt him, he said, although Price thought KFUN could be brought up to code for $50 a week. In a defiant letter on August 19, Thwaites accused Price of trying to be "judge-jury-and-executioner" and concluded: "We know that our problem, in the light of world events, is insignificant. Nevertheless, to us, whether we survive or not is 100% important! Moreover, there may be others who might feel as we do, that your threatened action is an unwarranted infringement upon Freedom of Speech and therefore a threat to our whole Democratic structure."[70]

The letter was unique. Never before had a publisher or broadcaster refused to do what the Office of Censorship had asked.

Price faced a dilemma. KFUN's unregulated broadcasts might inspire a broader radio rebellion. If the code were relaxed on the claim that Spanish was a semiofficial language, other stations might seek code exemptions for other reasons. On the other hand, if Price ordered mandatory censorship of KFUN to enforce the code, he did not know how he could justify withholding such censorship from the entire industry.[71]

He proceeded cautiously. He began by ascertaining that the KFUN transmitter's modest power was far too weak to reach across the ocean unless assisted by some atmospheric freak of nature. Under normal conditions, the signal disappeared within 300 miles.[72] However, the Mexican border was closer than that. Enemy agents theoretically could be listen-ing there.

Before the Office of Censorship could act, Thwaites appealed to the N.A.B., of which he was a member. He wrote a letter asking the group to support his defiance of censorship. He could not have anticipated that the strategy would backfire. The letter found its way to Willard Egolf, a law-yer who was the N.A.B.'s public relations director, who told the Office of Censorship about Thwaites's appeal on August 23. After speaking with Richards, Egolf said that he "recognized and respected [the Broadcast-ing Division's] position and felt there was nothing he could do but ad-vise Mr. Thwaites to conform." On that same day, Thwaites's lawyer ap-parently reached the same conclusion, refusing to represent KFUN in its battle against the censors.[73]

Price recruited Egolf to tell Thwaites about the legal authority that supported the Office of Censorship's requests. Although Price failed to record his remarks to Egolf, on August 24 he dictated a memorandum for possible use in resolving the conflict.[74] He noted that his talk with Egolf had followed the substance of his memo, which included copies of the First War Powers Act and Executive Order 8985. Price's memo said that if a broadcaster failed to conform to the *Code of Wartime Practices,* he would consider taking one or more of the following actions:

1. Imposition of a mandatory censorship involving the placement of censors in the offending radio station, with full power to act.
2. Enforcement of that clause of U.S. Censorship Regulations which requires that communications going out of the country be submitted beforehand to the Director of Censorship in Washington.
3. Recommendation to the Board of War Communications [techni-cally called the Defense Communications Board, which Roosevelt established in September 1940 under the authority of the Communi-cations Act of 1934 and empowered with wartime control over radio on December 10, 1941] that the Board exercise its power to modify or suppress the activities of the station.
4. Recommendation to the Federal Communications Commission that the station license be suspended.
    In case either one or two above were applied, and the station failed to submit all copy to Censorship, the failure might be construed as an attempt to evade Censorship and the penalties specified in Section 303 of the First War Powers Act invoked.[75]

Anyone convicted of evading or attempting to evade Section 303 by failing to submit cross-border communications to censorship faced a prison term as long as ten years, a fine as high as $10,000, or both. If the convicted person was the "officer, director, or agent of any corporation," the law authorized the U.S. government to seize "any property, funds, securities, papers, or other articles or documents, or any vessel, together with her tackle, apparel, and equipment, concerned in such violation."[76]

The next day, after Egolf spoke with Thwaites, the station manager wired the Office of Censorship that "regardless of our personal feelings," he would stop all Spanish programming on August 25.[77] Although the telegram read like an admission of defeat, Thwaites conceded only the battle, and not the war. He broadcast that he was being forced by federal bureaucrats to cancel Spanish programs. He and other Las Vegas civic leaders urged New Mexico's governor and members of Congress to pressure the Office of Censorship into reversing its decision. Thwaites apparently misrepresented the conflict to Governor John J. Dempsey, or Dempsey misunderstood. He asked Price on September 1 to explain a censorship rule that, in fact, did not exist. Why, Dempsey wrote, did Spanish-language scripts have to be submitted to the Office of Censorship for approval before they could be broadcast?[78] Price wrote back to point out that the censors had encouraged broadcasters to act as their own censors. As evidence, he enclosed a copy of the *Code of Wartime Practices* and said that all other American radio stations had complied with its requests.[79]

As Thwaites tried to mobilize public opinion in Las Vegas, Price tried to mediate the conflict with U.S. Representative Antonio Fernandez. The New Mexico congressman said Thwaites did not want a solution as much as he wanted to keep a political issue alive. Ryan had reached the same conclusion after discovering that both Thwaites and his wife could speak Spanish and easily act as KFUN's monitors. Before Fernandez's visit, Ryan had told Price in a memo that "KFUN is not cooperating because they are provoked by the Code's regulations."[80] The congressman urged turning the tables—in Price's words, "to put Thwaites on the defensive with his own listeners so that they would blame him instead of us for having suspended Spanish language broadcasts."[81] Price wrote Thwaites a letter, which Fernandez apparently released in New Mexico, urging KFUN to resume Spanish broadcasts. The letter said the station need only prepare and carefully follow scripts for any spoken program and, like all of the English-language stations, avoid the sensitive news items listed in the *Code of Wartime Practices*. Price closed by saying, "Please let me know at your earliest convenience whether you are willing to resume the Spanish language service which has been so highly prized by so many of your listeners."[82]

Thwaites surrendered. He wrote to ask a few technical questions about complying with the code and to explain that his protest had been "premised largely upon the fact that we could not saddle any more duties upon a key employee," apparently a reference to his wife. However, he said there was no question that he wanted to resume Spanish-language broadcasts. After receiving a six-paragraph letter of instructions from Price, Thwaites dropped his protest and said Spanish would return to KFUN on October 4.[83] Office of Censorship records do not indicate whether Spanish programming resumed that day. However, it had resumed by February 1944, when KFUN's broadcasts were recorded and sent to the Office of Censorship.[84]

Through careful handling of its feud with KFUN, the Office of Censorship solved one of the stickiest problems of voluntary censorship during World War II. If Thwaites had pressed his case, Price would have compelled the station to comply with the censorship code or go off the air. If the dispute had gone to court, Price might have had to reveal, and use, his "club in the closet" — the attorney general's opinion that had given him the authority to control domestic radio through the legal definition of broadcasting as an international communication. The original opinion, issued in response to Price's request for guidance about radiotelegraphy, had been expanded by the attorney general in September 1942 to specifically authorize the censorship director to suppress foreign-language broadcasts, particularly those that "may have a harmful effect on domestic morale" or pose a danger to the nation's security or war effort.[85]

Instead of legal restraint, however, Price had used public and peer pressure against KFUN. These two forces had changed the voice of radio during World War II, reducing the number of stations carrying foreign-language programs from about 210 in the spring of 1942 (up from 200 on December 11, 1941) to 128 in the spring of 1943.[86] Some had dropped German or Italian programs out of fear of offending their English-speaking listeners; others had stopped foreign-language broadcasts to avoid the costs of preparing scripts and paying program monitors. Those that remained on the air constituted the Broadcasting Division's main problem early in 1943. Yet, by July 24 of that year, Bronson, who had favored eliminating foreign-language broadcasting just three months earlier, said such broadcasts had been "cleaned up" and were "relatively quiet." Aside from the developing conflict with KFUN, he was correct. Foreign-language stations, which had violated the voluntary censorship code five times as often as other stations in September 1942, had policed themselves until, by the summer of 1943, their compliance record was the equal of any in the industry.[87]

GERMAN- AND ITALIAN-LANGUAGE PROGRAMS

Foreign-language broadcasters had been subjected to wartime scrutiny even before the Office of Censorship was organized. James Lawrence Fly, chairman of the FCC, sent FBI director J. Edgar Hoover a partial list of foreign-language announcers on December 16, 1941, and Hoover shared the list with Price a week later.[88] Price raised the issue on February 20, 1942, when he asked his Censorship Operating Board for opinions on stopping all German- and Italian-language domestic broadcasts. He volunteered to the group that he did not favor a shutdown. No one else at the meeting commented, and the matter was dropped. Foreign-language publications also continued printing. The Justice Department's Special Defense Unit read 650 foreign-language publications for sensitive or seditious items in February 1942. Price did not want to shift this huge task to the Office of Censorship. He urged the Justice Department to keep monitoring the foreign-language press, which it did for the rest of the war.[89]

Price considered radio a greater security threat than the print press, and his concerns about foreign-language broadcasting were reflected in the differences between the press and radio codebooks. While the press code had no special rules for foreign-language publications, an entire section of the radio code provided instructions for foreign-language broadcasters. The broadcasting code asked radio stations to keep full transcripts, either written or recorded, of all foreign-language programs, and to take precautions to prevent deviations from scripts.[90] The precautions aimed to prevent enemy agents from using commercial stations to send coded messages and to prevent announcers from spreading anti-American propaganda.

Radio stations' response to the code varied. In Massachusetts, WSPR in Springfield followed the code to the letter. However, WHYN in Holyoke decided that rather than comply with the foreign-language code, it would switch all of its Polish-language programs to English and heavily edit them. In addition, Milwaukee stations WTMJ, WEMP, and WISN dropped their German-language programs in the first half of 1942. The entertainment publication *Variety* noted that the "viewpoint of many in Milwaukee is that speaking German is bad propaganda for Milwaukee."[91]

When the code was updated in June 1942, the foreign-language regulations were tightened. The Broadcasting Division added a request that file copies of foreign-language scripts be accompanied by an English translation, and that each station monitor its broadcasts to prevent deviations from the script.[92]

The revised edition offered no explanation for the change, but it reflected concerns about code violations that had been raised at a meeting of foreign-language broadcasters at the twentieth annual convention of the National Association of Broadcasters on May 13. The war's impact on broadcasting had sent an electric charge through the convention's usually low-key discussions of issues facing the industry. A breakfast meeting of foreign-language broadcasters began innocently enough, when Lee Falk of the Office of Facts and Figures—which released government information and also concerned itself with morale—urged station managers to halt ad-libbing. Trouble started when broadcasters in the audience volunteered stories of their difficulties with Italian- and German-language announcers. One New York operator, unnamed in accounts of the meeting, said he had caught one of his announcers dedicating records to the captain and crew of a steamship leaving New York that night. When others at the breakfast meeting suggested reporting the announcer to the FBI, a conventioneer interjected, "Well, I would have done more than report him to the FBI. I would have killed him." Another broadcaster revealed that one of his foreign-language announcers had refused to read commercials for war-bond drives, saying his listeners did not care about such information. The revelations stunned the crowd. "It was so quiet you could hear a station break," a member of the audience later quipped.[93]

Members of the N.A.B. who represented stations that carried foreign-language programs formed a committee to address the laxity and indifference in foreign-language broadcasting. The group called itself the Foreign Language Radio Wartime Control Committee. It first met on the day after the acrimonious breakfast and agreed to coordinate an investigation of all foreign-language broadcasters in the United States. Arthur Simon, general manager of WPEN in Philadelphia, was named chairman.[94] The group agreed to have the nation's 5,000 foreign-language broadcasters fill out questionnaires that included questions about their personal histories, citizenship status, employment history, membership in organizations, and criminal history. There was a blank space for fingerprints.[95]

By June 6, 1942, the Foreign Language Radio Wartime Control Committee had printed its own code. It called on foreign-language broadcasters to observe the "spirit and letter" of the Office of Censorship's *Code of Wartime Practices*. It repeated the censorship code's statement that broadcasters were responsible for their programs' content and that all foreign-language programs must be scripted and monitored to avoid deviations. Then, Simon's code added that foreign-language broadcasters must submit their completed questionnaires to the committee for distribution to government agencies and cooperate with prodemocratic groups in selection of broadcast material. Furthermore, the code said, "No person will be employed whose record indicates he may not faithfully cooperate with the war effort."[96] *Broadcasting* magazine reported in July that Simon had sent stations a letter urging them to take precautions against hiring "undesirable" workers who had been fired from other foreign-language stations. The letter said that Falk, whose agency had been absorbed on June 13 by the OWI, would give any inquiring station manager a prompt answer on whether a potential employee had "a clean bill of health."[97]

Completed guidelines were routed to the OWI. Simon later told a congressional committee that the OWI never had authority over American radio personnel "and never should have had it," but in the summer of 1942 "it was impossible to get any [other] government agency who said it had responsibility of removing anyone from the air."[98] The Office of Censorship's interest in foreign-language broadcasts was limited to program content in mid-1942, and did not include the selection of appropriate announcers. Several radio managers wrote to the OWI that summer seeking an opinion about the patriotism of particular foreign-language broadcasters and the advisability of removing them from the air. Some Italian- and German-American broadcasts seemed to be subtle propaganda, they said, such as one Italian-language newscast that followed a report of a British retreat in North Africa with the "Victory March" from Verdi's *Aida*. According to the OWI's internal history, only once did the Foreign Language Division of the OWI Bureau of Special Operations request a broadcaster's ouster. "Our opinion was neither coercive, mandatory, or enforceable," and the FCC was not consulted about the option of removing any broadcast license, the OWI said.[99]

At the FCC, Fly was pleased that the committee had begun regulating foreign-language broadcasts, according to Arthur Simon. But the method of regulation was questionable. According to later congressional testimony, two lawyers in the FCC's legal division, Hilda Shea and Sidney Spear, began cooperating with the OWI to block the renewal of permits at stations with foreign-language broadcasters whom the OWI considered subversive. Simon discovered the connection when he tried to learn why many foreign-language stations were operating under temporary permits in 1942. He said that when the FCC refused to share personnel records with him, he turned to Falk for an explanation. According to Simon, Falk, the radio director of the OWI's foreign-language division, had been telling station managers to fire broadcasters, even though he lacked such authority. For example, Falk told Simon that newscaster Stefano Luotto of WGES in Chicago "was not the kind of person to be broadcasting." When Simon asked for "something definite" that would warrant Luotto's dismissal, Falk reportedly replied, "This office can't give anything definite. You've either got to take our word for it or you don't." [100]

To clear the air, Simon met with OWI director Elmer Davis and the Foreign Language Radio Wartime Control Committee. Simon argued that Falk had exceeded his authority, and Davis said he would ask the attorney general to decide who had the responsibility to remove subversive foreign-language broadcasters. [101] Francis Biddle delivered that decision at a meeting with Price, Ryan, Davis, and Fly on August 10, 1942. Only the Office of Censorship had such authority, Biddle said, and Davis and Fly concurred. They agreed that their agencies would provide pertinent information about foreign-language broadcasters to the Office of Censorship, which could examine an announcer's voice inflections and other subtle evidence in deciding whether to remove him or her. [102]

At the time, Price and Ryan had mixed feelings about taking on the new task. There were too many foreign-language broadcasters for any one office to police, Ryan said. The Broadcasting Division had a half dozen full-time employees, too few to monitor the 1,500 hours a week that were broadcast in twenty-nine languages besides English. [103] When Ryan's staff presented Price with a memorandum about trying to coordinate supervision of foreign-language radio with other government agencies, he returned it with his pencil-scrawled comments at the bottom: "We want all the help we can get but the Atty. Gen. says it is our job and if we don't move in on it radidly [sic], some one will take it away from us."[104]

Ryan assigned Robert Richards to lead a new section of the Broadcasting Division devoted to foreign-language broadcasts. Its purpose, Richards later wrote, was to "educate foreign language broadcasters to the necessity of observing the Code, and to remove from the air those who could not be so educated because of Fascist sympathies."[105]

After wading through the first batch of information the FCC provided to the Office of Censorship under their August 10 agreement, Richards gave Ryan a memorandum outlining the steps he proposed for control of foreign-language broadcasts. The FCC documents indicated that Italian, German, and Polish programs were the major part of foreign-language broadcasts in America. "Since the Polish people presumably are sympathetic to our cause, I believe we should concentrate our early efforts on German and Italian [programs] and limit those efforts to the cities which show the largest proportion of foreign language programs," Richards wrote. Richards then recommended that the Office of Censorship begin monitoring and analyzing foreign-language broadcasts and that the censors enlist the cooperation of the OWI and the FCC's Foreign Broadcast Intelligence Service, which prepared daily reports on overseas radio news and propaganda and also listened to domestic foreign-language broadcasts. He asked that the OWI send the Office of Censorship reports that formerly were routed to Falk. He also urged that the censorship codes be printed in Italian and German, that the Office of Censorship hire Italian and German translators, and that the FBI be approached about sharing its records on foreign-language broadcasters.[106] Ryan agreed to these suggestions and dispatched Richards on two fact-finding missions—the first to other federal agencies, and the second to New York and Philadelphia to interview the managers of Italian- and German-language stations.[107]

Richards completed the first assignment in a marathon of interviews that took him to three agencies in a single day. The first stop was the Foreign Broadcast Intelligence Service, where broadcast analyst David Truman agreed to share information with Richards's new section. At the time, in late August 1942, Truman's service was monitoring domestic foreign-language broadcasts only to obtain information for the FCC's legal department to use in broadcasting license renewal hearings. Richards had one reservation, which he described in a memorandum for the Broadcasting Division: "I believe there might be a tendency on the part of this section of the FCC . . . to take its work too seriously. I thought I caught a faint whiff of that old alley cat: government interference in free enterprise. I don't believe the Office of Censorship wants to be identified with any effort on the part of the FCC to go beyond its legal rights in supervising programming. . . . Briefly, the FBIS [Foreign Broadcast Intelligence Service] is offering facilities and advice. I believe we should use the facilities one hundred per cent, and file the advice."[108]

Next, Richards conferred with FCC attorney Spear, who Richards said "analyzes the analyses made by Mr. Truman." Richards found Spear both talkative and frank. The lawyer said he appreciated the Office of Censorship's interest in the foreign-language broadcasters and noted that he and Falk had been removing broadcasters on their own initiative. He said no one else had seemed to want to do the job. In a memorandum, Richards quoted Spear as saying:

> We worked it this way. If Lee [Falk] found a fellow he thought was doing some funny business, he told me about it. Then we waited until the station applied for a [re]newal of license. Say the station was WBNX and the broadcaster in question was Leopold Hurdski. Well, when WBNX applied for a renewal, we would tip off Lee and he would drop in on Mr. [W. C.] Alcorn, the station's manager. He would say, "Mr. Alcorn, I believe you ought to fire Leopold Hurdski." Then he would give Mr. Alcorn some time to think this over. After a couple of weeks, Mr. Alcorn would begin to notice he was having some trouble getting his license renewed. After a couple of more weeks of this same thing, he would begin to put two and two together and get four. Then he would fire Leopold Hurdski and very shortly after that his license would be renewed by the Commission. This was a little extra-legal, I admit, and I had to wrestle with my conscience about it, but it seemed the only way to eliminate this kind of person, so I did it. We can co-operate in the same way with you.[109]

Richards said the Office of Censorship mainly needed the information gathered by the Foreign Broadcast Intelligence Service's monitoring equipment. Spear agreed to provide it, along with copies of all FCC investigations that touched on foreign-language broadcasters.[110]

The final stop was at the OWI, where Richards spoke with Falk. Falk seemed reluctant to turn over the intelligence reports he had received from the FBI on various foreign-language broadcasters, but eventually he gave Richards the FBI's dossiers on one German announcer, William

Seuren, and four Italians—Giacomo Capozucci, Frank Polimeni, Michele Fiorello, and Raffaele Borrelli. He urged the immediate removal of Fiorello and Borrelli, but Richards examined their files and said he did not think the evidence—which he did not discuss in his accounts of the meeting—warranted their removal. However, he quoted Falk as saying that broadcasters whose backgrounds included suspicious associations should be taken off the air.[111]

Summarizing his meetings in a memorandum to Ryan and Price, Richards said none of his three contacts had mentioned the *Code of Wartime Practices* in discussions about removing broadcasters.[112] And compliance with the code was the censors' main concern about foreign-language broadcasting.

If Richards's discussions with Washington bureaucrats had suggested that Italian Americans and German Americans were being removed from the air with little evidence of whether their broadcasts actually endangered the nation's morale or defense, his tour of foreign-language stations removed all doubt. He talked on August 27 and 28 with Alcorn at WBNX in New York; Simon of WPEN in Philadelphia; Joseph Lang of WHOM in Jersey City, New Jersey; Mario Ferrari-Hutton of WOV in New York; and Griffith B. Thompson of WBYN in Brooklyn. Simon reported that he had fired two Italian-language broadcasters, Fiorello and Arcangelo Leopizzi, on August 24 on Falk's recommendation. The next day, he said, other employees of WPEN had told him that the two men were fascists. Richards wrote in a memo that the men were taken off the air "not because of what they broadcast, but because of what they were—or what their backgrounds represented them to be. Personally, I don't suppose they should be broadcasting; but if they're bad enough to be removed from the air arbitrarily, then I think somebody ought to arrest them." He quoted Simon as saying that if the Office of Censorship did not support WPEN and the OWI in the firing of the two announcers, "I'm going to blat to the press at the top of my voice."[113] Alcorn told Richards he had been badgered by the Bureau of Immigration and OWI into removing an Italian broadcaster, Lido Belli, even though he was convinced of Belli's loyalty.[114]

Price responded to Richards's findings in his careful manner. He set up a meeting with representatives of the OWI, FCC, and Foreign Language Radio Wartime Control Committee. They talked for four hours on October 27, 1942, in Washington and agreed that the Office of Censorship and the foreign-language radio committee would continue their roles, with the former maintaining primary responsibility for controlling foreign-language radio and the latter continuing to act as an unofficial liaison between the government and the radio stations. The FCC accepted the new task of investigating the background of foreign-language employees. It soon hired a staff of twenty-five to do the research and provide the Office of Censorship with reports. Lastly, the OWI agreed to provide more creative foreign-language programs to American radio stations. Before the interdepartmental agreement had cleared the air, both the Office of Censorship and the FCC had been checking broadcasts for subversive content, but neither agency had accepted responsibility for examining the personal histories of foreign-language broadcasters.[115]

The Broadcasting Division targeted twenty-one stations with heavy schedules of German- and Italian-language programs for the startup of its program-monitoring service. By late September, the *Code of Wartime Practices* had been translated into German and Italian and copies had been distributed to the broadcasters; later the codebook was translated into Spanish, Yiddish, and Polish. Censors began receiving scripts and program schedules from the stations and hired three translators who could speak Italian, German, French, Portuguese, Spanish, Polish, Yiddish, and Russian.[116]

When the Broadcasting Division wanted to monitor a station, it sent an order slip to the FCC's Engineering Division listing the station's call letters, the site of its transmitter, the name of the programs to be recorded, the languages used on the program, the days of the week to be broadcast, and the times that the programs started and ended. During one week, for example, censors asked the FCC to record eight programs in three languages on station WSAR in Fall River, Massachusetts, including "The Voice of Portugal" and the "Polish Hour."[117] The FCC ordered its nearest field unit—in Scituate, Massachusetts—to record the programs and mail the recording cylinders to the Federal Trade Commission building.[118] The translators compared the spoken word with its scripted version, which the Office of Censorship had requested from the station. Richards found the FCC cooperative and the quality of its cylinders "excellent."[119]

Richards's foreign-language service began with the most suspicious cases, including German-language programs on the East Coast. The FCC recorded the first foreign-language broadcasts for the Office of Censorship on September 21, 1942.[120] A recording obtained on that day started the Office of Censorship on a trail that ended four months later with

Price's decision to remove the first broadcaster from the air under his censorship authority.

REMOVING TWO BROADCASTERS FROM THE AIRWAVES

The translator for German-language programs noticed that Willie Seuren's script for September 21 did not match the recording of his broadcast that day over WTEL in Philadelphia. The script had Seuren, who broadcast twice a day, Mondays through Fridays, introducing a commercial for American war bond sales by saying, "Here is an announcement I take more real pleasure in making than any which I have ever made." The German-language broadcast lacked the statement entirely. This was a minor deviation, but it violated the code. The Office of Censorship notified station manager E. Douglass Hibbs, who investigated and explained that Seuren had deleted the phrase because he had used it before and believed it was becoming too repetitious and boring. Bronson was troubled. Seuren had admitted altering his script. How many times had he done it before, and might he do it again? Bronson had his answer soon. On October 19, he asked WTEL to submit more scripts. Again, the scripted war bond announcement was missing. Bronson acknowledged that its disappearance might have been an oversight. But more curiously, Seuren's script contained an announcement of a meeting of the German American League for Culture that featured a talk on "Underground Work in Central Europe."[121] It could be suspicious or innocent. The Office of Censorship had to know: How strong were Seuren's loyalties to the United States?

To supplement the meager information the Office of Censorship had received from the FCC, it hired a private investigative agency, the Hooper-Holmes Bureau, to check Seuren's background and ask questions about him in a German American neighborhood in Philadelphia called Olney. Bronson also received a confidential report from the FBI. Together they portrayed a man who had a questionable past, but they could find no hard evidence of pro-German sympathies since America entered World War II. According to the investigations, Seuren was born on August 10, 1897, in a suburb of Cologne and had served in the kaiser's army in 1916 and 1917. He, his wife, and eldest child emigrated to the United States in 1924 and settled in Philadelphia, where he began broadcasting to the area's German-speaking immigrants in their native tongue in 1930, first at WRAX and later at WIBG. In 1935, one year after becoming an American citizen, Seuren began operating for himself, opening the German American Broadcasting Company in Philadelphia. It placed programs on radio stations WTEL and WHAT. The latter station eventually dropped German broadcasts, but WTEL continued its association with Seuren, who scheduled airtime, helped develop programs, prepared scripts, and by 1942 broadcast his own programs between 7:30 and 8:30 on weekday mornings and 6:30 and 7:00 each weeknight.[122] According to Simon, whose WPEN station competed with Seuren's, he opened his program on WTEL by playing the "Horst Wessel Song."[123]

Hibbs called Bronson on November 17 to discuss WTEL's difficulty in complying with censorship requests concerning foreign-language scripts and mentioned that the FBI was investigating Seuren. While Hibbs believed Seuren was "behaving himself" on the air, he nevertheless told Bronson, "You know all of them Krauts' hearts is back in Germany" and said Seuren was no exception.[124]

By December 9, Bronson had decided that Seuren's background was "most questionable." In a confidential memo to Richards, Bronson presented his findings. The accusations against Seuren rested heavily on guilt by association and hearsay that could not be corroborated, although Bronson did not make this clear to his boss. According to a source in the FBI, whom Bronson did not identify, Seuren had joined the German American Zentral Bund of Pennsylvania on August 1, 1936, and his name had appeared on a June 6, 1942, membership list.[125] The Pennsylvania group, like other branches of the Bund nationwide, had expressed admiration for the changes wrought in Germany by the Nazis. Fritz Kuhn of New York City had founded the national Bund in 1936 by consolidating various groups of Nazi sympathizers. He gave the Bund its Nazi-like uniforms, swastika armbands, and crude anti-Semitic and anticommunist slogans. The German Nazi Party had repudiated it in 1938 as being "too radical," but Americans continued to link it with the Nazi philosophy.[126] Seuren also was reported to be a member of the German-American Vocational League, whose membership roll included two people who had been convicted of Espionage Act violations and a third who had aided a German spy. He also had testified as a character witness for the Reverend Kurt Emil Bruno Malzahn, who had been convicted in August 1942 of violating the Espionage Act. Furthermore, one WTEL listener had told the Office of Censorship that between 7:30 and 8:30 A.M. on June 5, 1941, Seuren had advised his listeners to buy German bonds instead of U.S. Defense Bonds because the former had a higher interest rate. The listener said Seuren had urged Americans on the same program to align themselves with the Third Reich. Investigators could not prove the listener's allegations, and even if true they would not have been treasonous because America was neutral in the summer of 1941. Seuren maintained his innocence, giving the FBI a sworn statement that he had been loyal to the United States since his arrival in 1924. His post as a Bund delegate and his defense of Malzahan had been business decisions, he said.[127]

Despite Seuren's denials and a statement from the FBI that it would "go no further than to say he was at least a questionable character," the Broadcasting Division decided to take him off the air. Price said Seuren's associations were "all bad."[128] Removing Seuren proved tricky. Price conferred with lawyers for the Justice Department about the proper legal procedure, as well as ways to stop Seuren's broadcasts without publicizing Francis Biddle's opinion that commercial broadcasts were international communications that Price could censor without restraint. He feared that releasing Biddle's memo, even if he used it against a man suspected of pro-Axis subversion, would frighten other broadcasters. The solution reached by the Justice Department and the Office of Censorship was patterned on the Post Office Department's method of rescinding second-class mail permits. Seuren would be allowed a hearing if he desired one. The Office of Censorship would act as a court, and Price would appoint three assistant directors to hear evidence from Seuren and his accusers. The three would make a recommendation to Price, which he would approve or reject. The procedure was designed to guarantee due process, but Price preferred to "avoid red tape if possible" and ease Seuren off the air without making a fuss. Price wrote Hibbs on January 18, 1943, to say his office had completed an investigation of Seuren, supplemented by an extensive review of his broadcasts. Price called Seuren's continued broadcasting "contrary to the best interests of the nation" and asked for Hibbs's cooperation: "Specifically, we recommend that Mr. Seuren's activity as an announcer be terminated and that any other connection, direct or indirect, he may have with WTEL which would afford him use of the station's broadcasting facilities, be concluded. . . . I know we can depend upon you for full cooperation, and hope this matter can be disposed of in this informal way without further action on the part of the Office of Censorship."[129]

Hibbs visited Price's office in Washington on January 28 to ask what evidence the Office of Censorship had against Seuren, who continued to protest his innocence. The meeting was more of a formality than a substantive exchange of information. Although Hibbs said he had requested the meeting to clear his conscience, in a September conversation with Richards he had been enthusiastic about the possibility of removing Seuren, saying, "If there is anything wrong with the guy, let me know. I want to shoot the gun."[130]

Hibbs did not need much persuasion. According to Price's account of the meeting, Hibbs asked what evidence the censors had against Seuren, and Price replied that it was sufficient to raise serious questions about the advisability of permitting Seuren to broadcast in German. "I assured Mr. Hibbs that if he was not willing to remove Seuren from the air on the basis of my simple recommendation, he was entitled to a hearing and could have one, but that meantime I did not propose to go into the evidence in detail or to express an opinion beyond what I already had said. I told Mr. Hibbs that I felt that in case of a question, national security should be given the benefit of the doubt."[131]

Neither Hibbs nor Seuren asked for a hearing. Seuren signed off for the last time at 8:30 A.M. on January 30.[132]

Perhaps in response to the difficulties with Seuren, the Office of Censorship codified its criteria for removing broadcasters from the air in the revised *Code of Wartime Practices for American Broadcasters* published on February 1, 1943. The addition had helped swell the codebook's foreign-language section to thirty-eight lines, up from five a year earlier. It said the president had given the Office of Censorship the responsibility to remove foreign-language broadcasters who, in the censors' judgment, endangered the war effort "by their connections, direct and indirect, with the medium." The censors' judgment would be based on "current material written for broadcast or broadcast over American facilities and past and/or present conduct of the individual, including evidence substantiating his sympathy with the regimes of our enemies."[133] It was the most restrictive rule in the code.

The FCC reports on foreign-language broadcasters were nearly useless, according to the Office of Censorship. Studies that the Foreign Broadcast Intelligence Service shared with the Office of Censorship relied on quantitative and qualitative analyses but gave no hard evidence of subversion or code violations. For example, a chart comparing German-language broadcasts of WBNX in New York with the CBS Radio network scaled their individual news items on a favorable-neutral-unfavorable spectrum and portrayed WBNX negatively. Broadcasting Division employee Charter Heslep, who said the analysis made him "groggy," nevertheless pointed out the logical error of this FCC evidence: The statistics compared a local broadcast aimed at a German audience with a nation-wide network broadcast. Naturally, he said, the WBNX broadcasts included more news about Germany. The Office of Censorship informed Foreign Broadcast Intelligence Service director Robert D. Leigh that his reports were of little use because they focused on propaganda while the censors were interested in national security. In April 1943, Leigh decided on his own to stop sending them.[134]

The FCC's investigations into broadcasters' backgrounds also had flaws. An FBI agent who evaluated the reports at Bronson's and Richards's request found two glaring weaknesses. First, they had no statement by the accused—not one of the individuals who had been investigated had been asked to defend the charges against him. Second, the reports were limited to the subjects' immediate circle, not their older acquaintances. The agent said petty jealousies and passions tended to be overrepresented among the comments of coworkers.[135] In addition, the Office of Censorship complained that the FCC was too slow in responding to requests for broadcaster background reports. Price had asked the FCC to send him background information on Raffaele "Ralph" Borrelli of station WPEN in December 1942, but FCC secretary T. J. Slowie did not send it until April 7, giving no explanation for the delay.[136] When it arrived, Price decided to ask for Borrelli's temporary suspension while his office completed its own investigation.[137] The Office of Censorship archives do not include the FCC's report, which also could not be found in the Federal Communications Commission's extensive archives. But the censorship records do contain the results of the independent investigation that Price commissioned by Hooper-Holmes. It said Borrelli, born in Italy in 1896, had emigrated to the United States at age three, joined the American army in World War I, and become a naturalized citizen and accomplished pianist. He had broadcast in Italian for twelve years, the last six of them at WPEN in Philadelphia. Informants had told the Hooper-Holmes investigators that Borrelli had been profascist before the attack on Pearl Harbor and had been a close friend of the Italian consul in Philadelphia.[138] Based on this report, Price told WPEN attorney Horace L. Lohnes on April 21 that the suspension would continue for the duration of the war.[139] By that time, Price's decision was academic. WPEN manager Simon had fired Borrelli on April 4, telling Richards that he had done so at the insistence of FCC attorney Hilda Shea.[140] Simon tried to discover Shea's evidence against the Italian American announcer, but she refused to tell him, he said.[141]

Borrelli complained to his sponsor, the wine merchant L. M. Renault and Sons; his union, the American Communication Association; and members of Pennsylvania's congressional delegation. He pointed out that many Americans had shared his love of Italy and admiration of the changes in the country before the outbreak of World War II. Since the start of the war, he had proved his loyalty to the United States by soliciting purchases of war stamps and donations to the American Red Cross.[142] His efforts came to naught. Price continued to insist that he had "no doubt as to the desirability of discontinuing Mr. Borrelli's broadcast activities." [143]

Price probably had Borrelli and Seuren on his mind when he gave his unvarnished, off-the-record talk with foreign-language broadcasters at the annual N.A.B. conference in April 1943, in which he told them that "their property [radio station] was in danger if they did not observe [the code]." [144] Simon, who was in the audience, seized on Price's remarks and decided to give the Foreign Language Radio Wartime Control Committee a new task. He appointed an unofficial group of "field representatives" to act as sectional liaisons between the Office of Censorship and foreign-language stations, in much the same way that the Press Division missionaries worked with publishers. The group voluntarily would help educate broadcasters about the foreign-language censorship code. According to the plan, the field representatives would attempt to rectify code violations on their own. If stations repeated the errors, the representatives would notify the Foreign Language Radio Wartime Control Committee. And, if the violations still were not fixed, the problem would be passed along to the Office of Censorship. The Broadcasting Division had the twenty field representatives visit all foreign-language stations in the summer of 1943. At Bronson's request, the representatives were to determine if the stations employed censors for foreign-language scripts and on-air monitors who understood the language being broadcast.[145] KGGM station manager Harry Burdick, who contacted Ernest Thwaites, KFUN's general manager, at Ryan's request, was the field representative for New Mexico. Another representative, Calvin J. Smith of station KFAC in Los Angeles, managed to persuade a California station to mail the censors its Spanish-language scripts after the Broadcasting Division had tried and failed.[146]

Representatives lived in all parts of the country. Price said he found the group helpful but not entirely effective—a comment he did not explain, although it may have been a reference to Thwaites's rebellion. If he was sincere in wanting to keep foreign-language programs on the air during the war, then he had to be disappointed during the summer of 1943 when at least seven stations halted such broadcasts. KWYO in Sheridan, Wyoming, curtailed its Polish programs in July because it had no one to monitor them; it targeted its Polish-heritage audience with English-language programs instead. WMTV in East St. Louis, Illinois, dropped Greek and Hungarian programs in the same month because it said it could not afford to pay a monitor, but Croatian and Polish programs continued. KIEV in Riverside, California, ended all foreign-language broadcasts on September 10, 1943, although the field representative filing a report gave no reason for the halt. Also ending foreign-language programs that summer were KFXM in San Bernardino, California; KGER in Long Beach, California; KRIS in Corpus Christi, Texas; and KABC in San Antonio.[147]

Code violations declined. Through the efforts of the field representatives and the Broadcasting Division, by October 1943 all foreign language stations were producing scripts and monitoring broadcasts.[148]

No major problems were recorded in foreign-language broadcasting in 1944 or 1945. When the revised *Code of Wartime Practices*, issued on December 1, 1943, retained the requirement for foreign-language scripts and monitors, Simon phoned the Broadcasting Division to ask for its cancellation. "Why can't we trust our own people?" he asked. Ryan and Simon discussed the issue four days before Christmas, and Ryan proposed loosening the code after Germany's surrender. Bronson had urged Ryan to continue foreign-language monitoring until then because he feared a return to poor compliance with the code and a rush of freelance censorship by government and military officials to fill the vacuum left by the Broadcasting Division.[149]

Hostilities ended in Europe on May 8, 1945. One week later, the final revision of the censorship code—the first in seventeen months—appeared. Although by then Ryan had left the Broadcasting Division, the new code incorporated his suggestions. Not only did it eliminate all foreign-language radio restrictions, it also loosened radio restrictions so the codes for radio and the print press were the same.[150]

Price, Ryan, and the radio industry had navigated through one of the most difficult censorship tasks of the war without imposing mandatory censorship. They had relied mainly on trust. In a democracy at war, trust can be a powerful motivator if participants know what is expected of them and believe the rules are fairly administered. Only once did Price appear to strain that trust, when he asked for Seuren's removal without presenting his case to the accused. Price noted privately that Seuren had questionable friendships and a history of participation in the Bund, yet little evidence exists in the archives that Seuren broadcast fascist ideology. Apparently no one pressed for proof that justice had been served, and Price devoted less than a paragraph to Seuren in his unpublished memoir. The minimal attention suggested that he either felt no need to discuss Seuren because the reasons for his ouster were obvious, or, like many autobiographers, he glossed over an episode that might mar his reputation. Why would Price not want the evidence in print? An airtight case against a Nazi sympathizer would have boosted the vigilance of other broadcasters. On the other hand, it might have embarrassed Hibbs, a station manager who had a history of cooperation with censors, at a time when Price and Ryan needed the cooperation of foreign-language radio.

Price seldom used his absolute power over foreign-language broadcasting. His restraint was notable considering the radio industry's reluctance to provide scripts and monitors, as well as FCC and OWI pressure for more control over foreign-language radio.

Pearson Said He Was Going to Tell Things He Could Not Write

Drew Pearson and His Secrets

Investigative journalist Drew Pearson gave an inauspicious after-dinner speech to a group of insurance agents at a New York City hotel in the spring of 1942. He talked about the war against Japan and outlined the damage to American ships and planes in the Pacific. He asked the audience to keep his talk a secret, implying that he was revealing information so sensitive that it should not leave the room. But it did. Reports filtered back to federal officials in Washington. As a consequence, Pearson was investigated by the Federal Bureau of Investigation on suspicion of violating the Espionage Act. He also was singled out as the only journalist required to submit all of his radio scripts to prebroadcast review by the Office of Censorship.

From this rocky beginning early in the war, Pearson and the Office of Censorship developed a grudging, mutual respect. Pearson, who staved off the espionage inquiry, came to understand and conform to the bureaucracy of censorship—so much so that he defended the censors to other journalists and "could rattle off the fine print in our rule book faster than we could," an assistant director of the Office of Censorship recalled.[1] The censors, in turn, kept a watchful eye on Pearson but slowly gained confidence in his ability to keep a secret. Pearson learned by mid-1944 of the attempt to develop an atomic bomb; censors cautioned him about the story, and he did not discuss the subject in print or on the radio until after the bomb was dropped on Hiroshima in 1945.

Pearson's relationship with the Office of Censorship demonstrates the extent of the government's effort to keep sensitive information out of the news media without compromising the First Amendment. The effectiveness and wisdom of World War II censorship can be judged not only by the relatively easy supervision of compliant journalists but also by the censors' more difficult handling of ones who were defiant or careless. Pearson, one of the most significant journalists of the twentieth century, sometimes was both.

Censors marked and filed copies of 145 of Pearson's wartime radio scripts, far more than for any other journalist. Those documents provide the most detailed, long-term description of the kinds of news and commentary that the government found objectionable. They are unlike most archives of the Office of Censorship, which are devoted to a single issue or contain a few documents relating to journalists who made inquiries to the censors or were chastised for recklessness. If most files provide snapshots of the censors in action, then the Pearson file is a photo album documenting censorship's evolution from the war's early months to its end.

Byron Price wrote in 1942 that he was having "a great deal of trouble" with radio commentators such as Pearson and Walter Winchell, whose syndicated newspaper column and Blue Network broadcasts were known primarily for Broadway gossip but also included military and government news stories.[2] Wartime censorship placed tough restrictions on Pearson's and Winchell's news-gathering and reporting techniques. They specialized in cultivating anonymous sources. But the censorship codes eliminated absolute anonymity for sources in news stories that compromised military security. Only an appropriate authority could release information violating censorship regulations, and journalists abiding by the code either had to name these authorities in print or on the air, or had to share them confidentially with the Office of Censorship. Since the appropriate-authority clause in the *Code of Wartime Practices* was ill defined early in 1942, it was not surprising that journalists who had built their careers on publishing leaks and rumors would cause censorship problems.

Pearson and Winchell met the challenge by couching some of their stories as speculation instead of hard news, and by finding authoritative sources in Congress and executive offices to give them scoops. "In Broadcasting we have found quite often that both . . . have been able to cite A.A. [appropriate authority] for stories which had been bottled up," John E. Fetzer, J. Harold Ryan's successor as Broadcasting Division director, said.[3] The Office of Censorship's own history noted that neither commentator deliberately violated the code,[4] but that assessment was based on a rather technical view of compliance.

Pearson respected the code but occasionally violated it when testing its boundaries. Winchell violated the code through his inability to understand it, telling the Broadcasting Division, "I can't figure it out!"[5] He asked the Office of Censorship in July 1942 and again in March 1943 to send him someone every week to screen his scripts shortly before his Blue Network broadcasts, but the censors declined to do for him what they believed they had to do for Pearson.[6] The decision was a pragmatic and political one. Winchell was a vocal supporter of the FBI, the president, and the navy, and he often received exclusive news leaks on important stories, such as the prosecution of eight Nazi saboteurs captured in summer 1942. Pressed by the print and broadcast censors to cite his appropriate authorities for stories that violated the code, Winchell once replied that he was under "secret orders" and that his scripts were being written by "government officials."[7] The censors were incredulous about many of his claims, such as the broadcast news story that American submarines were prepared to rescue the pope and that "a new, secret flame-throwing bomb" would create "acres of fire behind German lines," and their doubts were reinforced after he told them privately in 1942 that he fabricated his letters from listeners as a way to introduce his radio editorials.[8] Nevertheless, the censors handled Winchell more delicately than Pearson. "Our difficulty in the matter is the fact that Winchell finds himself in a position of being a close friend of [FBI director] J. Edgar Hoover and a little tin god as far as the Army and Navy are concerned," broadcast censor Eugene Carr told Winchell's network and Ryan.[9] If the Office of Censorship edited his scripts, it risked second-guessing Hoover or the president. In addition, the censors needed to avoid alienating the powerful and popular broadcaster. Fortunately for the Office of Censorship, Winchell professed his support for the code, and his violations nearly disappeared after the Blue Network began scrutinizing his scripts more closely early in 1943. Anonymous news leaks from the FBI continued to be aired in Winchell's broadcasts, but the censors were satisfied when the network vouched for their having been endorsed by appropriate authorities.

Pearson also received news leaks, but they often came from the enemies of Hoover, President Franklin Roosevelt, and other high-ranking officials. Pearson specialized in finding disgruntled sources in the president's administration who were willing to share inside information, often on the condition that it not be attributed to them. Many of the tips proved accurate, but some were embarrassing, as when Pearson and Robert S. Allen, his writing partner from 1932 to early 1942, reported six days before the attack on Pearl Harbor that the Japanese fleet had steamed out to sea, destination unknown.[10] That tip came from Pearson's friend Sumner Welles, assistant secretary of state. Other tipsters included officials in the army, navy, and Congress who disagreed with policies of the Roosevelt administration or wished to embarrass their enemies. Often, however, these tips proved to be speculation or wishful thinking.

Pearson had powerful enemies during World War II, including two at the very top. Roosevelt told Pearson in the summer of 1941 that "your batting average has been near the bottom of the League" and called him a liar in 1943.[11] Roosevelt was notoriously thin-skinned whenever Pearson, often through a tip from Welles, Vice President Henry Wallace, or Secretary of the Interior Harold Ickes, pointed out dissent within the administration. Also harboring a grudge was Hoover, even though Hoover's staff routinely gave Pearson leaks from FBI files in the 1930s in return for favorable publicity in Pearson and Allen's "Washington Merry-Go-Round" syndicated newspaper column.[12] Before America entered World War II, Hoover, acting under orders from the White House, informed Pearson on the activities of isolationists, whom Pearson exposed. Hoover also wrote him courteous letters—all the while criticizing him in private and calling his column "not . . . reliable." Particularly irritating to Hoover was a "Merry-Go-Round" item that said he used a distinctive and powerful perfume; he issued an aggrieved denial of this slur on his masculinity even though the item was true.[13] Hoover also wrote a defensive memo to the attorney general after the "Merry-Go-Round" accused Hoover of being a headline-grabber.[14]

Pearson also had powerful friends. In addition to Wallace, Ickes, and Welles, army chief of staff George Marshall supported Pearson's investigative journalism. Publicly responding to the backroom maneuvering of army and navy officials who complained about Pearson and discussed ways of silencing him, Marshall praised him as "one of my best inspector-generals." [15]

Officials in the navy and army attempted to learn his sources or catch him in an illegal act during World War II. The Office of Naval Intelligence shadowed Pearson in 1943 in attempts to end his secret contacts with naval sources.[16] In addition, the undersecretary of war told Pearson in 1944 that the journalist's phone conversations with Welles were being recorded, apparently at the order of the president.[17] Pearson believed that his phone was tapped and that the FBI kept him under surveillance during the war years.[18] Wallace wrote in his diary in 1944 that an authority had told him that Pearson was shadowed by Hoover's agents.[19]

Whether the FBI actually "shadowed" Pearson is not clear. A 1943 FBI memo denied that the bureau ever had placed Pearson under "technical surveillance," by which it meant a wiretap, but this left open the possibility of listening devices, physical surveillance by agents, and burglaries of Pearson's files to remove or copy documents. Pearson's FBI file includes memos that at one time had been locked away at his home. They were subsequently "extracted" by a person or persons whose names remain blacked out in the photocopies of Pearson's file that the FBI released in response to a Freedom of Information Act request.[20] It is known that agents in the bureau monitored Pearson's broadcasts and sent excerpts to Hoover, beginning on January 25, 1942.

The evidence indicates that Pearson was the focus of intense interest by federal agencies before and during World War II independent of any attempt to censor his newspaper column or Sunday radio broadcasts. Office of Censorship restrictions on Pearson merely supplemented a broad pattern of government scrutiny that occasionally bordered on harassment. Even before there was an Office of Censorship, Pearson clashed with federal officials who aimed to censor him, and censorship conflicts continued on and off throughout the war.

On December 12, 1941, after the attack on Pearl Harbor but before the creation of the Office of Censorship, Pearson and Allen distributed a "Merry-Go-Round" column in which they described details of the devastation of the Pacific Fleet. In particular, they pointed out that four heavy warships had been crippled and that most of the army's airplanes in Hawaii had been destroyed or damaged.[21] Secretary of the Navy Frank Knox and other federal officials had sought to suppress this kind of information on the assumption that the Japanese pilots would not have complete knowledge of the damage they had inflicted, and to avoid damage to American morale.[22] Martin Anderson, publisher of the *Orlando (Florida) Sentinel* read the column, which was scheduled for publication on the following day, and informed White House press secretary Stephen T. Early that he questioned whether it should be printed. Early, with Roosevelt's blessing, informed interim censorship director Hoover. The press secretary said that "if they [Pearson and Allen] continue to print such inaccurate and unpatriotic statements," the government would appeal to their subscribers and bar them from "all privileges that go with the relationships between the Press and Government."[23]

What happened next is unclear; details of Hoover's attempts to prevent publication of the "Merry-Go-Round" report on Pearl Harbor differ among the available sources. Hoover, in a memorandum to Early, said he shared information from the column with army and navy authorities, who told him that publication would be "highly prejudicial to the security and safety of the national defense." Hoover then tried to phone Pearson. Unable to reach him, he talked with Allen, who would soon enlist in the army and sever his connections to the "Merry-Go-Round." Allen agreed to ask the syndication clients to kill the column. About two hours later, Hoover said, Pearson phoned the FBI. Hoover's recollection of the call is bureaucratically phrased, yet pointed: "Mr. Pearson stated that he did not wish to be threatened in regard to this matter, and I pointed out to him I was not endeavoring to threaten him, but I was acting in my official capacity as temporary coordinator of censorship arrangements. . . . Mr. Pearson stated that he would take steps to eliminate from the article those portions giving the details of the losses in Hawaii."[24] According to Hoover's private memoranda, Pearson and Allen succeeded in preventing all papers from publishing the column.[25] Hoover's accounts of his talk with Pearson, which he shared with his FBI staff and Attorney General Francis Biddle, said he had cowed Pearson and "cut [him] short" when he protested the "threats" of censorship.[26]

According to Pearson, however, the conversation went entirely differently, with Hoover on the defensive. In his diary, Pearson wrote that Hoover called him, not vice versa, during the dinner hour, threatening to jail him unless he killed the Pearl Harbor column. "I told Edgar that he was nuts, that there was no law by which he could put me in jail. . . . He admitted all this, said that Steve Early . . . had called him up and asked him to throw the fear of God into me."[27] Although it is impossible to determine whether Pearson's or Hoover's version is closer to the truth, their conflicting accounts reveal both men to be self-confident if not strongly egocentric. This personality trait would continue to color Pearson's relationship with censors.

A second brush with censorship before the censorship codebooks were issued occurred in mid-December, when Pearson and Allen sent out a column mentioning the construction of a bomb shelter for the president's use. Roosevelt had asked that the story be suppressed for security.

As with the Pearl Harbor story, Pearson and Allen were able to prevent publication of the item in most newspapers. However, it appeared in the *Philadelphia Record,* specifying that the shelter beneath the White House would be connected by tunnel to the Treasury Building.[28] Early pointed out the column to Price but did not suggest how he should respond to it.[29] Interestingly, the original draft of the "Merry-Go-Round" column containing the story about the shelter had a veiled reference to the clash over the Pearl Harbor column. Deleted from the version sent to syndication clients, possibly to avoid damaging Pearson and Allen's relations with the FBI, was the sentence "J. Edgar Hoover . . . is now threatening newsmen regarding stories which the White House doesn't want published."[30]

According to the censorship archives, Pearson's first contacts with the Office of Censorship occurred in February 1942. Press Division censors questioned a draft of a newspaper column about the United States sending planes to China and the Philippines. Pearson agreed to rephrase one item but defended another as having been cleared by the White House and the army. When censor William Mylander objected, Pearson "launched [into a] vehement argument. In addition to trying to justify [the] story under the Code, he observed that if this office proposed to do anything about it, he'd 'get on your tail,' " and he dared the censors to "cite" him. Mylander, declining the chance to argue, debated the content of the Philippines story with an army colonel and other censors before telling Pearson that he should revise it or kill it. Pearson agreed.[31] That, however, was not the end of the conflict. On February 26, Pearson met with Price. According to the minutes of that meeting, Pearson was not belligerent or defiant. He expressed a willingness to abide by the censorship code but defended his stories as serving the "constructive purpose" of deflecting unfair criticism away from Roosevelt over the lack of military support for troops in the Pacific. Without giving ground, Price said that Pearson's column "was the type . . . which might be hit hardest by the Code, because it presumed to be 'inside' stuff; that all manner of dodges could be indulged in by any reporter who wanted to wreck the code." Left unclear was what would happen if Pearson and the Office of Censorship continued to clash.[32] Most likely, Price invited Pearson to call if he had any censorship questions while writing his broadcast scripts and newspaper columns. Pearson made such a request for guidance on three news items on the day after the meeting, and the Blue Network delivered a radio script two days after that.[33] Pearson underlined his willingness to comply with the censorship code in a follow-up letter to Price stating that journalists must, "no matter what happens, make the present code work."[34]

Still, material that the censors considered code violations continued to appear in Pearson's stories, including an account of sabotage at the New York Harbor that presidential secretary Edwin Watson referred to Price on March 6.[35] Throughout March, the Office of Censorship and Washington radio station WMAL, where Pearson's nationwide Sunday night broadcast originated, discussed establishing a regular review of Pearson's radio scripts but could not agree on details. Then came Pearson's New York speech.

THE *NEW YORK TIMES* ACTS AS INFORMANT

On the evening of April 14, Pearson addressed about 700 to 800 members of the National Association of Insurance Agents at the Hotel Pennsylvania in New York City. In the audience that night, taking notes on the back of a dinner program, was Russell B. Porter of the *New York Times*. Later that evening Porter typed a memorandum paraphrasing Pearson's talk and addressed it to the "Desk," presumably meaning his editors. The memo accused Pearson of attempting to circumvent domestic censorship regulations. "He told a lot of secret information, which the newspapers and radio are not permitted to publish," Porter noted. His two-page memo listed the alleged secrets, including many details of the Japanese attack on Pearl Harbor that were still being suppressed. He said Pearson had revealed that nine battleships had been "crippled," including six that sank. "Accordingly we have no striking power to interfere with the Jap navy in the Pacific," Porter wrote. He added that, according to Pearson, 300 American planes had been destroyed on the ground in Hawaii, 300 more met a similar fate in the Philippines the next day, one million tons of shipping had been sunk by the Axis during March, and the United States was sending planes to Alaska and China with the intention of launching bombing raids on Japan in midsummer. After detailing about a dozen other allegations, Porter summarized his reasons for writing the memo:

> At the beginning of his speech Pearson said he was going to tell things he could not write in his column or say on the radio, and that the newspapers could not print. He said he was sure anything he said in that room would not be published, and therefore could not help the enemy. . . .

However . . . it would seem to me that no one should be allowed to go around the country lecturing to large groups of people at public dinners, or even at one such event, and revealing as "inside stuff" information so secret and so useful to the enemy that the newspapers and radio are not allowed to publish it. It would seem that there is only a difference in degree involved. Certainly, no one can be sure that there was not an Axis agent or sympathizer in the room. Undoubtedly, nearly everybody who heard Pearson will repeat everything he said to show they have access to "inside stuff," and their words are bound to reach Axis agents somewhere, sometime. Even if the Axis already has the information, he has no right to publish what the newspapers can not publish, and he has no right to set himself up as the authority as to what he can and can not use in the way of military information at a public gathering.[36]

Porter conceded that much of what Pearson said had been the subject of gossip. He was concerned, however, about the likelihood of Pearson's reputation as a journalist adding legitimacy to the rumors. Porter suggested that the government either reveal as much information as it could without aiding the Axis or muzzle Pearson.[37]

The memorandum made its way to the publisher of the *Times,* Arthur Hays Sulzberger. The *Times* had grumbled about, but scrupulously followed, the voluntary domestic censorship regulations of the Office of Censorship since they were first established. For example, *Times* managing editor Edwin James told Price in February 1942 that the paper had obtained a detailed description of the losses at Pearl Harbor and wanted to print it; however, he complied with Price's request to suppress the story for the sake of national security and morale and continued to do so until the navy released its own version of the story ten months later.[38] Competitive concerns thus figured into the *Times*'s animosity toward Pearson—he was spreading, albeit by word of mouth, a story that the *Times* grudgingly had suppressed. For his part, Pearson was "a little contemptuous of big, powerful papers" such as the *Times,* according to his associate Jack Anderson, who was not surprised to learn of the *Times*'s role in Pearson's censorship troubles.[39]

Price phoned Early on April 24 to announce that he was forwarding Porter's memo, which "a newspaper publisher in New York" had placed in his hands. Price said Pearson obviously had disclosed military information, and he wanted Early's advice on a proper response.[40] Early left no record of whether he consulted with Roosevelt before responding; however, the magnitude of the actions he requested suggests that such a conversation took place. Early asked Price to send the memo to the attorney general, with an eye toward criminal prosecution and possible suspension or revocation of Pearson's "press privileges," which he did not describe.[41] He probably meant the accreditation that gave journalists regular access to the White House and other federal offices, such as the War Department. Considering Pearson's penchant for cultivating leaks and anonymous sources, the loss of his White House pass would not have hurt him significantly.

Price carried out Early's instructions the day he received them, sharing the memo with Biddle, privately naming Sulzberger as his source, and asking to be warned if Biddle should ever need to publicly identify the *Times* as the whistle-blower.[42] Apparently he was concerned about the damage to the *Times*'s reputation among the nation's journalists if Sulzberger were identified as having given evidence to the government about another journalist—even if that evidence suggested the possibility of an Espionage Act violation.

Biddle ordered an investigation of Pearson's remarks by the FBI. The inquiry lasted eight months. FBI agents began by interviewing Porter, who said he did not take complete notes because he had not planned to write a news story about Pearson's speech. The investigators then interviewed other members of the audience, some of whom contradicted Porter about Pearson's overview of battle damage as well as his summary of plans for a summer offensive. "It was indicated that Pearson's statements suggested only the possibility that such might happen and that the statements could have been regarded as predictions rather than actual operations contemplated by the War or Navy Departments," the agents wrote.[43]

Two agents interviewed Pearson in early May at his home in Washington. Pearson, responding to the agents' recounting of the speech point by point, said that almost all of his statements at the Hotel Pennsylvania previously had appeared in print or had been broadcast, the only exceptions being news items specifically cleared for release by the Navy Department or reviewed and found unobjectionable by the Office of Censorship. For example, he said, he had pointed out that there were nine battleships at Pearl Harbor and that all had been hurt and "some damage done." He did not say how many had been sunk, but he did reveal that the striking power of the Pacific Fleet had been compromised. He criticized the unidentified whistle-blower for getting overexcited by the talk and failing to gain a proper perspective. "With reference to allegations he had said he was going to tell things he could not write in his column or say on the radio, Mr. Pearson said he doubted he had said exactly that, but that he attempted to use some showmanship and to avoid making it look like a rehash of his writing and radio comments, which he accomplished by grouping incidents covering a considerable period of time into one situation," the agents told Hoover. Pearson "felt this was excusable" as a necessity to hold an audience's interest. His motive for giving the incendiary talk was to arouse the public to a wartime psychology, he said.[44]

The FBI gave Biddle the results of its investigation on May 14, 1942; investigators closed the inquiry without taking any action on December 17.[45] Neither the records of the FBI nor those of the Office of Censorship indicate a link between the investigation and the subsequent censorship of Pearson. However, one week after the attorney general received the FBI report, Pearson was ordered by his network to begin submitting scripts for his Sunday night radio news and commentary program to the censors' Broadcasting Division to have them screened on Sunday afternoon. Perhaps the idea was suggested by Press Division censor William Steven on May 3, when he argued on the phone with Pearson over several items in his script for that evening. After getting Pearson to agree to delete or reword every disputed sentence, he wrote a note to Press Division director John H. Sorrells: "Recommendation: That we quit this damn foolishness with P and A [Pearson and Allen] on the phone."[46] Price agreed. Writing in his wartime notebook, he said Pearson and Allen—who had left the partnership by that time—"were continually skating along the edge of the Code," but the Office of Censorship finally reached an arrangement with the Blue Network to let the censors screen their broadcasts in advance.[47]

The censors worked with publishers, syndicates, networks, and station managers to keep individual journalists in step with the censorship code. High-level mass media executives felt economic pressures to comply. If they were publicly identified as having violated the code or having been charged under the Espionage Act, they faced the possible loss of circulation or advertising revenue from readers who supported the government's prosecution of the war. These pressures were particularly acute at the network that supervised Pearson's broadcasts. NBC owned two networks at the beginning of World War II, the Blue and the Red. In 1941, the FCC, responding to Roosevelt's concerns about the concentration of power in the mass media, ordered NBC to divest itself of one of the two networks no later than April 1944. The Red was stronger financially, and so NBC began work in early 1942 to prepare the Blue for sale. The Blue Network was incorporated separately in January of that year and shopped to potential buyers. While trying to market the Blue as a strong, moneymaking venture, NBC did not want any trouble from Pearson that would drive away advertisers, listeners, or buyers.[48]

The Blue told Pearson on May 22, 1942, that he would have to be co-operative and submit a copy of his next script to the Office of Censorship by 1 P.M. on May 24, six hours before his broadcast. Pearson exploded in anger. He called Broadcasting Division director Ryan and protested that he was being unfairly singled out. Did the Office of Censorship hold Winchell or other radio commentators to the same standard? No, said Ryan, but the censors chose to look at some programs before broadcast "because of the nature of the subject." Pearson said he refused to submit his scripts in advance, arguing that he no longer chose to abide by the voluntary codes; Ryan countered that the network, not Pearson, was the censor of his program, and that the voluntary nature of censorship for radio was debatable. Ryan's account of the conversation did not indicate whether he mentioned licensing by the FCC or hinted at the opinion that Biddle had given Price four days earlier that authorized the Office of Censorship to take over any radio station. However, Ryan did tell Pearson, without elaboration, "There have been such things as programs being taken off the air."[49]

The threat stopped Pearson's defiance. He shifted his tactics, offering to compromise. Pearson and the censors agreed that he could deliver his script by 3 P.M. every Sunday. As promised, his next script arrived at the agreed-upon hour from the WMAL studio, and he continued to submit scripts throughout the war.[50]

The archived scripts begin in the first week of June 1942 and end on the Sunday before V-J Day in August 1945. Although Pearson was supposed to file a script for each week, twenty-two are missing or incomplete. After reviewing a script, a censor marked the items he found questionable and phoned Pearson or a manager at WMAL to ask about the apparent violations. Some items in the scripts crossed the censorship code and were removed or reworded to avoid the violation; others were acceptable because Pearson convinced the censors that the material was covered by various exceptions to the rules in the *Code of Wartime Practices*. The censor usually noted the applicable rule in the codebook for each item, Pearson's or WMAL's reasoning for including the item in the broadcast, the negotiations about whether the item could be broadcast in some form, and the final disposition of the item—whether it was deleted, reworded, or allowed to stand.

Of the 145 scripts on file, only twenty-two passed through censorship without objection. In one such instance, in January 1944, WMAL manager William Neel responded with black humor to censor Lester Halpin's verdict that Pearson's script was free from objections. Halpin noted, "He [Neel] thanked me and said it was nice to have known me, apparently insinuating that my lack of objection spelled the end of my censorship career."[51]

Censors objected to 11 percent of Pearson's news stories as well as 10 percent of the predictions he made at the end of his broadcasts. They sometimes objected to a statement presented as fact in the middle of a prediction, or to Pearson's predictions mentioning a subject that the Office of Censorship specifically had requested to remain off limits, such as speculation about invasion routes.

The percentage of items in Pearson's scripts to which the censors raised an objection decreased from 17.6 percent in 1942 to 11.8 percent in 1943. And it continued to drop, to 10.8 percent in 1944 and finally to 7.0 percent in 1945. The decline was the result of Pearson's growing familiarity with the code and the relaxation of the code's toughest restrictions beginning in late 1943, as the Allied armed forces began to gain dominance. Still, Pearson's continued submission of objectionable items until the end of the war demonstrates his willingness to continue to test the limits of censorship—and, sometimes, to continue to defy censorship when he believed defiance to be appropriate according to a strict reading of the code itself. When the censors insisted on deletions or revisions, Pearson complied but continued to voice objections in about one-third of the cases.

The news items and predictions that most commonly led to a censorship objection were those that dealt with war strategy—the future movements of troops, ships, and planes, plus diplomacy, invasion plans, and military intelligence. Such items would be especially sensitive to the accusation that they might provide the enemy with valuable knowledge in time to prepare defenses or countermeasures. Of the 300 objections noted in the wartime scripts, 107 fit this description.

Pearson's most common method of dealing with censorship objections was to delete or recast a portion of the news item or prediction, which he did in nearly half of the cases. In slightly more than 20 percent of the cases, Pearson was able to persuade the censors that his news story or prediction did not run afoul of the codebooks; the censors cleared these items because they had been previously published, had been cleared by appropriate authority, or upon further review did not actually violate the code. Finally, Pearson had thirty-nine news stories or predictions cleared by the censor when he revealed, in confidence, the "appropriate authority" who had agreed to violate the code by providing Pearson with the information in the belief that it would provide nothing useful to the enemy. In twenty-six of these cases, the source was an officer in the army or navy or an armed forces civilian such as the secretary of war or his assistant.

LEAKS AND LOOPHOLES

Pearson's network of military contacts enabled him to be the first to provide details on some important news stories. One involved the first raid on Japan. On April 18, 1942, sixteen army B-25s took off from the aircraft carrier *Hornet* about 800 miles east of Japan and bombed Tokyo and four other cities. The raid caused little damage but much confusion in Japan. In America, citizens speculated about how the raid had been carried out. The army and navy declined to reveal many details because they wanted to keep the Japanese guessing about America's ability to launch such attacks. Roosevelt added to the rumors by teasing reporters. He said that the bombers had taken off from "Shangri-La," the never-never land featured in the 1937 motion picture *Lost Horizon*.[52]

On October 25, Pearson received authorization from Assistant Secretary of War John McCloy and General Alexander Surles to describe where and how the bomber crews landed after the raid, although Surles removed a line revealing that the planes had lifted off the deck of an aircraft carrier. Surles, who was acting as appropriate authority for the release, personally marked out nearly every phrase that violated the censorship code. Thus, when the script finally arrived at the Office of Censorship, the only line that the Broadcasting Division asked Pearson to delete was a hint that Surles had overlooked about the future movements of Jimmy Doolittle, who had led the raid and returned safely to America.[53]

This episode illustrates the considerable cooperation among a journalist, the Office of Censorship, and two officials in the War Department to release a news story—albeit six months after the fact—to the public without compromising security. The censors would have questioned the entire story if Pearson had not obtained appropriate authority for its release, as journalists themselves were not deemed knowledgeable enough about national security to make such decisions. Noteworthy also is the degree of accord between Surles and the censors on which sentences in the *Hornet* story should be recast or deleted. This is not surprising, since the censorship codes were created with the input of military and government officials—again, because the censors themselves were not experts on national security.

If that was all Pearson had reported about the Shangri-La raid, his contacts with censors would suggest the degree to which government officials could exercise news management on a tough investigative journalist. However, Pearson was not content to end his reporting with only those details that had been freed by appropriate authority. In the final weeks of 1942, he pressed the army, which had carried out the Tokyo bombing, and the navy, which supervised the naval logistics, for more information. He had little success. The identity of the *Hornet* as the carrier remained secret until January 13, 1943, when Pearson finally revealed it in a speech at a small Southern university. He prefaced his remarks to an audience at Louisiana College in Alexandria by saying, "I think the American people are entitled to know this [the identify of the aircraft carrier] since the Japanese have known it all along." That was a reference to the announcement the previous day that Japanese radio, probably basing its reports on interviews with captured fliers, had named the *Hornet* as the source of the planes. Whether Pearson was reprimanded for the speech is not recorded in the censorship archives, but the editor of the Alexandria daily newspaper, which reported it, was admonished to try to follow the *Code of Wartime Practices* and not to accept Pearson as an appropriate authority. News of Pearson's speech reached the Associated Press desk in Washington, which killed the story after asking the Office of Censorship and Office of War Information about it. At about the time that the story was called to the censors' attention, Pearson tried to reprint the gist of his speech in the "Merry-Go-Round." Despite his attributing the story to Japanese radio, the Office of Censorship objected. The censors said that no military authorities in the United States had agreed to release the news, and besides, the Japanese possibly were unsure of the facts and were fishing for confirmation. The Office of Censorship asked Pearson's syndicate to kill the column item on the *Hornet,* and United Features did so. But the message could not reach all papers before publication deadline. A handful, including the paper in El Dorado, Kansas, printed the item; perhaps more damaging, however, hundreds of other syndication members learned of the details in the column and questioned why it had been suppressed.[54]

Why did Pearson try to tell the *Hornet*'s story? The most obvious answer is the one he gave in his lecture—that if censorship were intended to keep sensitive information from the enemy, the bureaucratic rules about the mechanism for the release of information became moot once the enemy demonstrated its knowledge. Furthermore, the sinking of the *Hornet* in September had been announced by the navy in October; thus, any Japanese interest in the ship as a potential platform for future raids had been eliminated. Pearson also cited, in memos to Price, his belief that the story had been cleared by appropriate authorities and that its phrasing was vague enough to warrant the label of acceptable speculation.

Pearson can hardly be blamed for utilizing the rules of censorship to his advantage, particularly when the information in question was already known to the enemy. The censorship code urged a ban on rumors that were spread "in such a way that they will be accepted as facts" and thus render aid and comfort to the enemy. The press and radio codebooks also requested that foreign military claims be carefully attributed. However, the codes did not forbid journalists from announcing other unsubstantiated stories as long as they were not presented as facts.[55]

Pearson exploited these rules to the fullest by sometimes taking stories he knew to be factual and spinning them to make them seem as if they were merely speculative. Such methods undoubtedly increased the percentage of predictions that later turned out to be accurate. For example, Pearson seized on this regulation on November 21, 1943, when he broadcast that "rumors have shot round the world" of an Allied summit meeting of Roosevelt, Winston Churchill, and Josef Stalin. "My own prediction is that they will go to an African town outside Cairo," he said. News of the president's travel was banned unless released by appropriate authority, but the Broadcasting Division cleared his story because it presented the information as a rumor and a prediction. Other journalists, including broadcaster Hilmar Robert Baukhage of the Blue Network, also had received censorship approval to speculate about Roosevelt traveling overseas.[56] "We had unobjected all along to speculation that a conference would be held," Jack Lockhart, the third director of the Press Division, wrote in a memorandum to Price on December 1, 1943. "What we had tried to sit on was the where and when of the conference. The Pearson broadcast gave the when only as the future and presented the where on the basis of personal opinion and prediction—which could be wrong."[57]

Price might have complained that this broadcast nevertheless gave out too much information about the movements of the commander in chief, or that the mention of the *Hornet* as the carrier that launched the Tokyo raid was a fact and not an opinion. However, what is fact and what is opinion can itself become a matter of opinion. Pearson benefited by stretching the interpretations of the rules right up to the point that security might be compromised. If he ever demonstrably crossed that line, of course, he would have to pay the penalties according to the Espionage Act.

The *Hornet* story also illustrates the potential for bureaucratic confusion in a system of self-censorship. Pearson followed further Office of Censorship requests to restrict news of the Tokyo raid in the spring of 1943, but he became upset when the *Cleveland Press* printed a detailed story on the first anniversary of the attack, which was followed by a general news release by the War Department on April 20.[58] Press Division censor Nathaniel R. Howard explained to Pearson that the censors had been "powerless" to halt the *Press*'s story because it had been cleared by a navy public relations officer in Cleveland, "a matter now giving the [Navy] Department Public Relations Office some annoyance."[59] In other words, the *Press* had interpreted the appropriate-authority clause of the censorship code to mean that a local naval official could release a story of national significance, whereas the Navy Department had reached the opposite conclusion. When thousands of journalists nationwide reached their own conclusions about how to apply the code, such confusion was inevitable. It had been foreseen early in the war. John Sorrells, the first Press Division director, had told Pearson in March 1942: "In the final analysis the only thing a newspaperman can do in wartime is to do what he thinks is right. If he gets scooped doing right by someone doing wrong, it is unfortunate, but in many instances, virtue is its own reward. Further, I think that all these things will balance out. You may kill something that another chap thinks is all right and you will get scooped; on the other hand, since all men do not see all things alike, you will publish something which another chap will kill out."[60]

And what of the cases in which the conscientious journalist brought a censorship question to Price's staff before deciding whether to publish or broadcast it? Bureaucracy again had the potential to work in favor of the censor, and against the journalist. If the story violated the censorship code and lacked an on-the-record source to act as an appropriate authority, the story would receive an unfavorable ruling. The censor might ask for the reporter's authority, confidentially receive the name, and then call that person for verification. The confidential source then might waver when confronted by a censor asking whether he or she was willing to take responsibility for violating the code. In another scenario, the censor might call his own contacts in other government offices to see if a questionable story had been freed for publication. Again, such efforts to verify authority for a story could lead to official denials. A censor "could call up various government departments and secure . . . denials, whether based upon fact or not, which could easily knock the guts out of a broadcast," Pearson wrote to the Office of Censorship in June 1942.[61] However, the Office of Censorship declined to censor stories that were known to be inaccurate. Accuracy often is difficult to assess, especially in news analysis, and demanding it would have damaged a voluntary censorship system built on cooperation. The Office of Censorship sometimes told journalists that official sources had expressed doubts about a story's veracity, but if the story did not violate the code, it offered no objection.[62]

ATOMIC SECRETS AND SHATTERED PRIVACY

The complexity of Pearson's relationship with the Office of Censorship can best be demonstrated by examining two extraordinary news stories. In one, the biggest story of the war, he cooperated fully and did not attempt to publish or broadcast what he knew. In the other, he revealed sensitive information despite pleas from Price.

It is evident from documents released in 1998 by the Lyndon B. Johnson Library that Pearson knew about the development of the atomic bomb long before President Harry S. Truman revealed its existence to the American public in August 1945. Pearson filed with his private papers a vaguely worded 1943 Office of Censorship memo about atomic research. The evidence that he understood the gravity of the memo appears in two letters—one filed in the Office of Censorship's archives, and the other in Pearson's papers at the LBJ Library. On June 6, 1944, Lockhart, who succeeded Howard as chief press censor, sent Pearson a registered letter acknowledging that Pearson knew of "several secret projects of major security importance" around the country and asking him to check any information about any such project with the Office of Censorship before mentioning it. The letter did not refer to atomic energy, but the implication is clear.[63] Direct evidence is provided in a follow-up letter in December 1944. Lockhart told Pearson, "You will recall . . . that I talked to you about the secrecy which must surround the Clinton Engineer Works near Knoxville, Tenn., and the Hanford Engineer Works near Pasco, Wash. We would like to see in advance of publication anything you write about these two projects."[64]

The Office of Censorship's archive on Pearson shows that he never attempted to violate its trust. The only hint that Pearson used his knowledge of the atomic bomb to his advantage can be found after the detonation of the first atomic device at Alamogordo, New Mexico, but before its use against Japan. On July 29, 1945, after the Trinity test but before the destruction of Hiroshima, Pearson broadcast a prediction that in retrospect seems too prophetic to have been simply an educated guess. After stating his opinion that Japan might suddenly develop a desire for peace, he reiterated previous predictions that the war in the Pacific would end in 1945. "I can't go beyond that," he added, "except to say that when peace with Japan comes it will come just as suddenly and unexpectedly as Pearl Harbor."[65] Pearson knew about the Manhattan Project, the plan to develop the bomb; given the text of his broadcast, it seems likely that he also had obtained a tip about its actual detonation in the New Mexico desert and had deduced its impact on the outcome of the war.

In another instance, Pearson defied Price's requests that he not use information from private mail that had been intercepted by postal censors and leaked to him. The letters were written by Vivian Kellems of Westport, Connecticut, co-owner of Kellems Products, which made a patented gripping device that simplified the installation of underground cables. A Republican and fierce opponent of Roosevelt's New Deal policies, she announced in January 1944 that she refused to pay her income taxes and urged other American business owners to do the same. Pearson, a supporter of Roosevelt despite his occasional criticism of the president's prosecution of the war, challenged her in his radio program by announcing that she had met Count Frederick Karl von Zedlitz in Buenos Aires, Argentina, and they had become engaged to be married. Von Zedlitz, Pearson revealed, was "an alleged Nazi agent" whom the British government listed as an operative for German business interests in neutral but German-sympathizing Argentina. "I suggest that the Justice Department investigate this strange love affair," Pearson said, "especially Miss Kellems's belief that the count is a man destined to become a leader of Germany after the war."[66] The Office of Naval Intelligence believed von

An aerial view, top, and the main entry gate, bottom, of the Oak Ridge plant, where work in developing the atomic bomb was done. Drew Pearson knew about the project as early as 1943, but he did not reveal the secret in his newspaper column or network broadcasts. National Archives.

Zedlitz to have been in contact with Nazi agents in the United States and to have formerly supervised the German propaganda office in Brazil.[67] U.S. postal censors read his mail to try to learn his intentions, and they shared summaries of his letters with the FBI, the State Department, and the Office of Strategic Services through an intelligence system established early in the war for just such a purpose. Pearson continued to harass Kellems by broadcasting personal excerpts from her letters. Although the Press Division found no objection to Pearson's Kellems broadcasts in the *Code of Wartime Practices,* Price began an ultimately futile inquiry to find the source of the embarrassing and illegal leak, writing to the heads of government agencies that received the intelligence summaries from intercepted letters. Such a leak violated the Office of Censorship's security regulations, which were designed to protect privacy yet gain valuable information for the conduct of the war. Despite the censorship office's personal appeals to Pearson to stop using the private information, however, he continued to do so until the source dried up that spring.[68]

GENERAL PATTON AND THE SLAPPING INCIDENT

Of all the stories that Pearson reported during World War II, the one that defines his place in wartime journalism was the revelation that General George S. Patton had slapped two American soldiers in Sicily in August 1943. Although the story was known to dozens of reporters in southern Europe and northern Africa in late 1943, they had censored themselves to prevent the story's circulation in the States. They feared that the story might damage morale, provide fuel for German propaganda, and possibly reduce Patton's effectiveness in future combat assignments. Pearson revealed the story in his Sunday night broadcast on November 21, 1943, after having shown the story to the Office of Censorship and the War Department. Neither office attempted to block it. Thus, some of the credit for one of the biggest scoops of the war must go to civilian and military censors who declined to oppose a story that had little to do with military security.

Patton, the flamboyant West Point graduate who carried pearl-handled revolvers and relished his "Blood and Guts" nickname, led the American portion of an Allied invasion of Sicily on July 10, 1943. The capture of the island took thirty-eight days and cost 20,000 Allied casualties.[69] On August 4, Patton dictated a diary entry to a sergeant that described a visit to the 15th Evacuation Hospital near Mistretta, where he had gone to visit some wounded men. He said that he had found a man "trying to look as if he had been wounded. I asked him what was the matter, and he said he just couldn't take it. I gave him the devil, slapped his face with my gloves and kicked him out of the hospital. Companies should deal with such men, and if they shirk their duty they should be tried for cowardice and shot." As the sergeant later recalled, Patton remained calm during the dictation and later edited the transcript to add the line, "One sometimes slaps a baby to bring it to." The soldier, Private Charles Herman Kuhl of Mishawaka, Indiana, had no evident physical injuries. Kuhl confirmed the details of the assault in a letter to his father.[70]

A week later, a similar incident occurred at the 93rd Evacuation Hospital near Sant'Agata di Militello. Finding another soldier suffering from combat fatigue, Patton asked the shivering man what was the matter. "It's my nerves," said the soldier, Private Paul G. Bennett of South Carolina, who had begun to suffer from nervous tension in the front lines after his wife had given birth back home. "Your nerves, hell. You are just a goddamn coward, you yellow son of a bitch," Patton said. He slapped Bennett and said, "Shut up that goddamned crying. I won't have these brave men here who have been shot seeing a yellow bastard sitting here crying." Bennett was struck so hard that his helmet liner flew off.[71]

The first slapping incident had been silenced. The hospital's medical staff did not report it to the chain of command, and no reporters were on hand to witness it. News of the second assault, however, quickly spread. Journalists Merrill Mueller of NBC and Demaree Bess of the *Saturday Evening Post* visited the 93rd Evacuation Hospital a day after Patton struck Bennett and learned the story from nurses and doctors who had been present. The story then circulated among the Allied armies in Sicily and the island's civilian press corps.[72]

Twenty Allied correspondents gathered at their camp for a discussion. Since they were accredited to cover military operations in a combat zone, any information they gathered and wished to send to the States would have to be submitted to military censors. But instead of trying to file a story on Patton's assaults, they decided to take up the matter with General Dwight D. Eisenhower, Patton's superior officer. The press corps respected Eisenhower for his candor and his willingness to keep journalists informed about the conduct of the war; journalists therefore found it "natural" to discuss the story with Eisenhower, according to CBS reporter Quentin Reynolds. Bess and Mueller wrote what they had learned at the hospital and appended the signatures of fourteen witnesses. They took the story to Eisenhower, who seemed appalled and said he had already heard another version of the story from a colonel at the hospital. A few days later, Reynolds, Bess, and Mueller talked with Eisenhower and were satisfied with the punishment he had imposed on Patton—a requirement that he apologize not only to the soldiers he had slapped but also to all of the witnesses and all of the officers and soldiers on hand. Patton carried out these instructions, and thus revealed to several thousand people an incident that the Allied correspondents had agreed to keep secret. Reporter Edward Kennedy of the Associated Press warned Eisenhower that the news would leak, and he asked permission to write a factual account in the press as an alternative to the inevitable gossip.[73] Eisenhower did not support Kennedy's plan. In his memoirs, he recalls telling reporters to "use their own judgment" on the Patton story.[74] However, he does not mention that he also had shared with reporters his belief that publication would embarrass the army and contribute to Axis propaganda. The correspondents treated Eisenhower's opinion as if it were a request to suppress the story, which they did.[75] Reynolds recalled that the approximately sixty journalists at army headquarters at Algiers believed they should follow the request for patriotic reasons. Every journalist agreed that publishing or broadcasting the story would only benefit Nazi propagandists, Reynolds said.[76]

For three months, nothing was published or broadcast about Patton's slapping of the two hospitalized soldiers. The self-imposed silence withstood rumors that circulated in America as soon as soldiers who had heard Patton's apology were sent home to recover from their wounds or had finished their combat duty. The *New York Times* heard a rumor, investigated it, and discovered it was true. However, the paper's editors did not submit a story to the Office of Censorship because they felt it would be suppressed.[77]

The rumors also reached the ears of Pearson. In November 1943, he was searching for a story that would uphold his reputation, which had come under attack in Washington. Roosevelt had called Pearson "a chronic liar" after he had published an attack on the policies of Secretary of State Cordell Hull and a spirited defense of Hull's assistant, Sumner Welles, who had been forced to resign.[78]

Pearson publicly defended what he had published and broadcast about Welles and Hull, but privately he fretted about some of his audience abandoning him. He conferred with Ernest Cuneo, his radio lawyer, who served the government as a liaison among British intelligence, the FBI, and the Office of the Coordinator of Information. Cuneo said a big, exclusive story would make people forget the president's criticism. And since his government job gave him access to military intelligence, he suggested Pearson broadcast a Patton story he had heard.[79]

Pearson apparently had no doubts about the story's authenticity. He discussed the details with the War Department, which declined to issue a denial.[80] Pearson's radio network took the story to the Office of Censorship. On the afternoon of November 14, 1943, WMAL's Neel sent Pearson's script to the censors' Broadcasting Division. The sixth and seventh pages included the following item:

> Algiers—General George Patton, nicknamed "Blood and Guts," will not be used in any European war theatre anymore. He was a bit too bloody for the morale of the Army. Inspecting an American hospital in Sicily, General Patton noticed several soldiers listed as "fatigue" patients. Fatigue means a case of nerves or shell-shock. Patton ordered one man to stand up. The soldier, out of his head, told the General to duck down or the shells would hit him. Instead Patton struck the soldier, knocking him down. The commanding doctor rushed in, told Patton that in the field Patton was in command of his troops, but in the hospital he, the doctor was in command of his patients. He ordered General Patton not to interfere. General Patton started to draw a gun, but was disarmed. He will not be used in important combat anymore.[81]

Censor Edward H. Bronson, who checked the script for possible violations of the *Code of Wartime Practices,* stopped when he read the Patton item. The Office of Censorship had a skeleton crew on Sunday afternoon duty, and Bronson engaged the other five employees on duty in a discussion of whether Pearson's story violated the voluntary censorship code. They disagreed, although Bronson did not record which of them favored eliminating the item. All agreed that the code had only a "somewhat tenuous" application because the story appeared to threaten morale but not military security. Bronson, who probably received the script at 3 P.M., had to reach a decision before the broadcast began at 7 P.M. He phoned Neel and a colonel in the War Department to ask their opinions. The former said the Blue Network was "very much upset" by the Patton story but had taken no action; the latter said the story was untrue and hoped the censors would suppress it. (In fact, much of the detail of

General George S. Patton, right, and General Mark Clark in Sicily in 1943 en route to the Tehran Conference, shortly after Drew Pearson revealed in a national radio broadcast that Patton had slapped American soldiers suffering from battle fatigue. The Office of Censorship did not object to Pearson's broadcast. Franklin D. Roosevelt Library.

the Pearson story was false, or at least unsupported by other evidence. Official documents do not mention a soldier cautioning Patton about incoming shells or Patton reaching for his gun. Furthermore, Pearson had left out one of the two slapping incidents entirely, and his prediction that Patton would be removed from combat command proved to be false.) Bronson finally called Price at home. Price felt no code application existed. He asked that the censors tell the network that they didn't personally like the story but that nothing in the code would block it.[82]

Despite receiving tacit approval, Pearson did not use the item in his broadcast that evening. The next script he submitted, for his broadcast the following Sunday, also did not include the item. However, at 6:45 P.M. on November 21, fifteen minutes before Pearson was to go on the air, Neel alerted the censors that the Patton story had been inserted in the script at the last minute. Halpin, on duty that night, asked

Neel to read the story over the phone. It differed slightly from the previous version, including a new introduction containing the words "I think," making it speculative. "On the basis of last week's action by this office, I had no choice but to clear it, which I did," Halpin told Ryan.[83] Since the final script of Pearson's broadcast of the Patton slapping incidents was never submitted in writing to the Office of Censorship, it was never placed in the agency's archives. Strangely, the FBI, which monitored Pearson's broadcasts and sent transcripts of interesting items to Hoover, also did not include a copy of the Patton story among the items it transcribed from the November 21 broadcast.[84] No verbatim transcript of the Patton item as Pearson read it over the air has been located.

Pearson had wanted a sensation to make the public forget Roosevelt's criticism, and his Patton broadcast produced one. Reporters in the United States swiftly sought confirmation. Secretary of War Henry Stimson decided that it would be best to minimize public comment, although privately he fumed that Pearson's report was "inflammatory" and "may do an enormous amount of harm." He dictated a three-point memorandum to the War Department to direct its response to reporters who tried to follow up on the broadcast. First, he said, the War Department had no official information. Second, if the story were true, it would be up to Eisenhower to decide on a response, and the War Department would endorse any action Eisenhower decided to take. And third, the rumors that Patton had been relieved were false.[85]

When reporters were given this information, they turned to Eisenhower's headquarters for more answers. Eisenhower's press aides at first imposed a blanket of censorship over the story. Then, a staff officer gave military correspondents an official statement but refused to let them cable anything other than the facts it contained. In the statement, the army denied that Patton had been reprimanded, as Pearson had reported. The army's announcement was a half-truth—although there had been unofficial criticism of Patton, no formal "reprimand," as the army defined it, had been filed.[86] Finally, two days after Pearson's broadcast, Eisenhower told his chief of staff to "tell the full truth," and the journalists in Europe and Africa who had kept their silence since August wired confirmation and details to their papers.[87]

In the United States, reaction in the news media to confirmation of the gist of Pearson's broadcast was supportive. The *Cleveland News* applauded the journalist for "prying out a story which never should have been hidden," while the *Mobile, Ala., Press* denounced the military cover-up as "conduct unbecoming an officer and a gentleman."[88] The *Waterloo (Iowa) Courier* editorialized that Pearson's record of repudiating official denials of his stories was building his reputation at the cost of public trust in government officials.[89]

Among the news organizations that initially had suppressed the story were the Associated Press and the *New York Times.* Kent Cooper, the AP's general manager and Price's former boss, complained that at least two of his correspondents had recited details of the slapping incident in confidence but had said a military "honor code" prevented publication. Cooper said it was unfair that "a radio commentator who has not bared himself to the privations and dangers of getting the news at its source," and thus has avoided the restraints of the "honor code," was able to break the story. Price replied that the Office of Censorship offered opinions about security but not ethics. "When a dispatch is presented to us, we ask ourselves one question only: Would publication or broadcast violate security," he said. "I do not mean to criticize in any degree General Eisenhower's censorship in the field in the case of the Patton incident. He was dealing with one set of facts and we were dealing in November with another set of facts."[90] The *Times* made a more pointed criticism in a confidential letter to Price. Managing editor Edwin James argued on November 23 that the paper's patriotism had kept it from breaking some of the biggest stories of the war, but Pearson apparently did not have the same motivations. James told Price:

> On February 8, 1942, we received the full story of Pearl Harbor. We asked you if we could publish it and you replied in the negative. And, so we sat on the story until some ten months later when the Navy gave it out. On every story we have received from a combat zone, we have carefully and meticulously referred it to Censorship. Now, Drew Pearson picks up a story that has been batted around for ten days or more. We did not even bother about submitting it to you because we thought you would say we should not publish it. And, if you had done so, we would have thought that you would have been right. . . . Aren't the newspapers being suckers?"[91]

Price replied by analyzing the *Code of Wartime Practices.* Technically, the clause on combat zone stories applied only to interviews and service-men's letters, he said, and was never intended to apply to information that traveled through official channels to the War Department and leaked out in the United States, as the Patton story did, unless the news violated another part of the code. Nothing in the press or radio codebooks requested suppression of news about the shortcomings of military officers, and he would oppose such a clause if it existed. "I would be sorry . . . to have American newspapers under any restraint as to the exposition of wrongdoing or fancied wrongdoing in high places. I am not currently in the newspaper business, but it seems to me that a part of the responsibility of newspapers in wartime is to expose official shortcomings so that they may be corrected," he said. If the *Times* had submitted the story to censorship, Price said, he would have passed it. The story's only major revelation, of Patton's character flaws, would be nearly useless to enemy propagandists because most American soldiers already knew about them.[92] James gave thanks for the censorship clarification, which he said would help guide the *Times* in reporting future stories. However, he noted privately to the paper's Washington bureau that he would keep a copy of Price's memo as ammunition for future conflicts over censorship.[93]

In the end, Pearson's story helped establish his reputation as an investigative journalist to be reckoned with; no simple denial would spell the end of a Pearson story. For this success, he owed a debt to the Office of Censorship, which chose not to interfere with a story that caused distress in the government and army but did not breach the censorship code. Price's decision not to keep the story from the American public ranks among his best as censorship director.

For Patton, Pearson's broadcast altered the arc of a brilliant military career. Outcry over the slapping incidents led to Patton playing a lesser role in the 1944 invasion of Europe than he might have otherwise had—commanding an army instead of an army group. Counterfactual reconstructions of history are dangerous but sometimes stimulating. Historians can only wonder where the Germans' surrender line separating Allied forces in the west and Soviet forces in the east—the line that eventually split Europe into two Cold War encampments—would have been drawn at the end of the war if Patton had supervised the assault along the entire western front, instead of just one section. However, it is pointless to argue that Pearson's broadcast was a turning point of the war in Europe. If the Office of Censorship had objected to Pearson's story in November 1943 and persuaded him not to broadcast it, the story almost certainly would have been released by some other source, with or without the censors' blessing, or become common knowledge through the gossip of soldiers who were rotated home from Europe. In a democracy that lacks a compulsory method of prior restraint, such a significant news story about a top general could not have remained secret forever, and Patton eventually would have been exposed.

In retrospect, Pearson presented one of the toughest challenges to wartime censorship and confounded easy distinctions between the two forms of censorship that Roosevelt established in December 1941—mandatory for certain types of information and voluntary for others. The censors' difficulty was to persuade Pearson to comply with censorship requests he found onerous. Short of threatening to invoke the FCC's ability to remove a radio license, seizing control of stations, or asking the Justice Department to initiate an investigation into possible violations of the Espionage Act—all drastic steps when aimed at a broadcaster whose radio and newspaper audience numbered in the tens of millions—there was little that the Office of Censorship could do other than appeal to reason and patriotism. Despite initial reservations, Pearson was willing to comply with the censorship code because the censors treated him intelligently. He was singled out among all World War II journalists, but he believed that, on the whole, the attention paid to his reporting was governed by the same rules that the censors applied to all other journalists. The censors realized that application of the *Code of Wartime Practices* must be evenhanded or it would jeopardize the willingness of journalists to comply with censorship requests. The same rules applied to the largest metropolitan daily papers and the smallest of weeklies, as well as to the national networks and the tiny radio transmitters in the remote corners of the nation. Pearson was savvy enough to realize that the best way for him to maximize his freedom to report during the war was to learn the codebook inside and out and to exploit its loopholes. More than three years of discussions about the censorship code gave Pearson and the censors an understanding about each others' work, even if the two sides did not always applaud the messy details. A rigid application of the censorship code gave Pearson a break by allowing him to scoop the world with his revelations about General Patton. It also allowed him occasionally to be scooped, as other journalists exploited the same rules to free their own sensitive news stories.

Occasional flare-ups between Pearson and the Office of Censorship left no lasting animosity. When Howard retired from the Press Division in June 1943, he congratulated Pearson for his record of compliance with censorship requests.[94] And Pearson returned the compliment. In a September 29, 1943, speech to the Overseas Press Club in New York City, he said the Office of Censorship was administered intelligently and "doing an extraordinary job."[95]

The President Is Making a Trip
The Press and the President's Travels

Byron Price received an urgent message on September 15, 1942, to report to the White House. Waiting for him in an upper hallway were the president's close friend and aide, Harry Hopkins, and Press Secretary Stephen T. Early. They appeared agitated and said they were having trouble making President Franklin Roosevelt listen to reason. He had decided to take a two-week trip across the country to examine the pace of wartime production and the quality of wartime morale. They knew that critics would attack the journey as politically motivated because it was slightly more than a month before the November 3 congressional elections. But a bigger concern, which had led them to summon Price from his office a few blocks away, was Roosevelt's plan to travel without reporters and to ask the nation's editors and broadcasters not to publicize his trip until he had safely returned to Washington. Early and Hopkins feared that the press would consider the request unreasonable and ignore it.[1]

Roosevelt's plan placed wartime democracy in a classic dilemma. Weighed against the president's need to be safe from enemy sympathizers, saboteurs, and spies was the citizens' right to monitor their elected leader. Only the mass media could provide the country with detailed, timely information to evaluate his performance. Roosevelt's decision to ask reporters not to publicize his trip created a rift in his normally friendly relationship with the press corps that continued until his death two and a half years later. Some reporters, including Walter Trohan of the *Chicago Tribune,* believed he abused the censorship code to cover up the frequency of his visits to his home on the Hudson River and his meetings with Lucy Mercer Rutherford, a former lover.[2] Yet as much as Roosevelt stretched the fabric of voluntary censorship, it did not tear.

As director of censorship, Price had control over communications crossing the borders. He also had the president's instructions and influence to help him coordinate voluntary censorship of radio, newspapers, and magazines. The single absolute check upon Price's powers was the commander in chief. When Price was summoned by Hopkins and Early, Roosevelt appeared ready to exercise his authority. Early told him that he and Office of War Information director Elmer Davis "have had our ears pinned back for suggesting that newspapermen go along, even if they do not write about the trip until it is ended. I hope that you can do something."[3]

Price and Early found the president in his study, plotting his route. His mood seemed less combative than Price had been led to believe. With a trace of his famous humor, Roosevelt said he might be recognized as he dropped in unannounced at defense plants, and Price's job would be to ensure that nothing was published or broadcast about his trip while he was away from Washington. Technically, this request was in accordance with the Office of Censorship's *Code of Wartime Practices*. Its predecessor, the World War I voluntary censorship bulletins of the Committee on Public Information, had asked newspapers to avoid stories about the movements of visiting diplomats and about threats to President Woodrow Wilson, but they did not take the extra step of banishing stories about the president's travels.[4] The extra precaution in World War II seemed necessary after the Japanese air raid on Pearl Harbor and the German submarine patrols off the East Coast had demonstrated America's vulnerability to attack. Roosevelt's trip would be the first major test of the censorship code's restriction on "movements of the President of the United States, or of military or diplomatic missions of the United States or of any other nation opposing the Axis powers—routes, schedules, or destination, within or without the continental limits of the United States."[5]

As Price listened to Roosevelt's plans, he looked for an opening to compromise. He waited until the president nearly had completed his railroad schedule before asking innocently if journalists were to accompany him. Roosevelt replied as Early had said he would: He wanted none. Why not? "If I took newspapermen along they would write that it was a political trip, and I am not going to see any politicians," he said. Price, picking up the thread of logic, replied, "If you are not seeing any politicians I certainly think you should take some disinterested reporters along so that they can testify to the facts afterward." Roosevelt agreed and started to say that Early would travel with him and report everything to the press afterward on October 1. But Early interrupted to decline. He said political enemies would not trust a presidential aide to report objectively. Reluctantly, Roosevelt conceded the point. Along with four navy photographers, he said he would accept one representative of each of the nation's three major wire services if they would agree to let him censor their stories personally. This compromise required the press corps to make greater concessions than the president, and Price feared that the plan would severely test voluntary censorship. As he left the White House, Price told the president, "If this one works, I won't worry about anything from now on."[6]

Early gave few details of the trip when he informed A. Merriman Smith of the United Press, Douglas Cornell of the Associated Press, and William Theis of International News Service on September 16. He said Roosevelt planned to leave Washington the next day, tour war plants and military installations, and return on October 1, and they would be the only reporters along for the ride. Pressed for details, Early revealed only that the first stop would be the Chrysler tank manufacturing plant in Detroit; beyond that, he did not even tell the reporters what type of clothes to pack.[7]

That night, the Secret Service took the three reporters to the basement of the Bureau of Printing and Engraving, one of the unpublicized railroad boarding stations Roosevelt used in Washington, Maryland, and Virginia. At the end of the waiting train was Roosevelt's personal car, the Ferdinand Magellan, which had been fortified for protection against enemy attack. The windows were bulletproof, the sides hardened to withstand the impact of an artillery shell, and the bottom reinforced with a foot of concrete and steel to absorb the detonation of any explosives that might lie in the railroad bed. The car also had the comforts one would expect for a traveling president. It had an office, a lounge, a bedroom, and a galley, as well as two elevators for a wheelchair. Between the Ferdinand Magellan and the engine were accommodations for the Secret Service, the president's staff members, and radio operators, a club car, a diner, and a room that before the war had been filled by about a dozen members of the traveling press corps. Settling into their nearly empty quarters, the three wire service reporters must have concluded that Roosevelt had stretched the truth when he told Early that if other journalists had been allowed to join the inspection tour, "the train would need more sleeping cars and it would be impossible to maintain any secrecy." More likely, the president was wary of a large press contingent making his information-gathering tour look like a political stunt.[8] Precedent was on his side. During World War I, President Wilson also had limited the press corps that traveled with him to three wire service representatives.[9]

Roosevelt liked to stay on good terms with journalists. Although he had many clashes with conservative publishers, he liked most reporters, who tended to be more liberal. As a young man, he had made the most of the opportunity to watch his distant cousin Theodore Roosevelt use his charisma and his bully pulpit to build favorable press relations, and he had tried his own hand as a journalist by editing the student newspaper at Harvard. When young Franklin went to Washington as Wilson's assistant secretary of the navy in 1913, he conducted his own news conferences and gained the favor of the national media by leaking information on the inadequate state of national defense.[10] Throughout his public career he continued to make himself available to reporters; as president, Roosevelt had 998 news conferences, an average of two a week. He often did not say anything noteworthy in answering pointed questions, but his readiness to banter with the press endeared him to journalists. However, the first months of 1942 had brought strains into the relationship. Since the start of the war, Roosevelt had used the censorship code to hide his frequent weekend train trips to Hyde Park, his home on the Hudson. The first secret retreat began on January 6 and ended five days later. William Hassett, one of Roosevelt's secretaries, recorded fourteen off-the-record trips to Hyde Park in his diary before the start of the September inspection tour.[11] Reporters familiar with the censorship code had ignored the trips. However, Smith's memoir of his travels with the president listed two violations early in 1942 by journalists unfamiliar with the censorship regulations. The student newspaper at Catholic University in Washington printed a story on February 5 that said the president had quietly boarded a train at the university station during the previous week. The editors promptly received a visit from the Secret Service and a lecture on protecting the president's safety. On another occasion, a *New York Post* columnist mentioned one of Roosevelt's trips, delighting in his mistaken belief that he had written a story unknown to the Washington press corps.[12]

Actually, the journalists who covered the White House knew when Roosevelt left his presidential home to head for his ancestral one. They knew the location of the out-of-the-way railroad sidings where Roosevelt entered and exited the Ferdinand Magellan, and they knew about his vacation retreats to Shangri-La, a camp in northern Maryland. Despite their self-censorship, rumors spread quickly in the small-town atmosphere of wartime Washington, and even the taxi drivers knew within the hour when Roosevelt had departed.[13]

The weekend journeys to Hyde Park lasted three to five days, and the president spent most of the time in seclusion. The September inspection tour would last fourteen days, and Roosevelt would be seen by thousands of Americans. Surely, if they saw the president they would expect to read about him in the paper or hear the news of his visit on the radio. Nevertheless, Price sent the nation's editors and broadcasters a confidential note on September 17 to ask them to avoid the story: "The President is making a trip to a number of war plants and camps. He plans to make no speeches or public appearances. He will be accompanied by representatives of the press services who will report on the trip in due course. Until they do, your attention is called to the code restriction that for reasons of safety nothing is published, locally or otherwise, about the president's movements or whereabouts except on authority."[14]

The note did not mention that the only appropriate authority for news of the president's movements was the president.

The next day, Roosevelt's train made its first stop, in Michigan, at the world's largest manufacturer of tanks. In a year's time it had sprung up amid a cornfield, spreading out to cover the equivalent of ten city blocks. Shortly after noon on September 18, Roosevelt took his accustomed seat on the right-hand side of his automobile, which had been unloaded from the train, and the driver started slowly down the length of the Chrysler building. The tank construction crews were startled when they glanced up from their tools and benches. "By God if it ain't old Frank!" a smudge-faced worker announced. The president smiled, waved, and asked questions.[15]

Roosevelt rode outdoors to the arsenal's testing grounds to witness a demonstration of a new all-welded tank. To the consternation of the Secret Service, the driver of a thirty-two-ton M-4 Sherman tank headed straight for the president's car before braking ten feet short. Roosevelt was unfazed. "A good drive!" he said.[16] He then inspected the Ford Motor Company's Willow Run bomber plant and chatted with two

President Roosevelt, in the car at far right, tours an Alcoa plant in Vancouver, Washington, during his secret inspection tour of war production in September 1942. Press Secretary Stephen T. Early is at left in the white hat. Next to him, left to right, are Admiral Ross McIntire; Roosevelt's daughter, Anna Boettinger; and Secret Service agent Frank J. Wilson. Franklin D. Roosevelt Library/U.S. Navy.

midgets whom the company had hired for assembly work in the B-24s' cramped tail sections.[17] At the end of the day, not a word had been broadcast or printed about the president's arrival.

The Secret Service, in charge of presidential security, established a pattern to prepare each day's schedule. At 3 A.M. an agent would place two calls—one to the governor of the state where the president's train would stop, and the other to the owner of the factory the president wanted to inspect. The train would arrive without fanfare, the president would conduct his tour while seated in his car, and the three wire service reporters would write and file their dispatches for later publication.[18]

A security leak occurred on the second day of the journey, which included tours of the Great Lakes Naval Training Station near Chicago and the Allis-Chalmers Manufacturing Company in Milwaukee. The president of Allis-Chalmers, Walter Geist, met the presidential party and told Early that the wire services had phoned the factory the night before to ask about the president's arrival time. Early "hit the ceiling" but later learned through the Secret Service that railroad employees were the source of the security breach. Roosevelt's transit of the Midwest also was noted by two weekly papers in Michigan, one weekly in Ohio, and one daily in Woodstock, Illinois, but censorship records do not indicate how the Office of Censorship discovered these code violations or responded to them.[19]

From state to state, the president's train chugged along. Roosevelt visited a night shift at the Federal Cartridge Corporation plant in New Brighton, Minnesota. On September 21, he dropped in on a thousand naval officers, sailors, and recruits at the nation's newest naval training station, which had been established at a lake in northern Idaho to ease congestion at coastal naval bases. He inspected battle-tested warships in Washington State and tried to swear the 5,000 workers at the Puget Sound Navy Yard to secrecy. "I am not really here . . . my cruise is not published in the papers, so just remember that for about ten days you haven't seen me." Roosevelt then drove through downtown Seattle, effectively putting his appearance before thousands of civilians "off the record."[20]

Radio stations ignored the story.[21] Only one newspaper took note. The *Aero Mechanic,* a weekly publication of the Boeing Aircraft Company union, printed thousands of copies on September 24 headlining Roosevelt's visit to the Boeing factory in Seattle. The editor, W. N. Mahlum, had received the *Code of Wartime Practices* in the mail but had overlooked its restrictions about the movements of the president. He said he had not received Price's special memo about the ban on publicity of the president's tour. A navy public relations officer accompanied Mahlum to the post office to prevent the mailing of 14,000 copies. More than 4,000 already had been distributed among workers inside the Boeing plant, and Nathaniel R. Howard of the Press Division asked the union president to appeal for their return.[22] The Secret Service, the FBI, the post office, and the army also helped round up copies. Howard told the editor he could release the edition after Roosevelt had returned to Washington.[23]

A day after leaving Seattle, Roosevelt was in Portland, Oregon, to study Henry Kaiser's rapid ship construction methods. At the Oregon Shipbuilding Corporation's yard on the Willamette River, Roosevelt observed the launching of a 10,600-ton Liberty freighter, the *Joseph N. Teal,* ten days after its keel had been laid. After the ceremony, the cry of "Speech! Speech!" went up from the crowd of shipbuilders, and a microphone was placed in the president's hands. The politician in him could not resist. "You know, I am not supposed to be here today," he said. "You are the possessors of a secret which even the newspapers of the United States don't know. I hope you will keep the secret because . . . like the ship that we have just seen go overboard, my motions and movements are supposed to be secret."[24] The shipbuilders laughed. But the wire service reporters, who stood a few feet away while Roosevelt was talking, disliked being the butt of a joke and powerless to respond.

Roosevelt's timing could not have been worse. The day before the president's visit to the Kaiser shipyard, twenty journalists in the nation's capital had submitted a petition to Early, Price, and Davis. They demanded to know why only three of their peers had been permitted to accompany the president and suggested that a larger press corps would pose no safety threat. The petition acknowledged the danger of publicizing Roosevelt's itinerary in advance but suggested that reports about cities he already had visited should be acceptable and could boost public morale. It expressed outrage at the imposition of "involuntary censorship."[25]

When the petitioners visited the Office of Censorship, Price said he disagreed with them, stressing the paramount importance of protecting the president. He said their complaint about the size of the traveling press pool was beyond his jurisdiction because he did not accredit journalists. Furthermore, he said he could not see much difference between their request to delay stories of Roosevelt's actions by a day or two and the president's request for a two-week blackout.[26] That ended the discussion. Privately, however, Price sympathized. In notes that he never placed in his wartime notebook or his memoir, Price said Roosevelt "greatly abused" the immunity from press coverage that he could invoke at will when he traveled.[27] A kinder analysis appeared in Price's memoir, which said the president gave unyielding support to the Office of Censorship except for his "blind spot" and "nonsense" about his own movements. "I never thought that FDR really wanted to wreck it [the censorship code], as nearly as he came to doing so," he wrote. "I think he was only having fun according to the complicated pattern of his congenital inconsistency."[28]

Roosevelt's remarks at the Kaiser shipyard aggravated the petitioners' already foul mood. After being rebuffed by Price and teased by the president, they began seeking recruits to increase pressure on the White House. They rounded up additional signatures in Washington but tried without success to get signatures from managing editors outside the capital. Eventually, the petition contained thirty-five signatures.[29]

Meanwhile, the Ferdinand Magellan continued its descent of the Pacific coast. On September 24, Roosevelt inspected a submarine at the Mare Island Navy Yard, on the north end of San Francisco Bay, and spoke with a wounded Marine who had killed thirty-six Japanese at Tulagi. Moving to a naval supply depot and embarkation station in Oakland, the president greeted thirty-three men in wheelchairs who were recovering from wounds suffered in major Pacific battles. At Long Beach, he toured the Douglas Aircraft factory, a producer of bombers and the giant C-54 cargo planes. Workers were stunned when Roosevelt's green car slowly passed through the building, but they recovered to cheer and wave.[30] "Why doesn't someone tell me these things?" one of the plant's executives asked about the visit.[31]

The president spent the next evening with his son John, a junior lieutenant in the navy, at his home near San Diego. Then, Roosevelt headed east. His train stopped at Uvalde, Texas, allowing him to chat with John Nance Garner, his vice president from 1933 to 1941. The president visited airfields and army bases and inspected the new Consolidated Aircraft bomber assembly plant in Fort Worth. The plant manager told the traveling wire service reporters that the factory building, so huge that it was difficult to stand at one end and see the other side, probably contained the longest straight assembly line in the country. Just how long they were not told; the plant manager said the length was a military secret.[32]

The nation's papers and radio stations continued to censor themselves while Roosevelt's train headed home, and Price began to prepare for the petitioners making their protest public. He started by speaking at the Southern Newspaper Publishers Association annual convention in Hot Springs, Arkansas. He complained that editors "have done a poor job of informing the people why some information has to be withheld."[33] Off the record, Price polled the assembled editors on whether they supported his office's restrictions on news of presidential movements. In a memo to Early, Price reported the results: "Every publisher to whom I talked supported completely the position of the Office of Censorship." Some had helped keep the story of the presidential inspection tour out of the smaller papers and the weeklies in their regions, Price said, and were proud of their success.[34]

Criticism of the press ban finally surfaced publicly, but in a veiled way. Two days before the end of Roosevelt's journey, the *Buffalo Evening*

News reported that the voluntary censorship "honeymoon" was nearly finished. The *News* did not disclose the subject of discord but said reporters soon would be free to publish the details. The unnamed censorship conflict was "ridiculous," it added, and unless rectified could kill voluntary censorship.[35] Arthur Krock, chief of the Washington Bureau of the *New York Times,* alluded to the controversy on the next day. Under a headline that said an important news item had been banned, Krock said many Washington reporters considered the suppression "unnecessary as well as unfair."[36] Despite the grumbling and the hints, no journalist publicized Roosevelt's trip prematurely.

A rebellion appeared likely at the president's next press conference, scheduled for the afternoon of October 1, when the protesters planned to present their petition. Having gauged the mood of journalists outside Washington when he had spoken at Hot Springs, Price urged Early to have his boss take the initiative and open the press conference by praising journalists' cooperation.[37]

Roosevelt's routine before his biweekly press conferences was to meet Early to discuss the questions he should expect. On October 1, Early told him that reporters would attack the censorship imposed on his tour. He apparently also mentioned Price's suggestions about commending the nation's press. While they chatted, the announced starting time for the press conference passed.[38] A few reporters pounded on the door to be let in. When the door finally opened at 5:05 P.M., the press corps found Roosevelt in shirtsleeves at his desk. Davis, "looking glum," occupied one of the chairs at the rear of the room, according to the Press Division's William Mylander, whom Price had sent to monitor the meeting. The crowded room was hot and smoky.[39] But reporters had no opportunity to begin the conference by pressing Roosevelt with questions about their letter of protest, which Roosevelt had received from Early or Davis. At the cry of "All in," signaling that the last of the reporters had come through the door, Roosevelt launched into a statement summarizing his tour, "which you can now print because obviously I am here." At the end of the summary, which provided little news beyond what the wire service reporters were preparing to release in stories that Roosevelt had reviewed but had decided not to censor, the president lauded the journalists whom he had left behind for "the fine way in which they have cooperated in delaying the publication of the news about my trip until it was over." He addressed congressional criticism that the trip had partisan political undertones and then deftly shifted the focus to the press. He implied that some reporters were under orders from their editors to sabotage his administration. Most reporters, he said, wrote the wartime news objectively, but "there is an unfortunate minority of news stories which just 'ain't so.' They just are not based on fact. And more than that, they tell people in the country things that are not in existence. Some of them are honestly written. Some of them are written for other reasons, which perhaps we need not go into. They represent a minority, but at present they are doing infinite harm to the country. . . . The greatest of fense of course is . . . among the commentators, and the columnists, in both the press and the radio."[40]

Elizabeth May Craig, the Washington correspondent for a group of Maine newspapers, tried to get the president to specify who had hurt the war effort and how they had done it. "Mr. President, I am not quite clear in my mind. What is the complaint about the press?" she asked.

"May," Roosevelt responded, "ask the press."

"I mean your complaint about us. . . . I mean it quite seriously."

"I would ask the press," Roosevelt said. "They all know."

"Well," Craig said, "I don't."

"I think it's very simple. I am saying that about certain elements in press and radio that are hurting the war effort. And we all know. . . . You people know better than—even better than I do who the fellows are, who the owners of the papers are. You know far better than I do."[41]

Comparing Roosevelt's two statements about the press made the implication clear. Journalists who had cooperated with the voluntary censorship ban deserved praise, but a few—unnamed—were harming the war effort.

Fifty-five minutes after the news conference began, reporters who had expected to give their petition to the president walked away mumbling and angry, never having presented their formal complaint. They settled for releasing it in the next morning's newspapers, expecting that it would run alongside the belated coverage of the president's inspection tour.[42] It said the protesters did not question the desirability of keeping Roosevelt's itinerary a secret but questioned "whether, and why, the national interest required that nothing concerning the trip be published until it had been completed." In addition, it asked why only three wire correspondents had been allowed to accompany the president and warned of the danger of a news blackout:

We believe this kind of suppression undermines confidence, not alone in the newspapers, but in the government. When so many people have personal knowledge of such an important event as the visit of their President, and see nothing about it in the newspapers until a long time afterwards, doubts are inevitably raised as to the consequences and authenticity of other news emanating from the government. . . . In short, we are disturbed at what appears to be, intentional or not, a creeping censorship, and we respectfully request a reconsideration of this policy as it might apply to any situation in the future.[43]

Commenting editorially on the two-week tour and subsequent press conference, the nation's newspapers split into two camps. The first, and larger, group congratulated itself for supporting the president's ban on premature disclosure of his movements, albeit with some grumbling over the need for it. *Los Angeles Times* managing editor L. D. Hotch-kiss said, "The president is entitled to and must have absolute protection under all circumstances. But preventing millions from learning what tens of thousands already knew does not seem to fit in with sound protection measures." David Lawrence, editor of *United States News,* added that whenever the president's life is involved, "the customary rule is to err on the side of suppression."[44] The second group of papers expressed emotions ranging from surprise to outrage. The *Richmond Times-Dispatch* ran an editorial cartoon of "John Q. Public" reading a newspaper and wearing a huge pair of black blinders. The caption said, "All I Know Is What I Read in the Papers."[45] A *Chicago Tribune* editorial likened Roosevelt to a fictional Arabian prince who visited his kingdom incognito, but it pointed out that the undercover president traveled with a "brass band." The *Tribune* sarcastically described the tour as "the biggest secret in history" because "probably less than half the people in the communities thru which he passed have been talking about it."[46]

Price received two significant showings of support, from reporters and ordinary citizens. First, thirty-three Boston journalists wrote to Roosevelt and Price on October 4 to endorse the censorship restrictions on presidential travel.[47] Second, the Blue Network asked its listeners to phone in their opinions on whether secrecy surrounding the president's trip had placed free press and radio in jeopardy. Although the poll had no statistical validity—people who are most agitated about a subject are more likely to respond—the results heartened Price and his staff. Out of 1,395 respondents, only 91, or 6.5 percent, disapproved of the ban on reporting the president's just-completed tour.[48]

Realizing the public's mood, the White House press corps dropped its protest. No reporter raised the issue at any subsequent presidential press conference. Roosevelt sealed the matter, at least in the public arena, when he addressed the American people directly in a fireside chat on October 12. Without mentioning the *Tribune*—a paper he despised yet read every day—Roosevelt rejected the brass-band image of his trip. He said his critics found it easy to say that a president should travel "with a blare of trumpets, with crowds on the sidewalks, with batteries of reporters and photographers." But, he said, "I can tell you very simply that the kind of trip I took permitted me to concentrate on the work I had to do without expending time, meeting all the demands of publicity. . . . One of the greatest generals of American soldiers, Robert E. Lee, once remarked on the tragic fact that in the war of his day all the best generals were apparently working on newspapers instead of in the Army. That seems to be true in all war."[49]

Similar blankets on news coverage attended Roosevelt's trips out of the country, to conferences in Casablanca and Tehran in 1943, and Yalta in 1945. The White House controlled the release of news originating overseas from the president's meetings with Allied leaders; the Office of Censorship's role was mainly to police the "embargo"—the informal agreement under which the news stories were distributed simultaneously to media outlets around the country but were held from publication or broadcast until a stated time.[50]

Throughout the war, Roosevelt continued his trips to Hyde Park. After his September inspection tour, he allowed wire service reporters to accompany him only once before the end of 1942, when he returned to his official residence to vote in the November congressional elections. During that trip, he decided to go on the record for the five minutes it took to be carried up the steps to the town hall, vote, and leave.[51] The reporters, who had no need to check with the Office of Censorship about a story Roosevelt had cleared, promptly dispatched a short report saying Roosevelt had voted at Hyde Park. At 12:35 P.M. on election day, Bill Neel of WMAL radio in Washington called to alert the Office of Censorship that a story on the Associated Press wire said the president had voted at Hyde Park. According to an in-house memo, the call sent three people scurrying for an authoritative confirmation: James Warner, the office's liaison to the Washington press corps; Charter Heslep, the Broadcasting Division staff member who previously had served as night news editor for NBC in New York; and William P. Steven, a Press Division aide who formerly was managing editor of the *Tulsa Tribune*. Within ten minutes they had traced the story to the three wire service reporters in Hyde Park, ascertained that the president personally had approved its release, and cleared it for broadcast on WMAL.[52] If it seems ludicrous that three men would rush to confirm a story that said the president had voted in his hometown, it nevertheless underscores the censors' attempt to be consistent. Price's strictest rule was that no exceptions should be made to the comprehensive coverage of the censorship code—no matter how seemingly innocuous—without an official acting as appropriate authority.

That was the last presidential trip to include reporters for four months. When the wire service correspondents protested their exclusion and asked to tag along on more visits to Hyde Park, Roosevelt told Early to relay a reply: "What do you want to do—watch me take a bath or go with me to the toilet?"[53] Brief automobile rides in the Virginia and Maryland countryside and even journeys that took Roosevelt a few blocks from the White House were blacked out, as if he had traveled to a combat zone. Washington radio stations that announced plans to dedicate the Jefferson Memorial in April 1943 were asked not to mention that the president would attend.[54]

"YES, THE *ADVERTISER* KNOWS THAT HE WAS HERE"

Early in 1943, the White House press corps had heard rumors that Roosevelt was planning a long trip that would include a visit to Warm Springs, Georgia, the spa where he relaxed and received treatment for the paralysis of his legs. The wire service reporters composed and sent Roosevelt a poem asking to be included in the entourage. Roosevelt agreed and, not to be outdone, replied in verse:

> Your touching deep desire
> Arouses in me fire
> To send a hasty wire
> To Warm Springs in the mire
> To scrape the roads,
> Break out the corn.
> The gals is waiting
> Sho's yo born.

to the press associations only. none other need apply.[55]

The Office of Censorship sent out a confidential memo about the upcoming trip and asked the Press Division missionaries to ensure that the weekly papers saw it. The note said not only that the president soon would begin another off-the-record journey, but also that the press pool had been expanded beyond the representatives of the three wire services.[56] Two New York reporters, Bert Andrews of the *Herald Tribune* and William H. Lawrence of the *Times,* had asked Roosevelt and Early to open the train to all White House correspondents who normally traveled with the president before the war. Roosevelt and Early suggested a compromise to the two reporters: Let the White House Correspondents Association select six members for the journey. Andrews and Lawrence, both members of the association, quickly picked themselves. Then they chose William C. Murphy of the *Philadelphia Inquirer,* Roscoe Drummond of the *Christian Science Monitor,* Raymond P. Brandt of the *St. Louis Post-Dispatch,* and Dewey L. Fleming of the *Baltimore Sun.*[57] All six reporters had signed the petition protesting Roosevelt's censorship of his September tour.

The selection angered some reporters who had been passed over. One threatened to violate the voluntary censorship code. Warren Francis of the *Los Angeles Times*'s Washington bureau called the Office of Censorship at 8:08 P.M. on April 8, 1943, to say he was writing and sending to his paper a dispatch reporting that Roosevelt soon would leave the White House for another cross-country inspection tour. "We are going to disregard the code for tonight, and I want to know what the penalty is and who will suffer, the correspondent who writes the story or the paper which prints it or both," he told Frank C. Clough of the Press Division. Clough gulped and said he would have to reach Price or Howard, his immediate supervisor, for such a ruling. Clough phoned Howard at home—he did not know where Price was at that hour—and told him to expect a call from Francis about violating the prohibition on publicizing the movements of the president. When the phone rang, Howard, who in the meantime had found and spoken with Price, listened while Francis explained the *Times*'s reason for its plan of defiance. He said the managing editor, Hotchkiss, was upset that his paper had not been chosen to fill one of the extra six correspondents' seats on the president's train. Twice, in September and April, the *Los Angeles Times* had been excluded from the president's train, and Hotchkiss was threatening to retaliate for the snub by announcing Roosevelt's secret trip. Howard, recalling the conversation in a memorandum for the Press Division's files, said he asked Francis to deliver a personal message to Hotchkiss: "[I]f the *Times* went out to sabotage voluntary press censorship over a single incident like this we would sock the *Times* with everything we had."[58]

What constituted "everything" that the Press Division could throw at an offending newspaper? There is no way to know with certainty, for it never had to confront a deliberate violation by a newspaper that had been asked to avoid a story. The print press had been free from licensing since the eighteenth century and was more powerfully protected by the First Amendment than radio. The main weapons policing voluntary compliance were public scorn and competitors' wrath. If the *Times* had pressed the issue, the Office of Censorship could have done little more than publicly cite it, warn it that any news that violated the Espionage Act might result in prosecution by the Justice Department, and urge the rest of the nation's news outlets not to destroy voluntary censorship by following the violator's lead. Fortunately for the censors, the *Times* backed down, although no details of its decision making exist in the Office of Censorship's records. Francis contented himself with writing a story describing the "injustice in hand-picking six special reporters for an impending White House assignment." He showed the story to Howard, who rephrased six sentences to delete references to "developments involving President Roosevelt" that would allow "opportunities [for six journalists] to be first-hand witnesses." He then cleared the story, along with a similar one prepared by the *New York Daily News*, another paper that would not have a reporter on the train.[59]

Roosevelt's train left Washington on April 13 and headed south toward Parris Island, South Carolina, where the president witnessed soldiers training with Garand rifles. Further stops occurred in Georgia, Alabama, Tennessee, and Arkansas. In a departure from the rules of his September inspection tour, the president allowed the traveling press corps to file day-old dispatches, datelined "Aboard the President's Train." The president made an on-the-record visit to Mexico on April 20. In addition, the silence about his movements was broken twice. The governor of South Carolina, ad-libbing on April 14 into a microphone over station WSPA in Spartanburg, said, "By the way, I have just talked with the president of the United States and it will interest you to know that he is now within the boundaries of your state." The Broadcasting Division thereupon asked the Secret Service to tell governors and other high officials who might see the president that any communication about his movements would be subject to censorship unless Roosevelt cleared its release.[60]

The other leak occurred on April 16, the day after Roosevelt's train swung through Montgomery, Alabama. He visited Maxwell Field to watch an overhead formation of 108 training planes from Gunther Field and the synchronized takeoff of eighty-four advanced training planes from Craig Field. The presidential party then watched 4,000 cadets perform calisthenics and play volleyball, basketball, and other games.[61] In a front-page story, the Montgomery newspaper said: "Yes, the *Advertiser* knows that he was here yesterday. . . . Nearly everybody else in Montgomery knew he was here—when he arrived and when he departed. If the details of all that are still interesting when the lords of free speech in Washington decide to let the news be printed, the *Advertiser* will print such part of the details as it may remember at the time."[62] Price wired a complaint to the paper; the ensuing explanation persuaded him that the story was an editor's attempt at humor while the publisher was out of town.[63]

Considering the Office of Censorship's problems with censorship of Roosevelt's movements, it is understandable that Price confided in his notebook that the 1944 presidential campaign made him nervous. Despite unanimous endorsement by the Editorial Advisory Board in January 1943 of censorship of presidential trips,[64] no president could campaign for reelection and remain off the record. Some freedom to report Roosevelt's movements would be necessary. Price's job became more complicated when Roosevelt, five months after he privately had revealed his plans to some members of the press, revealed at a press conference on July 11, 1944, that he would seek a fourth term.[65] Shortly after the conference, the representatives of the AP, United Press, and International News Service as well as a radio "pool" reporter, Carlton Smith of NBC, were told to pack for a five-day train trip to San Diego, where Roosevelt would broadcast his acceptance of the Democratic Party's nomination before sailing for Hawaii to confer with General Douglas MacArthur.[66] Price sent a confidential memo to editors and broadcasters on July 13 stating that Roosevelt soon would leave on a trip and reminding recipients of the appropriate clauses in the press and broadcasting censorship codes. Four days later, Roosevelt sent a note to the convention in Chicago, stating his preference for Harry S. Truman as a running mate. The note said he expected to be "away from Washington for the next few days." On the basis of this information, the *Chicago Tribune* asked the Office of Censorship if it could "speculate" in print that Roosevelt would be in Chicago soon.[67] The Press Division said no. The president never appeared at the convention. His train stopped briefly in the Chicago switching yards on July 15 to allow him to confer with Democratic Party chairman Robert E. Hannegan, but that fact was not reported until six days later.[68]

When the president reached San Diego, Roosevelt's naval aide, Admiral Wilson Brown, informed the four traveling reporters that they must use a Washington dateline on their stories about the nomination acceptance speech the president planned to give on the next evening, July 20. They protested that it would be a lie to imply that Roosevelt had spoken from the capital. A. Merriman Smith told presidential secretary Grace Tully that he would not misinform his readers. Tully ushered Smith into the president's bedroom, where Roosevelt chuckled at Brown's order and said, "Oh, damn, that's a lot of nonsense. I say in the first paragraph of my speech that I am speaking from a West Coast naval base. Why not use that for a dateline?" Smith, on behalf of his colleagues, agreed.[69]

Roosevelt's last campaign afforded the public few opportunities to see him. In his acceptance speech in July, he said his busy schedule as commander in chief meant "I shall not be able to find the time" to campaign.[70] He then vanished from view on his Hawaii-to-Alaska tour. Ultimately he was away from the White House, and off the record, for thirty-five days in July and August. He had no press conferences during the trip, whereas his usual schedule would have called for ten. When Roosevelt returned to the White House and to public scrutiny on August 18, Thomas E. Dewey, the Republican candidate, told reporters he did not wish to comment on "Mr. Roosevelt's holiday."[71]

In limiting his public appearances during his reelection campaign, Roosevelt followed a play-it-safe strategy. Successors to Roosevelt often campaigned for reelection by acting presidential, signing bills on the White House lawn, and posing for photographs while avoiding overexposure and the risk of a public blunder. A key question about the 1944 campaign is whether Roosevelt used censorship to minimize his public appearances or whether his security required secrecy. He had a legitimate need for censorship in the Pacific because of the possibility of submarine attack. However, wartime censorship hid more about Roosevelt than just his itinerary. Trohan believed Roosevelt twisted the code to lessen gossip about his pale complexion and sunken skin, which testi-

Roosevelt, addressing a crowd at Soldier Field in Chicago in October 1944. The president used the Code of Wartime Practices *to hide his movements when he did not want publicity and overrode the censorship regulations when he thought it suited his purposes. Franklin D. Roosevelt Library.*

fied to his worsening heart disease, and to cover up his 1944 visits with Rutherford near Newark, New Jersey.[72] Their World War I affair had nearly wrecked Roosevelt's marriage, and despite promises to his wife that he would never see Rutherford again, he clandestinely had reestablished contact by July 1944.[73] When reporters for New Jersey papers and Washington correspondents asked the Office of Censorship for permission to report Roosevelt's train halting near Rutherford's estate in mid-September 1944, they were refused.[74]

Smith of the United Press observed that the president used security "like winter underwear" in the 1944 campaign, taking it off when he wanted publicity and putting it on when it suited his purposes.[75] The Press Division had to respond to reporters who argued that the censorship code's rule on reporting presidential movements had been or should be abrogated during the campaign. The censors responded by reiterating the president's need for security in wartime, reminding reporters that the code had been in effect before the campaign, and pointing out that more news had been cleared about presidential movements during the campaign than in earlier months.[76]

In fact, Roosevelt did use censorship for private purposes unrelated to

Roosevelt, in the car at lower left, does some last-minute campaigning on November 6,
1944, in his native Duchess County, New York. Roosevelt's off-the-record trips between
Washington, D.C., and Hyde Park prompted syndicated newspaper columnist
Westbrook Pegler to publicly threaten to violate the censorship code. Franklin D.
Roosevelt Library. ·

the war. The temptation was too great for him not to exploit the political
advantages of shielding his physical deterioration from voters as well as
hiding his rendezvous with Rutherford from his wife. Historian Doris
Kearns Goodwin suggests that the burdens of war and his failing health
had increased Roosevelt's need for rest and relaxation that he could not
find in the sexless partnership he had created with Eleanor after she had
discovered the 1918 affair. Trohan, in an interview, recalled a cruder analysis of Roosevelt's need for female companionship: Early rejected Trohan's requests for permission to report Roosevelt's train and car trips
in the company of Norwegian Princess Martha, a wartime guest of the
White House, by telling him, "After Eleanor, he's entitled to some femi-
ninity."[77]

Roosevelt would have to have been a saint to forego the personal
benefits of censorship. But, when he misused the censorship code to hide
his ill health and his meetings with Rutherford, his fault was more the
shortcoming of a tired and overburdened leader than the evil of a political
schemer. Rare indeed would be the politician so honest that he paraded

his faults before the electorate or waged an exhausting campaign when a less stressful strategy would be as effective. As for his health, Roosevelt could not have predicted his death in April 1945, although he must have harbored doubts about his ability to survive a fourth term. He suffered an angina attack on August 12, 1944, and was too weak to maneuver on his braces in the next month.[78] Roosevelt adhered to the letter of the censorship code while he undermined its spirit. If his actions helped him win reelection and maintain continuity in the prosecution of the war, his motives are understandable even if they were of questionable ethics. His misuse of censorship would have been heinous if it had hurt the war effort, but the end of the war four months after his death suggested that no harm was done. What would have happened if he had lived is unknown.

Roosevelt made his last trip overseas in the winter of 1945. After his return from an Allied summit at Yalta, the Office of Censorship faced the only instance in which a reporter publicly vowed to ignore the ban on news of presidential travel. On February 20, Westbrook Pegler, whose column appeared in the *Washington Times-Herald* and was syndicated nationwide by King Features, threatened to report Roosevelt's next trip to Hyde Park without waiting for the news to be released by the White House. He argued that the Secret Service kept Roosevelt as safe on the Hudson as he was on the Potomac. Furthermore, Pegler said, Roosevelt had used censorship to hide excessive campaign spending in 1944 and other unpleasant facts. Someone should "smash the secrecy" and "defiantly" challenge Roosevelt, he said.[79]

By 12:50 P.M. that day, Price had read the column and sent a telegram to Pegler's syndication editor, J. V. Connolly of New York. Pegler could violate the code only if King Features allowed him to do so, Price said. "I feel sure you would not take any such step . . . without considering that once the code is deliberately broken none of us can forecast what the consequences may be." At the least, he continued, Connolly should delay any action by Pegler until Price could confer with his Editorial Advisory Board about reporters' dissatisfaction with the code on presidential movements. Connolly wired that he agreed.[80]

Meanwhile, Price conferred with Jonathan Daniels, who was the acting press secretary and would officially replace Early on March 24. Price said many journalists disliked the code's application to Hyde Park trips, but Pegler was the "noisiest" complainer. Daniels wrote in his memoir that Price appeared anxious to appeal to Roosevelt to loosen his travel restrictions. If Roosevelt did not, Price feared that voluntary censorship would crack. He told Daniels that if that happened, the White House would be to blame because the president's secrecy was excessive.[81]

Washington journalists expected a showdown. Like Pegler, many believed the code had been abused. However, Pegler found no journalists willing to join his public protest. "If the newspapers take into their own hands the decision of what does and does not involve security, it seems to me that voluntary censorship will be destroyed and we're apt to have something worse," *Washington Evening Star* associate editor Benjamin McKelway said.[82] McKelway, who had taken censorship matters into his own hands as a member of the American Society of Newspaper Editors' Washington Committee that had endorsed an ill-advised blackout of the 1943 international food conference, evidently had developed his appreciation of the voluntary code.

Price summarized the standoff in memos to the nation's editors and to the president. To the press, he said he was aware of the depth of dissatisfaction with the code on presidential movements. He revealed that he had asked for advice from his advisory board and that none of its members had recommended any change in the code. Price concluded by reminding editors and publishers that they would decide, as voluntary administrators of the code, whether any of their employees would violate it."[83] To the president, Price admitted facing an "incipient rebellion." The advisory board that had endorsed the censorship code also had recommended that it be more intelligently applied to the timely and safe release of information about the president's movements. Armed with this endorsement, Price made three requests: First, routine trips to Hyde Park should be removed from the secret category by White House disclosure as soon as the journey either way had been completed. Second, in all other cases the facts should be disclosed as soon as the trip was completed and the president had returned to the White House. Third, on future trips the principal White House correspondents should be permitted to accompany the president, releasing their dispatches at the end of the trip or as the White House might specify.[84]

Roosevelt met Price halfway. He agreed to announce his returns to Washington but not his arrivals in Hyde Park. As Daniels explained to Price, announcing that Roosevelt was in Hyde Park would imply that he would travel from New York to Washington within a few days, which would compromise security.[85]

Roosevelt's concession worked; the rebellion faded. Fulton Lewis Jr.

broadcast over the Mutual network on March 8 that for the first time during the war, Roosevelt's return from Hyde Park that day had been announced quickly to the press corps.[86] Daniels explained to reporters that as the tide of the war turned in the Allies' favor, some of the stricter censorship rules had become unnecessary. "We felt that where security was not involved, security should not be invoked," he said.[87] Except for special occasions, however, such as the April 20 opening of the United Nations conference in San Francisco, Daniels said, the president's schedule would still not be announced in advance.

Roosevelt never went to the conference. His death on April 12 put Truman in office, and the rapid collapse of the German war machine brought a decrease in concerns about presidential security. Truman was one of the most visible presidents, taking brisk walks daily around downtown Washington for the exercise and fresh air. After Germany's surrender was announced in May, Price talked to him about censorship. At Truman's request, Price immediately sent him a draft of three options for a censorship code revision on presidential travel. Truman picked the least restrictive.[88] Price informed editors of the change on May 9, and the new rule was incorporated into the May 15 edition of the *Code of Wartime Practices* that combined the press and radio regulations. In keeping with the simplifications evident in the four-page rule book—the last and shortest of the war—the code on presidential movements was cut to one sentence banning advance information on his routes, times, and methods of travel.[89]

The end of hostilities with Japan erased the need for the voluntary censorship code in mid-August 1945, and with it, the contention over the appropriate level of press and radio secrecy about the president's travels. The presidential clause in the censorship code probably was the most unpopular one among journalists, especially in the Washington press corps. Many reporters clamored for greater access to news about the president and his diplomatic and military aides, but in the end they did what they were asked to do.

The Highest Considerations
of National Security

Military Secrets and the End
of Censorship

Three-year-old Pat came home nervously excited from day care on May 18, 1945, and repeated a story she had heard. "There are red balloons with wires on them. Don't touch them or they will blow up and kill you and your mother too," she said. "They are in the sky. . . . They blow up and make a noise." The story seemed fantastic, but the girl's fear was genuine. While playing in the yard, she heard a car backfire and ran into the house screaming, "Balloons!"[1]

Her family called the city desk at the St. Paul, Minnesota, *Pioneer Press and Dispatch* to repeat her story. What had scared the child? they asked. Was there a kernel of truth in her story? Someone at the newspaper's city desk took notes on the conversation, and as similar reports were phoned in during the next two days, they were added to a file. Editor J. R. "Russ" Wiggins compiled three dozen messages from callers expressing concern about the balloons. He sent the list to Byron Price, who had asked editors and broadcasters in January not to publicize the appearance of Japanese balloon bombs that had first been sighted on November 4, 1944, at San Pedro, California. Wiggins did not reveal what he had told the callers; presumably he had confirmed the existence of the balloons and explained that he had been asked not to write about them. Perhaps he also had mentioned an Office of Censorship bulletin of March 28, which said the censors had no objection to news accounts of damage and casualties from balloons that did not indicate the cause.[2]

The balloons had been publicized briefly in December 1944, after a second sighting near Kalispell, Montana. Two timber cutters found what they believed to be a parachute painted with Japanese characters and attached to what looked like a bomb. They reported it to a mail carrier on December 11, and the message eventually reached the FBI office at Butte. Agents took the balloon and its unexploded bomb to a garage for safekeeping. On December 15, newspapers in western Montana began seeking permission to publish stories about the balloon. Since this kind of story appeared to be covered by the "intelligence" section of the *Code of Wartime Practices,* which restricted news about "operations, methods, or equipment of the United States, its allies, or the enemy," the Office of Censorship ruled that the story would require an appropriate authority for release.[3] For three days, the FBI and army debated who had jurisdiction over Japanese balloon attacks. On December 18, the FBI bowed out. When no other government agency objected to publicity about the Kalispell balloon, the Office of Censorship released the news for publication and broadcast. Balloon stories appeared nationwide. Some were highly speculative. *Newsweek* suggested in January 1945 that the balloon had carried passengers; it did not mention the bomb.[4] Two weeks later, it said three balloons had been found—one in Kalispell, one in an undisclosed site in Oregon, and a third in an unidentified location—and suggested that the balloons had been launched by Japanese submarines.[5] The government also was confused. On January 2, a reporter asked President Franklin Roosevelt if the balloons could be part of a "spy offensive." Roosevelt replied that he had no more information about the balloons than the White House press corps. "Obviously, the first thing we've got to do is to find out the origin,"[6] he said. By that time, the FBI had translated the Japanese writing on the Kalispell balloon, which included details about the factory shifts that made it.[7] As more balloons arrived, government investigators unraveled the mystery. The balloons had been launched from the Japanese main island of Honshu and were intended to cause panic and start forest fires. Their effectiveness was limited because they did not always explode and the forests they aimed to set ablaze were unlikely to catch fire during the winter and early spring, when the launchings occurred.[8]

Publicity about the Kalispell balloon, coupled with the knowledge that another, unpublicized balloon near Thermopolis, Wyoming, had exploded but caused no damage on December 6, prompted the army to seek a blackout. Scary rumors had surfaced, including forecasts of widespread fires and the possibility of saboteurs entering the country in gondolas. The *Portland Oregonian* and the national wire services agreed to

Paper balloon and
ballast-dropping
device, inflated
for testing.

*A Japanese balloon bomb. Domestic censorship of news of Japanese balloon bombs, such
as this one captured and inflated for testing, may have played a role in civilian deaths
in Oregon in 1945. Six Sunday school picnickers were killed by an explosion during the
news blackout.* National Archives.

an army request on January 1, 1945, and prevented publication of a story
on a balloon that had drifted near the city's power plant on that day.
That disposed of news about one balloon; what the Office of Censorship wanted was a clear, nationwide policy before more arrived. After
the Office of Censorship had a conference on January 4 with military
officials and the FBI, Price issued a confidential bulletin to editors and
broadcasters describing the balloons as a method of enemy attack involv-

ing military security. He said that only the War Department could act as appropriate authority and release news about them. The army's Western Defense Command, in charge of military operations on the Pacific coast, notified Price's office every time it verified a sighting or found part of a balloon or its cargo. By May 12, the list of such "balloon incidents" had grown to 150, from Sonora, Mexico, to Alaska. That number eventually would total 285, about 3 percent of 9,300 balloons known to have been launched.[9]

A balloon that landed on Gearhart Mountain in south central Oregon resulted in the only deaths from enemy attack on the U.S. mainland during World War II. It killed five Sunday school children, ages eleven to fifteen, and Elsye Winters Mitchell, the pregnant wife of the minister of the Bly Christian and Missionary Alliance Church, on May 5, 1945. A navy bomb expert who examined the evidence surmised that the balloon had been on the ground "for some time" because its bag had become mildewed and several of its metal parts had rusted. He believed that one of the victims had dropped or kicked a thirty-three-pound high explosive, causing it to detonate, but a survivor of the detonation, Rev. Archie Mitchell, told reporters that the blast occurred when one of the children pulled part of the balloon. Four incendiary bombs, which did not explode, were safely defused. Officials asked journalists to maintain the news blackout. Accounts of the deaths in Oregon papers referred to an explosion "of unknown origin."[10]

After the Oregon incident, residents of western states pressured the War Department for protection from enemy attack, according to the Office of Censorship's internal history, which did not mention how they knew that a danger existed.[11] Apparently the six deaths and numerous sightings of balloons had bred rumors. A "wave of fear" spread among loggers and campers in Oregon in mid-May, the Associated Press reported later that year.[12] G-2, the army intelligence office, decided that the best way to calm citizens' fears and respond to the enemy threat was to read a short statement about the balloons to schools, civic clubs, and other groups west of the Mississippi River, where nearly all of the balloons had been sighted. The education campaign began sometime between the day after the Oregon explosion, May 6, and May 15, when the Office of Censorship became aware of it. The G-2 statement warned of balloon attacks, urged schoolchildren not to pick up strange objects, and said newspapers and broadcasters had agreed to suppress publicity. However, the army had not consulted the Office of Censorship before beginning. When the censors learned of the campaign, they said it would be difficult to continue the press and radio news blackout.[13]

They were right. Price recalled that his office was "inundated" with indignant complaints about the education campaign from editors and broadcasters.[14] Wiggins believed the press blackout was contributing to wild rumors. In the choppy, short sentences of a journalist in a hurry, he gave Price a summary of reports that citizens had phoned to the *Pioneer Press and Dispatch:* "West coast heavily damaged. Parts of San Francisco wiped out. Several sections of North Dakota devastated. Number of persons killed in Western Minnesota. Balloons are filled with gas and when they let go folks anywhere near are killed. Balloons are filled with high explosive. Is it true that we are being Robot bombed?" Callers were "scared, curious, calm, and furious," he said. The *Pioneer Press and Dispatch* investigated and discovered the army's word-of-mouth campaign in schools and civic buildings.[15] Instead of quietly spreading information and calming nerves, the campaign had a reverse effect, especially among the young. Facts became distorted as schoolchildren remembered them imperfectly and shared them with parents, friends, and neighbors. Much like the childhood game of "telephone," the story became less recognizable as it was told and retold. The education campaign would not have presented a problem if anyone wishing to check the original message could have turned to an authoritative source, such as a news release. But since there was no such record, the truth remained elusive. Wiggins argued that rumors would continue unless the news could be published.[16]

Price complained on May 15 about the military's balloon education program to General Clayton Bissell, director of army intelligence. According to Price's memoir, he told Bissell that either the army would have to make a public statement about the balloons or he would expose the G-2 educational program.[17] He said he could not ask journalists to ignore information being spread throughout half of the United States, particularly when it was widely misunderstood. Bissell, whom Price considered to be sympathetic to voluntary censorship, had him repeat his complaints to the G-2 staff. After much discussion, Bissell had Price draft a public statement for the War Department, disclosing the existence of the balloons without revealing details that would benefit Japan. The statement aimed "to reassure the nation that these attacks are so scattered and aimless that they constitute no military threat. . . . The chance that any given place could be hit . . . is only one in a million."[18]

G-2 examined Price's proposed memo for three days without returning it. Price learned that while the army favored the release, the navy did not. That was odd, he wrote in his memoir. Why would the navy want to block a news release about balloon attacks that had reached the Midwest? On Saturday, May 19, he made an appointment for two days later to see Admiral R. S. Edwards at the Navy Department, who had vetoed the memorandum. Over the weekend, censorship of news about Japanese balloons showed signs of cracking. On Sunday, the Office of Censorship got the *New York Daily News* to kill a proposed column that said that "a Chicago newspaper" planned to publish a story soon about Japanese balloons in the Midwest. The Press Division phoned newspapers in Chicago and learned that the *Tribune* had a story ready to publish, based on an interview with an army colonel. Price spoke on Sunday afternoon with the *Tribune*'s Don Maxwell, an old friend, and they agreed that the paper would wait forty-eight hours before publishing, giving the Office of Censorship time to try to overcome the navy's objections to Price's news release.[19] Although Price's memoir does not indicate the likelihood or consequences of the *Tribune* publishing the story before he could issue a statement, he probably wanted to avoid the protests that usually occurred when one newspaper printed an item that others had suppressed.

When Price met with Edwards the next morning, the admiral insisted on continuing the blackout. He thought the proposed news release would "kill Americans," according to Price's memoir, but Price did not elaborate. He asked Edwards to leave the issue to his boss, Admiral Ernest King. Later that day, King overruled Edwards and approved the news release that had been held up for three days. The army and navy issued a joint statement about the balloons at 3 P.M. on May 22. Shortly after noon, Theodore F. Koop, who had become director of the Press and Broadcasting Divisions on May 1, 1945, asked the wire services to distribute a confidential note alerting editors to the upcoming release and asking them to continue withholding any news about the balloons that would help Japan target them, such as the number and location of their sightings.[20] The bulletin said a balloon had killed six people, but it gave no details about the victims or their location. It urged journalists not to contribute to hysteria and said the War Department would continue to be the only appropriate authority for news about specific balloon incidents.[21]

For a week, the Office of Censorship suppressed attempts to link the army-navy news release to the casualties in Oregon. Then, on May 31, the censors decided that numerous authorized statements to reporters by

army officials had made it impossible to continue suppressing the site of
the six deaths, and they endorsed the mention of Lakeview, Oregon, near
Gearhart Mountain.[22] The Associated Press quickly put a story on the
wire that named the victims and included an interview with Mitchell, the
pastor whose wife had died in the blast.[23] The Office of Censorship continued the restriction on specifying the location of balloons for the rest
of the war but offered no objection to generalities such as "the western
part of the United States." After censorship ended on August 15, 1945,
many papers published the details of nearby balloon sightings during the
previous nine months.[24]

The news blackout had kept Japan from learning about the balloons'
progress after launching. The enemy could not know whether they had
caused death and destruction or had fallen harmlessly. If the balloons
had caused panic, Japan might have benefited from that knowledge and
stepped up production or launched a propaganda campaign. However,
the story was suppressed and panic was averted. Japan had no way of
knowing that the balloons were nearly useless as a weapon, and for six
months it invested expensive resources into their manufacture that otherwise might have been diverted to other weapons.

The news of Japanese balloon bombs was a major story unanticipated
by the original *Code of Wartime Practices*. Suppressing it required civilian
and military censors to recognize it as a potential security risk and to create a strategy to keep in check the public's curiosity. While the balloon
bombs posed a special challenge because they were seen and discussed
throughout the West, other major stories were suppressed without difficulty. In the winter of 1942, the Office of Censorship asked journalists
to "lay off" stories of Japanese cruelty to Allied prisoners of war. Press
Division director John H. Sorrells explained in a memorandum to his
assistant Nathaniel R. Howard on February 24 that publicity might in-
cite reprisals against people of Japanese ancestry in the United States
and provide Japan an excuse for more cruelties.[25] On another subject,
five weeks later, Price informed journalists that the restrictions on stories
about prisoners of war did not apply to news of the forced relocation of
Japanese Americans. While the internment of enemy aliens was covered
by the censorship code, he said, journalists were free to publicize the federal government's internment of American citizens of Japanese ancestry,
which had been done out of fears about their loyalty.[26]

Other news stories unforeseen at the start of the war that effectively
were suppressed included those about new treatments for malaria that

simplified tropical warfare and the accuracy of German rocket attacks on England in the autumn of 1944. Because the V-1 and V-2 rockets were unmanned and imprecisely targeted, a news blackout on their detonation sites kept Germany unaware of the degree of their effectiveness. The Reuters agency thanked American journalists in the first week of December 1944 for complying with civilian and military censorship requests restricting combat zone information.[27]

Closer to home, the Office of Censorship allowed domestic publication of news of racial violence, approving wire service stories on November 27, 1942, about a gunfight between white military police and black soldiers in Phoenix and on December 28, 1942, about a riot among black and white soldiers in Vallejo, California.[28] However, it asked cable and postal censors to delete racially inflammatory statements that might be twisted by Axis radio propaganda.[29]

RADAR AND THE ATOMIC BOMB

Two of the biggest wartime secrets were radar and the atomic bomb. They were the only news subjects in which the Office of Censorship refused to recognize a code violation by a radio station or publication as a condition for the general release of the same information nationwide.[30] Yet, they were too newsworthy to be smothered by censorship, and numerous stories attributed to government and military authorities were published or broadcast. The Office of Censorship's suppression of news of these subjects took divergent paths. Price fought military and government attempts to impose a complete blackout of stories about radar because much had been written about it before the war, Axis nations had developed their own forms of radar and obtained knowledge from downed Allied aircraft, and the basic radar information usually submitted for censorship review posed no clear danger if it were published. In mid-February 1943, the Joint Chiefs of Staff ordered a ban on written, oral, and pictorial publicity for army and navy experimental projects, including pure and applied science in electronics, chemistry, biology, and physics that had "present or potential use for military-naval purposes."[31] The Office of Naval Operations informed all navy offices of the ban on February 16, and the adjutant general's office informed all army offices on the following day.[32] The total suppression of news about radar had a boomerang effect. Journalists prohibited from publishing or broadcasting stories involving radar concluded that if the technology was worth an extraordinary effort to keep secret, it must be newsworthy.[33]

According to Price, the Joint Security Control Board initiated discussions with the Office of Censorship and the Office of War Information on a revision of the army's and navy's radar news policy. The talks culminated in a statement prepared by Nicholas Roosevelt of the OWI that contained all of the information that the government felt comfortable revealing about radar. Howard reviewed the proposed statement on April 17, 1943, and wrote Price, "It would let us peg the radar issue close to where we have it, and I told Mr. Roosevelt we were entirely satisfied."[34] The army and navy approved the 800-word statement, which the OWI released on April 25, 1943. It described radar's history, the scientific principles on which it was based, and its military uses in locating planes and ships. It devoted only a paragraph to radar's role in Allied military operations in World War II, mentioning its contribution to the battle of Britain. The statement concluded that publicity about radar developments beyond those listed in the news release might help the enemy. Thus, "it has been decided that no further items on the subject will be released until the Army and Navy are convinced that the enemy already has the information from some other source."[35]

On July 27, the president, the only authority to whom the director of censorship by law had to answer, endorsed a continued ban on radar news other than what had been released in the report.[36] Invoking "the highest considerations of national security," Price informed editors and broadcasters on July 29 that public discussion of radar was "causing increasing concern" in the government. All items mentioning what he called the "secret weapon" had to be cleared by the Office of Censorship or an appropriate government authority.[37] In a private memorandum on the same day to the heads of the Press, Broadcasting, Cable, and Postal Divisions, Price said censorship policy would serve to discourage all publication about radar and delete from outgoing cables and mail all mention of military electronic devices.[38] Still, leaks continued. When General George Strong, the head of army intelligence, phoned Price at Christmas 1943 to begin his ultimately unsuccessful bid for military control of domestic censorship, his complaints included the Office of Censorship rule that an appropriate authority could release information about radar. "He could not understand how we could stand aside when authorized spokesmen violated security," Price recalled.[39] The Office of Censorship counted seventy-eight army, navy, and government-authorized violations of the censorship code in 1943, including three releases on radar by high-ranking officials—General H. H. "Hap" Arnold, James Byrnes, director of war mobilization, and Lieutenant Colonel James Roosevelt, the president's son.[40]

In the winter of 1944–45, Axis reversals as well as a spate of appropriate-authority releases about radar that had not been cleared by the War and Navy Departments prompted Price to seek a revision of the radar censorship policy to make it less restrictive. He did not succeed. The War and Navy Departments continued to suppress references to radar in stories submitted for their approval.[41] On February 6, 1945, Price wrote to the Joint Security Control and the public relations offices of the army and navy to complain that the policy was unreasonable and could no longer be defended. It kept from enemy intelligence considerable information it already knew. The following month, he told White House chief of staff William Leahy that a radar policy revision was "long overdue."[42] While the army and navy were continuing their blackout on radar, the Office of Censorship by the end of February had dropped its objections to radar items except references to specific characteristics, experiments, new uses, tactical operations and limitations, and countermeasures. Finally, by March 26, the Office of Censorship converted the army and navy to its position that general information about radar no longer posed a security threat, although the office's internal history did not say why the armed services had changed their position.[43] After months of negotiations, in July 1945, the Joint Chiefs of Staff approved a new policy on radar publicity. The statement was released for publication on August 15, which, by coincidence, was one day after Japan agreed to surrender. The radar news that journalists had clamored for was lost amid the news of the war's end.[44]

Like the development of radar, the possibility of splitting the atom was widely discussed in public before the start of the war, but much less so afterward. In 1939, when war began in Europe, American scientists stopped publishing information that might have military value, and during the next year editors of scientific journals began informally asking the National Academy of Sciences to clear articles that might contain sensitive information.[45] However, articles about atomic research continued to be printed by popular magazines. On September 7, 1940, "The Atom Gives Up," an article by *New York Times* science reporter William L. Laurence, appeared in the *Saturday Evening Post*. The article explained research into atomic fission as an energy source, and Laurence, who understood the significance of atomic energy in wartime, expected it to cause an uproar in Washington. Instead, he heard nothing. He later learned that early in 1943, officers in charge of security for atomic research asked libraries nationwide to take the magazine off their shelves.[46]

Responsibility for research into the military uses of fission was shared in 1942 by the Office of Scientific Research and Development, led by Vannevar Bush, and the War Department, whose Army Corps of Engineers handled construction. On August 11, 1942, the research and development project was designated the "Manhattan Engineering District" or "Manhattan Project," names chosen to avoid arousing curiosity. Leslie R. Groves officially took charge of the project on September 23, on the same day that he was promoted to brigadier general.[47]

Groves's method of maintaining security over the project was to control the flow of information among the members of his team. "Compartmentalization of knowledge, to me, was the very heart of security," Groves wrote in his memoir. "My rule was simple and not capable of misinterpretation—each man should know everything he needed to know to do his job and nothing else." Army intelligence, headed by General Strong, supervised internal security for about the first year of the project, Groves wrote, before responsibility shifted to the Manhattan Project's own security staff, led by John Lansdale.[48]

On February 13, 1943, Bush proposed broadening the project's security net by bringing all news of military atomic research under the provisions of the censorship code. According to an army history of the bomb project, Strong and Groves at first expressed "serious reservations" about the war's biggest secret being subjected to voluntary censorship regulations. Strong told General W. D. Styer, chief of staff to the Army Services of Supply, that subjecting the atomic development project to voluntary censorship "might be more detrimental than otherwise."[49] Nevertheless, the Office of Censorship had to be informed about the project. The subject could no longer be avoided by March 1943, when the army expressed concern about newspapers publicizing construction contracts near Oak Ridge, Tennessee, and Pasco, Washington.[50] Lieutenant Colonel Whitney Ashbridge of the Army Corps of Engineers notified Press Division director Howard of the government's atomic research on March 30, 1943, and asked for a complete press blackout in a letter to Price on the next day.[51] Howard replied that publicity about the project could not be completely suppressed, noting that much of the information that appeared in the Tennessee and Washington papers had come from public records. It would be impossible for construction projects employing thousands of workers on 70 square miles in Tennessee and 600 square miles in Wash-

General Leslie R. Groves. As director of the Manhattan Project, Groves initially had "serious reservations" about subjecting news of atomic research to the voluntary censorship code of American newspapers and radio. National Archives.

ington to be blacked out, and Howard feared that attempts to enforce a mandatory censorship would backfire by arousing journalists' curiosity. He suggested a less conspicuous course of action: have the Office of Censorship send a confidential note to editors and broadcasters in Tennessee and Washington directing attention to the censorship code's clause on new or secret weapons. Price said in his memoir that the implication would be clear to editors near Pasco and Oak Ridge that the note referred to the giant factories. However, Groves objected that a draft of the letter prepared by Howard revealed "entirely too much," and it was not until the end of June that the Office of Censorship and the Manhattan Project agreed on a way to approach editors and broadcasters without specifying that secret war experiments were under way.[52] Howard's insistent persuasion wore down the army's reluctance to a censorship plan.[53] On June 25, Strong, Howard, and the OWI's Elmer Davis agreed upon a confidential note to editors and broadcasters nationwide that would draw attention to atomic research without mentioning the work in Tennessee and Washington. Strong asked how many people would see the note and "whistled through his teeth" when Howard gave an estimate of 25,000. Then, Strong suggested camouflaging the importance of uranium, a crucial element in bomb production, by hiding it among a list of harmless elements. Howard thought that "a swell idea," and they drafted a note listing several obscure elements.[54]

The Office of Censorship sent the note on June 28, 1943, to all of the nation's newspapers and radio stations. It said:

> The *Codes of Wartime Practices for the American Press and American Broadcasters* request that nothing be published or broadcast about "new or secret military weapons . . . experiments." In extension of this highly vital precaution, you are asked not to publish or broadcast any information whatever regarding war experiments involving:
>
> Production or utilization of atom smashing, atomic energy, atomic fission, atomic splitting, or any of their equivalents.
>
> The use for military purposes of radium or radioactive materials, heavy water, high voltage discharge equipment, cyclotrons.
>
> The following elements or any of their compounds: polonium, uranium, ytterbium, hafnium, protactinium, radium, rhenium, thorium, deuterium.[55]

The note created neither a bang nor a whimper. Most editors and broadcasters read it but did not grasp its significance. On August 11, 1945, after atomic bombs had been dropped on Hiroshima and Nagasaki and the ban on the mention of uranium lifted, *Editor & Publisher* published an article recalling the June 1943 note, saying it "sounded like Greek. . . . But the request was followed. Science writers had been discussing U-235, U-238 and cyclotrons. That stopped immediately."[56]

The Associated Press was one of the few organizations that questioned the note's meaning. AP staffer Bill Beale told the Press Division on June 30 that the wire service's New York headquarters was curious about what the note was intended to hide. William Steven of the Press Division was reluctant to elaborate. "Under some prodding," Steven wrote in a memorandum for Howard, "I gave him this much: The note covers some things the War and Navy Departments are working on; if and whenever these projects or products come into use, undoubtedly the AP will know."[57]

News of the secret project appeared in three ways. First, some journalists had never seen or understood the memorandum and publicized atomic experiments without consulting the Office of Censorship. Second, some editors and broadcasters believed their stories were allowed by the code, but in fact they were not. Third, appropriate authorities, including government officials, became sources for news even though Groves and Strong wanted a total blackout.

In late July 1943, neither the *Schenectady (New York) Gazette* nor *Business Week* magazine sought censorship clearance for items that referred to uranium and "the Army's most secret project" at Oak Ridge, respectively.[58] Neither publication apparently realized the significance of the June memorandum, but the Office of Censorship quickly brought it to their attention. Newspaper columnist and Blue Network commentator Walter Winchell, who had problems understanding the code, violated the ban on news of secret experiments in February 1944. In his broadcast, Winchell had threatened to "expose the whole business" if the army did not give him details of the secret project. The Broadcasting Division called the Blue Network in New York and secured a promise that it would allow the censors to see any Winchell script dealing with the subject before it aired.[59]

Other broadcasts proved more dangerous. One of the worst leaks of the war, according to John Fetzer, who became director of the Broadcasting Division on April 15, 1944, occurred in a nationwide Mutual network broadcast by Arthur Hale. About two million listeners heard his "Confidentially Yours" program on August 15, 1944, in which he said the army would split the atom and soon create a weapon. He also referred to Pasco, Washington. The Office of Censorship found that two procedural errors had been made. The first occurred when the Transradio Press Service, which prepared the script for Hale, failed to check it for code violations. The second was that Hale had not been made familiar with the code. Hale responded to inquiries by the army by saying he hoped the Germans had heard him and would surrender.[60] "I had my greatest fight with the military then and there," Fetzer recalled. "They wanted to move in and install censors in every radio station in the country." The Office of Censorship talked the military out of the idea, he said, and asked for the destruction of all recordings of Hale's broadcast.[61]

Confusion arose over the wording of the June 1943 note to editors and broadcasters because it applied to "war experiments" and the use of radioactive materials and cyclotrons "for military purposes" but not to possible peacetime uses of atomic power. This ambiguity led the Broadcasting Division to clear a Westinghouse Company radio script in October 1943, only to have its decision questioned by the Press Division and the army. The problem centered on the Broadcasting Division's literal interpretation of the memorandum in deciding to approve a script that revealed little about the military potential of the atom and yet provided saboteurs with a valuable target. Broadcasting Division director J. Harold Ryan wrote Price on October 19 that two weeks earlier, the Westinghouse Company voluntarily had submitted a script for pre-broadcast review. Prompted by the press censors, the radio staff decided to ask Westinghouse to delete eighteen lines, he said. Later, the Broadcasting Division reviewed the script on its own and concluded that most of the deletions requested by the Press Division related to the benefits of peacetime atomic energy, as opposed to war experiments, the discussion of which the June memo had banned. The broadcasting censors decided that Westinghouse would not violate the censorship code if it merely deleted the word "cyclotron" from two pages as well as the phrase "and, as the men of Westinghouse have found, the bombardment of uranium may yet lead to the creation of a new fuel which, though the size of a walnut, will give off as much energy as 1250 tons of good bituminous coal." They approved a description that said an atom smasher in Pittsburgh was five stories tall, involved in work more valuable than manufacturing gold, and left substances radioactive. According to Ryan, the broadcasting censors notified Westinghouse of their editing decisions on October 7, and the longer version of the script aired within the next twelve days, on a date that Ryan did not specify.[62] He also asked Price to clarify whether there was a difference in censorship rules depending on whether a story pictured atomic power as destructive or beneficial. He said he feared that the Broadcasting Division had been imprudent and was curious about the opinion of Jack Lockhart, his counterpart in the Press Division. Price gave Ryan's note to Lockhart on that day after scrawling at the top, "Mr. J. H. Lockhart Your comment Pls."[63]

Lockhart responded, "I may be scared of this subject by what I have been told by Nat Howard and others, but I feel we have nothing that is hotter, or more important, than it at present." He added, "If I were the enemy, there would appear to be no more vital target for sabotage in this country than this Westinghouse laboratory and similar atom-smashing equipment elsewhere."[64]

The Westinghouse broadcast angered Groves, who sought to tighten the policy on radio news about atom smashing. Lansdale and a lieutenant from army intelligence arrived at the Office of Censorship on the after noon of October 21 to discuss the broadcast and the importance of the Manhattan Project. After they told Price and Lockhart that atomic re- search was a "hot" subject, Price informed his staff members that they should be "most cautious" in handling any reference to atom smashing.[65] As with radar, the Office of Censorship did not accept prior publication or broadcast as a reason for the general dissemination of news of atomic research.[66]

More surprising than the Westinghouse broadcast was an item in the *Minneapolis Morning Tribune* on August 24, 1944, that said "all known explosives are popgun affairs compared to the dreadful power sub-atomic energy might loose." The item, reporting that the War Pro- duction Board had imposed controls on the sale of uranium, appeared in a column of Washington gossip beneath the names of five corre- spondents—including that of William Mylander, a former member of the Press Division who had returned to journalism. Mylander's man- aging editor was William Steven, another alumnus of the Press Division. Both men, along with reporter Nat Finney, who wrote the item, called the board's report on uranium an appropriate authority for the item. Frank C. Clough of the Press Division disagreed. He told Steven that the item "did chisel into the Production clause of the code and the special [June 1943] request."[67] Groves was so upset about the item that he visited *Tribune* owner John Cowles and convinced him to halt such leaks.[68]

Without getting clearance from Groves or his aides, several high- ranking military and government officials released atomic research in- formation that journalists could publicize according to the appropriate- authority clause. One such leak occurred on December 11, 1943, when General Tom Frazier, Tennessee's Selective Service director, mentioned the work at Oak Ridge. In discussing a news release about a draft appeal board for the eastern part of the state, he said, "Within the area of the new appeal board is the Clinton Engineer Works, in secret war production of a weapon that possibly might be the one to end the war." The Associated Press put the story on its news wire at 12:24 P.M. Fifty-nine minutes later, the Office of Censorship learned of the item when the *Knoxville News-Sentinel* called to ask if it could be published. The censors called Lansdale, who asked Frazier to withdraw his consent for publication, and shortly after 2 P.M. the AP issued a bulletin asking its subscribers not to publish the story. Presses already had begun printing the edition of some afternoon newspapers, but most newspapers removed the item at substantial cost. "Very little publicity" resulted from Frazier's remarks, the Office of Censorship's history said.[69]

Leaks of any kind concerned Groves, whose office compiled a list of 104 published references to the Manhattan Project and related subjects and sent it to the Office of Censorship in September 1944. The list began in 1939; seventy-seven of the references had occurred since the issue of the confidential note in June 1943. Lockhart replied that while the total was high, "I cannot help but remember how many thousands of opportunities there were for references to the project or the purposes of the project within the same period of time. That these references have not been made is a tribute to . . . voluntary censorship."[70]

Despite Groves's many complaints about news leaks, he respected the work of the Office of Censorship and Lockhart in particular. Lockhart, the former managing editor of the *Memphis Commercial Appeal* who served as director of the Press Division from June 26, 1943, to May 1, 1945, was Groves's first choice to write the press releases that would be issued after the atomic bomb was used in war. According to Groves's memoir, Lockhart "felt that he could not be spared from his present assignment, and suggested that we get someone who had a better background in scientific reporting."[71] He recommended Laurence, the *New York Times* science writer. Laurence had tried and failed to win Price's and Lockhart's approval in December 1943 and August 1944 for the publication of stories about the explosive power of uranium-235. After the second refusal, Laurence's editor told Lockhart that the reporter would "commit suicide" if the *Times* were scooped, and although the sentiment surely was hyperbolic, Lockhart probably felt that Laurence had earned the rights to one of the biggest stories of the war.[72]

In the spring of 1945, Groves invited Laurence to work on a secret war project. The *Times* agreed to give him a leave of absence, and Laurence accepted the job. He soon learned that he was the official historian of the atomic bomb. He visited the secret sites in Tennessee and Washington, as well as the Los Alamos, New Mexico, research and assembly laboratory. At Pasco, Laurence discovered that one of the unpublicized Japanese balloon bombs had landed on power lines of the plant that produced plutonium. Although it did not explode, it produced a short-circuit and cut electricity to the plant for part of a day.[73]

In the summer of 1945, as final preparations were being made for a test detonation in the New Mexico desert, the Manhattan Project contacted the Office of Censorship to make plans to censor news of the blast. No one was certain how powerful it would be, and Price envisioned potential difficulties in suppressing the news. "If you blow off one corner of the United States, don't expect to keep it out of the newspapers," he told a Manhattan Project official, whom he did not identify. He suggested that press releases be prepared for immediate distribution as soon as the bomb was detonated.[74] Groves gave Laurence the task of writing four official statements, ranging from a report of a loud, bright explosion that caused no damage to a catastrophe involving hundreds of deaths, including those of many top scientists. Laurence, whom Groves had told to witness the explosion, realized that the last of the four, if it were printed, would be his obituary.[75]

When the bomb exploded at 5:30 A.M. local time on July 16, 1945, near Alamogordo, it produced a light bright enough to be seen 200 miles away. One of the four official statements was released as planned, attributing the blast to an explosion of an ammunition dump.[76] Some journalists in New Mexico, not satisfied with the press release, began interviewing witnesses who had seen or heard the blast. The army feared these stories might reveal too much, and as a result the Press Division phoned the Washington, D.C., offices of the news wire services and asked to examine any witnesses' stories before they were put on the wire or published. The AP submitted the first such story at 3:15 P.M. It quoted a blind woman 150 miles to the north of the detonation site as asking her brother-in-law, "What's that brilliant light?"[77] Two of Groves's staff officers, Lansdale and William A. Consodine, argued that the Office of Censorship should suppress that story and others, but the censors countered that attempts to black out news of what seemed to be a routine explosion would spark journalists' curiosity. They had learned this lesson when attempts to ban radar news early in 1943 increased interest in the subject. After Price and censor James Warner advised that a big explosion often resulted in publication of conflicting and fantastic first-person accounts, Lansdale and Consodine agreed to drop their opposition to the stories. The story appeared throughout New Mexico, but East Coast papers ignored it.[78]

On the morning of August 6, Consodine told the Office of Censorship that the White House would issue a special statement at 11 A.M. that Hiroshima had been bombed. The censors prepared a note to editors and broadcasters ending the restrictions on writing about secret war experiments and atomic research. However, the note, issued at 11:30 A.M. Washington time, said that "in the interest of the highest national security," editors and broadcasters should continue to withhold news of the secret methods by which the bomb was devised, assembled, and detonated.[79]

As the story blossomed into one of the biggest in history, the Office of Censorship's Press Division received nearly fifty inquiries within twelve hours on a variety of subjects regarding atomic energy. Callers included the *Chicago Tribune*, which gained approval for an editorial on atomic explosives, and the AP, which received permission to locate and interview Danish atomic scientist Niels Bohr.[80] The Office of Censorship cleared nearly all of the stories; it withheld judgment on a few until journalists could supply details, and it only offered one immediate objection, to portions of a *Tribune* story that lacked appropriate authority for details about the bomb's midair triggering device and the size of its explosive core.[81]

On August 9, a second atomic bomb was dropped on Nagasaki. In the war's final days, the army and the White House asked if the Office of Censorship would consider asking journalists to continue censoring themselves about the atomic bomb after the wartime censorship agency closed, but Price refused to do so. His reasons were stated in a letter to a curious citizen in Houston on August 14: "I have seen so many incidents in which Censorship did harm that I was determined I would do what I could to get rid of it as soon as the harm began to overbalance the military benefit."[82]

On the day he wrote the letter, Japan agreed to halt hostilities. The atomic bomb, whose development had been censored for more than two years, had brought a swift end to the war. Groves thanked Price and his staff on that same day for their efforts over the last two years, and he asked Price to share his gratitude with the entire American news media for their cooperation.[83]

The "Little Boy" atomic bomb. The detonation of the atomic bomb over Hiroshima on August 6, 1945, prompted fifty inquiries to the Office of Censorship within twelve hours. Only the most sensitive information about the bomb's manufacture and detonation remained secret. National Archives.

A final news story that had not been foreseen by the writers of the censorship codebooks was about the Soviet Union's entry into the Pacific war. Although it actually happened in August 1945, the possibility first was discussed in the spring, and it presented one last challenge for censorship. Army chief of staff George C. Marshall called Price to the Pentagon on March 28, 1945, to tell him a secret: Soviet premier Josef Stalin had promised in the previous month at the Yalta Conference that Soviet troops would enter the war against Japan two or three months after the end of the war in Europe. "The General's recital of this information evidenced him great anxiety," Price wrote in his notebook.[84] Marshall said Japan must not learn of the Soviet plan to transfer troops from Europe to eastern Asia. He feared that gossip might help Japan guess the truth, prompting it to attack first or to strengthen key portions of its defenses. He asked Price to limit speculation by the press and radio. "I said I would be glad to help," Price recalled, and during the next six days they collaborated on a note to editors and broadcasters that cautioned journalists of the possible danger of speculation about Soviet-Japanese combat.[85] On April 5, Price visited Marshall's office and secured his final approval for the note's wording. Before returning to the Federal Trade Commission building, he stopped at General Clayton Bissell's Pentagon office to examine a captured Japanese balloon bomb and was informed that the wire services had just reported that the Soviet Union had denounced its 1941 nonaggression pact with Japan. He hurried to issue the note. "Of course I had no thought that speculation could be suppressed," he noted. "The memorandum was issued, in part, for the record, but with the hope that some good might result."[86]

Marshall had carefully phrased the note: "Reports or discussion of expectations or probabilities involving future war plans may be of great value to the enemy. For example, published or broadcast speculation or statements regarding the probable intentions of Soviet Russia toward Japan . . . could possibly lead to a Japanese attack on Russia. Whether such a speculation or prediction were true or false, the military interests of the United States would be damaged and the war's sacrifice of American life might be prolonged. Please weigh the consequences and consult the Office of Censorship."[87]

The note caused a flurry of resentment. Some journalists interpreted it as an attempt to control opinions. Others argued that the note stifled justifiable demands for the Soviets to open a second front against Japan, just as in 1942 when the Soviets had asked its allies to open a second front against Germany. The Office of Censorship received what Price called "a few protests," although Theodore F. Koop, the Press Division's final director, characterized the reaction as a great "bewilderment."[88]

I. F. Stone complained in *PM* that there could be no security concerns in such speculation, especially since "the Japanese are speculating a great deal more than we are."[89] George M. Cox, editor of the *Mobile, Ala., Register,* complained of the restrictions in a letter to Price on April 6. He would be glad if American editorials started a Soviet-Japanese war, he said, and thus "take some of the pressure off our boys in the Pacific." Price replied that Cox would change his mind if he knew the facts available to the nation's military commanders as well as their "very deep anxiety." He added that he had issued the note "with my eyes completely open, after full consultation, knowing that my position would be misunderstood by some, but hoping that my action would render some help at least to the Army and Navy. I still hope so."[90]

The protests died within a week. Speculation about a Soviet attack on Japanese troops declined but did not end. After discussions with the Joint Chiefs of Staff, Price issued a second note to editors and broadcasters on May 11 to try to halt the talk. The note, distributed by the major news wire services, revealed that the original request had been made by Marshall and Admiral King. They had warned that "any prediction . . .

of action in the field might set off developments which would very seriously disrupt the military plans of the United States and prolong the war greatly. This may be difficult for you to understand, but remembering the help you have given heretofore we take hope that you will trust our word in this matter."[91]

The request quieted the speculation as well as any lingering criticism. True to Stalin's word, the Soviet Union declared war on Japan on August 8, 1945, three months after Germany's capitulation.

THE END OF CENSORSHIP

Throughout the war, Price told journalists that he wanted censorship to last no longer than necessary.[92] On November 20, 1943, he received the endorsement of the Censorship Policy Board for his suggestion to ease censorship when the threat to national security decreased and to shut down his office as soon as possible after the war ended.[93] The fighting ended at different times against Germany and Japan, and censorship consequently shut down in two waves. On May 8, 1945, when Germany surrendered, Price canceled all program restrictions of the radio code. Restrictions on news of production and prisoners of war also were eased on that day. In addition, with the approval of the War Department, the Office of Censorship cleared the identification of all military units in Europe as long as publications and broadcasts did not indicate their future movements. The next week, the censorship codebooks for radio and the print press were combined in a final edition that deleted or relaxed about twenty clauses.[94]

On June 27, 1945, Price sent President Harry S. Truman a proposal to declare an end to voluntary censorship of press and radio on the day that the defeat of Japan "is formally and officially announced." Every member of his Censorship Policy Board, he said, agreed with his request.[95] Truman responded on July 3, telling Price to send him a directive for his signature "when the appropriate time arrives."[96] During the rest of July and early August, Price's staff prepared copies of what he called "our V-J Book," containing instructions for postal and cable censorship stations, as well as the Office of Censorship headquarters, on ending censorship and preparing documents for storage. He pressed his administrative staff to complete the book quickly because he knew, but did not say, that the Soviets would enter the war on August 8 and that Groves had told him to expect the atomic bomb to be dropped soon. The V-J—Victory over Japan—books were mailed on August 3.[97] Price announced publicly on August 13 that press and radio censorship would end one hour after Truman announced victory.[98]

On the next evening, Japan told its armed forces to stop fighting, but it was unclear to Price whether the end of hostilities was the same as the end of the war. He did not know whether to try to close the Office of Censorship immediately or wait for a formal declaration. On the morning of August 15, Price called Truman's presidential press secretary, Charles G. Ross, to inquire when the formal surrender would occur. Told to expect a two-week delay, Price asked that his directive to end censorship be placed immediately before the president. No doubt he recalled his public pledge and felt awkward at the prospect of delay. Ross took the document to Truman "at the first opportunity," and he signed it at 3 P.M. Censorship officially ended when the signed document arrived at the Federal Trade Commission building at 5:28 P.M.[99]

In a bulletin sent to thousands of editors and broadcasters nationwide after he received the document, Price canceled the code and praised all for having followed it. "You deserve, and you have, the thanks and appreciation of your Government. And my own gratitude and that of my colleagues in the unpleasant task of administering censorship is beyond words or limit." An AP photographer posed him in front of his office door, tacking up an "Out of Business" sign, although the office remained open through November 15 to finish its record keeping.[100]

Accolades soon appeared in print nationwide. Many attributed the success of voluntary censorship to the man who directed it. The *New York Times* editorialized, "Every newspaper man knows how sadly he suffered when it became his duty to ask that news be suppressed. Throughout the war he did his best, usually with success, to see to it that censorship was not unreasonable."[101] *Editor & Publisher* said, "We have never heard anyone in the newspaper business contradict the statement that Byron Price conducted the Office of Censorship in a competent, careful and wholly patriotic manner."[102] Five hundred journalists belonging to the White House Correspondents Association, the National Press Club, the Gridiron Club, and the Overseas Writers Club rewarded Price with a scroll of thanks at a Washington reception on September 6, 1945. Truman, who presented the scroll, said it honored a "good public servant."[103]

Price's analysis of why his office succeeded was contained in a plan for future wartime censorship that he gave Truman on August 24, 1945. He noted that he based his recommendations on his having served longer as censor—forty-four months—than anyone in the nation's history, and he hinted at his distaste for the job. "It should be understood that no one who does not dislike censorship should ever be permitted to exercise censorship," he wrote. Much of the twenty-five-page document concerned technicalities of organizing and staffing a censorship office. Price advocated a duplicate of his censorship system to be created upon the declaration of war and to be directed by a civilian who had served in the military. However, he prefaced the recital of administrative minutiae with an endorsement of voluntary censorship of press and radio, arguing, "[I]t is precisely here that the entire operation will face its greatest danger of fatal error and consequent disruption."[104]

Price's personal records made no mention of a response by Truman. The president evidently thought highly of Price, though, because he had asked him on August 19 to be his personal representative and to examine the conditions of the Allied Occupation of Europe. Price spent ten weeks in Austria, France, Belgium, the Netherlands, Czechoslovakia, and western Germany. He made his report to Truman upon his return in early November, notably complaining about French efforts to block the re unification of Germany. His return was just in time to requisition the Office of Censorship's government-issued Ford for its final official trip, to take his personal belongings home from the Federal Trade Commission building on November 15.[105]

He declined most job offers, including one to become dean of the School of Journalism at the University of Kansas.[106] Instead, he took a job as vice president of the Motion Picture Producers and Distributors on December 4, 1945, where, among other duties, he sought to improve labor-management relations in Hollywood.[107] He felt he had to leave his beloved Associated Press, telling Cooper that the AP's administrative changes and wartime personnel losses had made him fear that he would be unhappy if he returned. "The ranks have been closed, quite naturally and properly," he said.[108] In addition, it would have been awkward to return to an organization in which newspaper clients would make requests of him, in contrast to a wartime relationship that had reversed their roles.

Price served at the United Nations as assistant secretary general for administrative and financial services from 1947 to 1954.[109] He then retired and moved to Chestertown, on Maryland's Eastern Shore. He stopped playing golf at the Washington Golf and Country Club and the Scarsdale, New York, Country Club and devoted his attentions to growing irises.[110] President John F. Kennedy phoned him at Chestertown during the Cuban missile crisis of October 1962 to ask him to become director of censorship if the naval quarantine of Cuba turned into a shooting war with the Soviet Union. He could not refuse, he recalled, but he did not relish the idea. He was seventy-one years old and had not worked as a journalist since 1941.[111] In 1975, he and his wife, Priscilla, moved to Hendersonville, North Carolina. She died in 1978, and he suffered a heart attack and died on August 6, 1981, at the age of ninety.[112]

Conclusion

Byron Price's legacy was a paradox: contributions to long-term press freedom that came from a handful of press and broadcasting censors. Perhaps the greatest of these contributions benefited radio rather than the print press, and involved actions that Price refused to take. In declining to seize control of radio stations in 1942 despite receiving the attorney general's approval to do so, Price made radio an equal partner in the news media's effort to inform the public about the conduct of the war. Price's decision preserved radio's freedom to report the news robustly and critically. Furthermore, he treated with restraint the most potentially dangerous broadcasters, those who spoke the languages of America's enemies.

Such restraint was evident at censorship's beginning, and at its end. Price's office in 1945 had defused the criticism of the ban on Soviet-Japanese speculation, and gained the cooperation of the press, by issuing an appeal to patriotism and trust in government, frankly admitting that the rationale was difficult to understand but emphasizing his trust in voluntary censorship. Price's faith in journalists paid dividends as they returned their trust. The *Richmond, Va., News Leader* editorialized that while Price's request to avoid speculation about a Soviet invasion made little sense "in the abstract," it deserved full compliance because of his record as censorship director. "He has asked nothing for which there was not ample reason—and he always has asked it reasonably!" it said.[1] The *Bismarck, N.D., Tribune* echoed its appreciation of Price's gentle persuasion: "If Mr. Price had 'ordered' a cessation to Russo-Japanese speculation the uproar would have been terrific and the order would have been challenged[,] but as long as he merely 'asked' that this policy be adopted there was no question about it."[2]

Patriotic appeals, openness, and faith in the reasonableness of journalists during a bitter war were keys to the Office of Censorship's success.

The censors had recognized these keys when they issued the wartime practices codes and supplementary notes to editors and broadcasters. In writing the codebooks, the censors tacitly endorsed trust in the military and the government by allowing congressmen, army and navy officers, and other high-ranking authorities to censor themselves, and to choose when to violate the censorship code by releasing sensitive information to the news media according to the appropriate-authority clause. Furthermore, the censors made journalists themselves responsible for following the codebooks, and for choosing whether to ignore any censorship request. The codebooks rested on a foundation of openness by revealing, as much as possible, the reasons for censorship requests and encouraging journalists who had questions or complaints to talk to the censors. And, ultimately, the codebooks were impotent without faith. Lacking the legal authority to force journalists—at the very least, print journalists—to submit their stories to censorship, the censors requested compliance. The codes enabled each journalist to be responsible, in a small measure, for the success of censorship.

Some journalists doubted this faith in World War II. Many military and government authorities doubted it, too. This was especially true during the first ten months of 1942, when the navy severely censored news of ship sinkings, and the *Chicago Tribune* published its Midway story. This faith was strongly questioned as late as December 1943, when General George Strong attempted to have the military run domestic censorship in hopes of safeguarding the 1944 invasion of Europe and curtailing news of radar.

The Office of Censorship, however, maintained its faith that journalists would censor themselves as long as they believed that the reasons for censorship were legitimate. When faced with a major challenge, the censors tried to bolster their case through mediation and compromise. On the one hand, Price pressed government and military authorities to stop withholding information that had no security value, and he occasionally overruled official attempts to keep certain topics secret. That reduced the perception that censorship was being misused, and thus lessened the danger of violations. On the other hand, Price continually reminded journalists of the danger of revealing secrets, which improved their compliance with censorship requests that they found questionable.

Price balanced the benefits of unfettered journalism with its attendant responsibilities. If the government took control of the press, he said in a tribute to the Bill of Rights on February 21, 1945, at the Library of

Congress, "all of our freedoms would be in instant peril." However, he said, a free press cannot endure when it abuses its freedom, adding, "The people, in due course, will see to that."[3] During his tenure, he charted a middle ground between the anarchy of total press freedom, which might reveal secrets to the enemy, and the alternative of total control, which might ruin the democratic principles that the nation was defending. To urge both press and government toward a golden mean, he appealed to reason. That, in turn, required faith in the reasonableness of both parties.

He was heartened when the press scrutinized the conduct of the war, even though his censorship duties kept much of what they learned out of print and off the air. To him, their vigilance was evidence that the press would emerge from the war with its freedom intact. In the spring of 1944, journalists asked the Office of Censorship to clear stories related to the upcoming invasion of Europe. "Always, the answer is no," he had said. "But I like to see those articles arriving regularly for they indicate enterprise on the part of the reporters, without which journalism would be in bad shape."[4]

What might have happened to the press and the nation if voluntary censorship had failed, and mandatory control had taken its place? No one can say. However, Jack Lockhart, the Press Division's third director, believed that laws lacking popular support always are quickly broken. He once said that any compulsory form of censorship would have been doomed, like Prohibition, the 1920–33 federal ban on the manufacture, sale, and transportation of alcoholic beverages that was widely ignored. "Evading it would become a sport, a sport having the sanction of a great body of public opinion," he said. "I know that anyone who wants to can beat the censor. The essence of the success of voluntary censorship lies in convincing everybody that they don't want to beat the censor." Theodore F. Koop agreed. He wrote in the Office of Censorship's history that voluntary censorship works most efficiently when it is compatible with American aims and traditions.[5]

Among these traditions are the dynamic tensions between individual liberty and group equality. Under the rules of voluntary censorship, each journalist had the liberty to report a sensitive news story, resulting in a short-term gain at the expense of others who suppressed the story or were ignorant of it. However, to violate the censorship code would conflict not only with the needs of the military and government, whose potential defeat might jeopardize freedom, but also with the value of equality. Each journalist claimed the rights of the First Amendment, and each demanded that censorship give no one an advantage in exercising those rights. At least, they demanded that their competitors enjoy no advantage over them. Censorship would be equitable or it would be ignored by the highly competitive news industry.

Price did have flaws. Among them was his habit to preach high ideals but occasionally compromise them in their administration. He could not see, or refused to acknowledge, that the Office of Censorship did not always follow its rules to the letter. For example, Price disregarded the rule calling for candor when he dismissed Willie Seuren and Raffaele Borrelli and did not announce or state his reasons for the firing. He violated the rule requiring impartiality and consistency when he asked only Drew Pearson to submit scripts before broadcast. Price worked toward what he perceived to be a greater good, sometimes choosing the most pragmatic—but not always the fairest—means to the end.

Fortunately, Price's flaws were not fatal to censorship. He must receive credit for herding the independent-minded institutions of the American press and radio safely through World War II and leaving them as free as they had been before the attack on Pearl Harbor. Identifying the milestones of this success is difficult, though. It is impossible to know about the battlefield disasters that never happened and the ships that were never sunk because potentially dangerous news stories were kept from publication or broadcast. Numerous leaks occurred, but the fact that such mistakes occurred cannot be blamed exclusively on the Office of Censorship. Many violations stemmed from ignorance of the code as well as the inexperience of journalists hired to replace reporters, broadcasters, and editors who joined the armed forces or became combat zone correspondents. Furthermore, military sources, whom Price refused to censor, accounted for many of the leaks.

It is more striking to list the assaults on the First Amendment that did *not* occur during World War II. The Office of Censorship avoided a military takeover of civilian censorship and declined to seize control of radio. It censored no editorial opinions and silenced no criticism of the administration, other than endorsing the revocation of second-class permits of six publications that the Justice Department had deemed seditious. It made no demands of the press—only requests, sometimes strongly worded. It did not allow censorship to expand unduly during the war or censorship regulations to continue after they had lost their military purpose.

Four factors contributed to these successes: popular support for the

war, military and government support for civilian-run censorship, journalists' support for voluntary codes, and Price's acumen as censorship
administrator.

The first is perhaps the most significant. America entered the war after
a devastating sneak attack at Pearl Harbor. Thirty-three minutes after
Roosevelt asked for a declaration of war against Japan on December 8,
1941, Congress granted its approval with only one dissenting vote.[6] The
feeling that the United States had been unfairly attacked created a near-
unanimity of purpose. Bolstering this mood were patriotic and militaristic appeals, such as the American and British declaration of altruistically
worded war aims in the Atlantic Charter, issued August 11, 1941, and repeatedly endorsed throughout the war, and Roosevelt's demand at Casablanca for unconditional surrender by the Axis powers.[7] Also supporting
the public's militaristic mood were the constant reminders of the cost
of combat, from the U-boat attacks along the coastline to the unprece-
dented number of American battle deaths—at 292,000, they were five
times the total of the first world war. World War II was "The Good War,"
to use oral historian Studs Terkel's phrase. Those who did not see it that
way were few, and their most extreme voices, such as *Social Justice,* were
silenced. Perhaps other voices would have risen against the war if it had
dragged on longer. Opposition almost certainly would have increased if
the war had gone badly. It is instructive that two of the most serious discussions of intentionally violating the censorship code occurred in the
troubled year of 1942, and one of them, by the *New York Times,* reflected
concerns that the navy was hiding the severity of its losses from the public. Price's memoir also indicates that his greatest difficulties occurred
in the first two years of the war, before victory appeared to be assured.
He noted that after defeating Strong's attempt to take control of censorship in December 1943, he faced only "misunderstandings" for the rest
of the war and no high-level opposition.[8] The decline in major conflicts
about censorship indicated both a refinement of administrative proce-
dures, which eliminated early mistakes, and a decrease in concerns about
censorship as America's wartime fortunes steadily rose. Fortunately for
Price, the public supported censorship. Periodic wartime surveys consistently found that two-thirds of the people agreed that they were given as
much information as possible and disagreed with the idea that "the government could give us more information about the fighting in this war
without helping the enemy." Public opinion researchers Herbert Hyman
and Paul B. Sheatsley, who reported those results, said only one Ameri-

can in ten thought World War II censorship was too strict and only two in ten thought it was not strict enough.[9] In between those extremes, the silent majority endorsed the censors' work.

Second, the Office of Censorship was fortunate to have the support of numerous sympathetic officials. In the military, supporters of voluntary, civilian censorship included Ernest King, George Marshall, William Leahy, and General Dwight D. Eisenhower, who said in April 1945, "Public opinion wins wars, especially in democracies. Public opinion must be honestly and fearlessly informed."[10] In government, Price's strongest supporters included two presidents. Stephen T. Early told him on August 31, 1945, that the Office of Censorship, "from the time of its creation to its ending, was never a source of worry or trouble to President Roosevelt or to President Truman. . . . There were many who favored and actually advocated compulsory censorship. Their plans were ready. Except for President Roosevelt's strong faith in you and his insistence upon a voluntary system, the advocates of compulsory censorship might have succeeded."[11]

Third, journalists supported voluntary censorship not only because they, like other Americans, supported the prosecution of the war, but also because they feared the alternatives if civilian censorship failed. Options might have included screening of stories before broadcast or publication, or the adoption of a punitive war-secrets law such as the one drawn up by the Justice Department in February 1942.

Fourth, Price was "widely respected as an evenhanded, canny and unflappable administrator,"[12] according to his *New York Times* obituary. He was an ideal person for his job. His skills as a personnel manager, developed at the Associated Press, helped him recognize how far he could press his case for voluntary censorship with journalists and bureaucrats before they rebelled. His extensive background had prepared him for the role of liaison between the wartime government and the press. He had served in the army in World War I and known many military and government officials through his three decades in journalism, and he knew the newspaper industry from composing room to boardroom. Yet he did not become arrogant or narrow-minded. It was a testimonial to his personality and administrative skills that as chief censor he made many more friends. "The wisdom and the logic of Price was the success of the whole thing," recalled John Cosgrove, a journalist who did administrative tasks for Koop but was not a press or radio censor. "He had people around him who were dedicated to the service they were doing. There was just a whole lot of common sense and logic in these guys."[13]

Price's most important trait was his judgment. He knew that voluntary censorship required the cooperation of officials in wartime agencies, and he worked with them to keep their censorship requests reasonable. He also realized it would be illogical to allow a civilian censor to alter a military decision on a faraway battlefront and release information that a commander considered dangerous to his troops.[14] Thus, in December 1941 and January 1942, he arrived at common sense decisions allowing appropriate authorities and combat zone commanders to exercise some control over the news. Despite Price's having made these decisions in haste, they remained in effect throughout the war.

Censorship was "far from perfect," *Editor & Publisher* editorialized on March 4, 1944, yet it said Price was universally praised. In the following month, John S. Knight, head of the Knight newspaper chain and the Office of Censorship's liaison in London, told a reporter that Price had "the best-run bureau in Washington. . . . All he is interested in is seeing that the American press gets its full due."[15]

There could be no better accolade for a censor who worked for press freedom.

Notes

OF   Office File, Franklin D. Roosevelt Papers, Franklin D. Roosevelt
              Library, Hyde Park
OWI   Office of War Information, Record Group 208,
              National Archives Annex, College Park
PPDP   Personal Papers of Drew Pearson, Lyndon B. Johnson Library, Austin
PSF   President's Secretary's File, Franklin D. Roosevelt Papers,
              Franklin D. Roosevelt Library, Hyde Park
ROC   Historical Reports on War Administration,
              Report on the Office of Censorship
STE   Stephen T. Early
STEP   Stephen T. Early Papers, Franklin D. Roosevelt Library, Hyde Park
USSL   United States, *Laws, etc. (United States Statutes at Large)*

INTRODUCTION

1. Tocqueville, *Democracy in America,* 2:96–97.
2. For an oral history and a study of soldiers' motivations in the front lines, see Ambrose, *Citizen Soldiers,* and Glad, *Psychological Dimensions of War.*
3. Goodwin, *No Ordinary Time,* 356–59.
4. Don Anderson to E. P. Adler, Mar. 20, 1942, box 3, folder 4, DAP. Anderson's correspondence with Wisconsin newspapers concerning compliance with the censorship code is in box 7.
5. STE to Kent Cooper, Dec. 31, 1941, box 14, "Price, Byron" folder, STEP.
6. Trohan interview.
7. Clough, "Operations of the Press Division," 222.
8. Harry S. Truman, "Citation to Accompany the Award of the Medal of Merit to Byron Price," box 7, folder 4, BPP.
9. STE to BP, Aug. 31, 1945, box 14, "Price, Byron" folder, STEP.
10. American Civil Liberties Union, *Liberty on the Home Front,* 45.
11. James F. Byrnes, inscription, box 7, folder 5, BPP.
12. NRH, "Editor's Column," *Cleveland News,* Aug. 21, 1945.
13. BPM, 223.

CHAPTER ONE

1. BP to Francis Biddle, Mar. 19, 1942, box 367, "Point-to-Point Circuits" folder, OC.
2. BPM, 341–42.
3. Sypher, "No Snoops Stops Scoops," 38.
4. "Intercepts," 12.
5. Louis J. Hector to Lloyd Cutler, May 11, 1942, and Oscar S. Cox to Francis Biddle, May 18, 1942, box 64, "Radio Censorship Opinions" folder, Oscar S. Cox Papers, Franklin D. Roosevelt Library, Hyde Park.

6. BP, "How Can Censorship Help Win the War?," 229–30.

7. "Proceedings of the National Press Club Off-the-Record Forum on Press Censorship," Mar. 14, 1941, box 1, "Censorship 1941" folder, OF 1773.

8. BPM, 327, 329.

9. BP, "News Dissemination in Wartime," 158.

10. Barnouw, *History of Broadcasting*, 2:156. According to Title VI, Section 606(c) of the Communications Act of 1934, "Upon proclamation by the President that there exists war or a threat of war . . . the President may . . . cause the closing of any station for radio communication and the removal therefrom of its apparatus and equipment, or he may authorize the use or control of any such station and/ or its apparatus and equipment by any department of the Government under such regulations as he may prescribe, upon just compensation to the owners." See *USSL*, vol. 48, pt. 1, pp. 1104–5.

11. Landry, *This Fascinating Radio Business*, 245.

12. Doan, "Organization and Operation," 209.

13. Cable Censor, San Francisco, to District Intelligence Officer, Twelfth Naval District, Feb. 17, 1942; H. K. Fenn to BP, Mar. 19, 1942; and James Lawrence Fly to BP, Apr. 3, 1942, box 367, "Point-to-Point Circuits" folder, OC.

14. BP to James Lawrence Fly, Apr. 6, 1942, box 367, "Point-to-Point Circuits" folder, OC.

15. BPN, 1:90.

16. Francis Biddle to Franklin Roosevelt, May 18, 1942, "Exhibit U," *HOC*, 1:n.p.; BPN, 1:91; *Federal Radio Commission v. Nelson Brothers*.

17. BPM, 341–42.

18. Rosenman, *Public Papers*, 10:575.

19. BPN, 1:94.

20. HMJD, bk. 529.

21. BPM, 344.

22. Barnouw, *History of Broadcasting*, 2:169.

23. James Lawrence Fly, "Broadcasting As an Instrument of Democracy," Feb. 12, 1941, box 10, "Fly, James Lawrence" folder, LMP.

24. BPM, 344.

25. Grover, "Radio Censorship in Wartime," 38.

26. "Proceedings of the Censorship Policy Board, Meeting of May 19, 1942," HMJD, bk. 529. Radio stations had lost revenue from weather broadcasts, on-street interviews, and quiz shows that were knocked off the air by the censors, who feared that they could be exploited by enemy agents. In addition, stations in 1942 erroneously expected ad revenue to decline as consumer goods became scarce. Instead, wartime profits led to an advertising boom.

27. Office for Emergency Management, "Public Radio-Telegraph Traffic Within United States Closed by DCB," May 28, 1942, box 367, "Point-to-Point Circuits" folder, OC.

28. "Proceedings of the Censorship Policy Board, Meeting of May 19, 1942."

29. BPN, 1:94–95.

30. Koop, *Weapon of Silence*, 177.

31. The Office of Censorship completed its own historical analysis in accordance with a presidential directive of Mar. 4, 1942. The document ordered the "assembly and analysis of the administrative developments in each of the major fields of war administration exclusive of the strictly military." World War II mobilization had been hampered by the lack of detailed documentation from federal agencies in World War I. See Conn, *Historical Work in the United States Army,* 79–80.
32. Creel, *Rebel at Large,* 160.
33. Creel, *How We Advertised America,* 17.
34. Mock and Larson, *Words That Won the War,* 6–7.
35. Creel, *How We Advertised America,* 74–75.
36. Mock, *Censorship 1917,* 48; Creel, "Open Secrecy," 205, 207.
37. Creel, "Plight of the Last Censor," 34.
38. *USSL,* vol. 40, pt. 1, p. 219.
39. Chafee, *Government and Mass Communications,* 294–95; Washburn, *Question of Sedition,* 12.
40. Rogers, "Freedom of the Press," 178.
41. *USSL,* vol. 40, pt. 1, pp. 413, 426.
42. Stevens, *Shaping the First Amendment,* 49.
43. *USSL,* vol. 40, pt. 1, p. 553.
44. Washburn, *Question of Sedition,* 13. An appendix in Chafee, *Freedom of Speech,* 387–94, lists defendants who were prosecuted for speech that would be permissible in peacetime.
45. *United States ex. rel. Milwaukee Social Democratic Publishing Co. v. Burleson.*
46. The Supreme Court's 1931 ruling in *Near v. Minnesota ex rel Olson* limited the potential use of "prior restraint" to narrow issues of security and safety. Prior restraint would have simplified information control, at the expense of popular opinion, by blocking publication of stories deemed too dangerous by the government.
47. W. Preston Corderman, "Planning for the Operation of Postal and Wire Censorship," BPN, 1:n.p.
48. A. Smith, *Thank You,* 64; Steele, *Propaganda in an Open Society,* 34–35; Winfield, *F.D.R. and the News Media,* 29–31, 115.
49. Orrin E. Dunlap Jr., "Sentries Posted on the Radio," *NYT,* June 9, 1940, sec. 9.
50. Grover, "Radio Censorship in Wartime," 24–28; "Orders Radio Operators to Prove Citizenship," *NYT,* June 20, 1940; "The FCC to Add 'Policemen' to Patrol Radio under National Defense Program," *NYT,* July 7, 1940, sec. 9.
51. Short, "Hewing Straight to the Line," 167, 172.
52. CBS commentator Boake Carter lost his program in 1938 because his attacks on British foreign policy and Roosevelt upset the White House and his sponsor, General Foods. See Culbert, "U.S. Censorship of Radio News in the 1930s," 173–74.
53. "Free Press Urged in Peace of War," *NYT,* Oct. 3, 1939; "Sense and Censorship," 98.
54. Purcell, "Wartime Censorship in Canada," 93, box 6, folder 4, BPP.

55. Harry Chandler to Jesse H. Jones, May 11, 1940, and Stephen T. Early to Chandler, June 13, 1940, box 8, "Newspaper Publicity, World War II 1940" folder, OF 463 c.

56. Steele, *Propaganda in an Open Society*, 102–3.

57. Roosevelt, *Complete Press Conferences*, 14:131.

58. Rosenman, *Public Papers*, 8:461.

59. "Virtual News Censorship Set by War Department," *NYT*, June 14, 1940; Morrissey, "Disclosure and Secrecy," 10–12.

60. Frank Knox to David Lawrence, Dec. 31, 1940, box 64, "Frank Knox" file, David Lawrence Papers, Princeton University, Seeley G. Mudd Library, Princeton.

61. HMJD, bk. 348.

62. "Secret Spilled."

63. Turner Catledge, "Reporters Fingerprinted in Capital in Move to Check on Naval News," *NYT*, Feb. 6, 1941.

64. "Knox Asks People to Protect Navy," *NYT*, Feb. 9, 1941.

65. Roosevelt, *Complete Press Conferences*, 17:141–42, 146–48.

66. Koop, *Weapon of Silence*, 162.

67. "British Battleship Here, 20-Foot Hole in Her Side," *New York Herald Tribune*, Apr. 7, 1941; "Battered British Battleship Here," *New York Daily News*, Apr. 7, 1941; "Hands Across the Sea—And Pals Along the Bar," *New York Daily News*, Apr. 7, 1941; "Seen from Three Ferries," *New York Daily News*, Apr. 8, 1941.

68. "Damaged British Battleship Here for Repairs," *New York Daily News*, Apr. 7, 1941.

69. "British Battleship Here, 20-Foot Hole in Her Side."

70. "Crowds View British Warship," *New York Daily News*, Apr. 8, 1941; "Censorship, of Which the Less Is Better," 88.

71. ASNE, *Nineteenth Annual Convention*, 149.

72. Siebert, "Federal Information Agencies," 31.

73. Rosenman, *Public Papers*, 10:120.

74. "Small Publishers Reported Hit Hard," *NYT*, Apr. 23, 1941.

75. Roosevelt, *Complete Press Conferences*, 18:149.

76. "Secrecy Asked on Allied Aid Shipping," *NYT*, May 21, 1941; "Post Office Stops Mail Ship Listing," *NYT*, May 29, 1941.

77. "Knox Curbs News of Navy Actions," *NYT*, June 12, 1941; Siebert, "Federal Information Agencies," 31.

78. "Knox Hints Navy Has Shooting Right in Sea Lane Patrol," *NYT*, July 10, 1941; "Churchill Assails Talk by Wheeler," *NYT*, July 10, 1941.

79. McKay, "Civil Liberties Suspended"; "Mr. Knox's Censorship," 45. Many people of Japanese ancestry lived on Bainbridge Island and were the publisher's friends. The paper thus was less prone than others to anti-Japanese hysteria.

80. "Censorship Changes"; "Visiting Navy."

81. Steele, *Propaganda in an Open Society*, 108; Jeffery Smith, *War and Press Freedom*, 149.

82. Corderman, "Planning for and Operations of Postal and Wire Censorship."

83. Joint Board No. 325 (Serial 681), "Plan for National Censorship of International Communications (As Amended)," n.p., "Survey of Censorship Practices and Plans," box 10, "Censorship" folder, LMP.

84. Corderman, "Planning for and Operations of Postal and Wire Censorship."

85. BPN, 1:9; Koop, *Weapon of Silence,* 23.

86. Davenport, "You Can't Say That!" 19, 62.

87. Lowell Mellett to William J. Cheney, Charles Colebaugh, and Thomas H. Beck, Mar. 27, 1941, box 10, "Collier's . . . Davenport" folder, and Mellett to Frank Tripp and Grover Patterson, Mar. 6, 1941, box 15, "Newspaper Publishers Committee" folder, LMP.

88. Davenport, "Impregnable Pearl Harbor."

89. Steele, *Propaganda in an Open Society,* 90, 106.

90. "Censorship Intent Denied by Mellett," *NYT,* Feb. 27, 1941.

91. Francis Biddle, notes of Nov. 7, 1941, box 1, "Cabinet Meetings, 1941" folder, FBP.

92. HMJD, bk. 462.

93. Biddle, "Private Diary," 72.

94. HMJD, bk. 462.

95. Jeffery Smith, *War and Press Freedom,* 159; Knightley, *First Casualty,* 272.

96. Corderman, "Planning for and Operations of Postal and Wire Censorship."

97. "West Coast First to Go on Wartime Basis."

98. Roosevelt, *Complete Press Conferences,* 18:349–54.

99. Rosenman, *Public Papers,* 10:525.

100. Francis Biddle, notes of Dec. 7, 1941, box 1, "Cabinet Meetings, 1941" folder, FBP.

101. Franklin D. Roosevelt, "Memorandum for the Secretary of State, Secretary of the Treasury, Secretary of War, Secretary of the Navy, The Postmaster General, Chairman, Federal Communications Commission," Dec. 8, 1941, box 1, "Censorship 1941" folder, OF 1773.

102. JEH to Edwin M. Watson, Dec. 9, 1941, box 14, "Justice Department/FBI Reports 1941" folder, OF 10 b.

103. "In Re: Censorship," Dec. 9, 1941, and JEH to Edwin M. Watson, Dec. 10, 1941, box 14, "Justice Department/FBI Reports 1941" folder, OF 10 b.

104. Ibid.; BP, memorandum on censorship activities as of Feb. 15, 1942, box 1, "Office of Censorship 1941–42" folder, OF 4695; "Industry Takes Its Place in War Program"; Landry, *This Fascinating Radio Business,* 254. These records do not identify the stations that broadcast programs in Japanese before Dec. 7, 1941.

105. Kahn, *Codebreakers,* 527; BPN, 1:2.

106. Farago, *Game of the Foxes,* 656–57.

107. Corderman, "Planning for and Operations of Postal and Wire Censorship."

108. Toledano, *J. Edgar Hoover,* 173.

109. JEH, "The Present Practices in the Field of Censorship and Related Activities," Dec. 11, 1941, box 1, "Censorship 1941" folder, OF 1773.

110. Biddle, "Private Diary," 72; Kenneth G. Crawford, "FDR Picks AP Editor as

Censor," *PM,* Dec. 17, 1941; Lowell Mellett, "Memorandum to the President," May 5, 1941, box 5, "White House 1941" folder, LMP.

111. Francis Biddle, notes of Dec. 12, 1941, box 1, "Cabinet Meetings, 1941" folder, FBP; Walker, *FDR's Quiet Confidant,* 112.

112. Lowell Mellett, "Memorandum to Stephen T. Early," Dec. 19, 1941, box 11, "Correspondence—Mellett, Lowell" folder, STEP.

113. STE to "K.C." [Kent Cooper], Dec. 31, 1941, box 14, "Price, Byron" folder, STEP.

114. BPM, 204; BPN, 1:164; Walker, *FDR's Quiet Confidant,* 112.

115. BPM, 208; BP to STE, Dec. 15, 1941, box 1, "Office of Censorship 1941–42" folder, OF 4695.

116. Roosevelt, *Complete Press Conferences,* 18:369–70.

117. Frank L. Kluckhorn, "President Appoints Byron Price to Direct Wartime Censorship," *NYT,* Dec. 17, 1941.

118. "Censorship Chief."

119. "Nice Going, Mr. President!"

120. BP, interview by Raymond Henle, Mar. 21, 1969, box 5, folder 9, BPP.

121. Crawford, "FDR Picks AP Editor as Censor."

122. *USSL,* vol. 55, pt. 1, pp. 840–41.

123. Rosenman, *Public Papers,* 10:574–75; untitled news release, Jan. 10, 1942, box 2, censorship folder, Frederick S. Siebert Papers, Archives Division, State Historical Society of Wisconsin, Madison.

124. "Byron Price Sworn as Censorship Head," *NYT,* Dec. 21, 1941.

125. BPN, 1:70.

126. Koop, *Weapon of Silence,* 19.

127. Martha Ellyn, "Platter Chatter," *Washington Post,* July 17, 1942.

128. Burgeron, "Censor Who Fights for Freedom of the Press," 31; "Byron Price Collection," City Book Auction, Dec. 1, 1954, box 7, folder 6, BPP; "Where Are They Now," box 4, folder 6, BPP.

129. "This Is America's Director of Censorship"; BPM, 35–36.

130. Price was a first lieutenant, and later captain, of the 52nd Pioneer Infantry from 1917 to 1919. He was shelled near Verdun on Sept. 26, 1918. See BPM, "Miscellaneous Pages."

131. "Cecelia Ager Meets the Censor," *PM,* Apr. 20, 1942.

132. Knebel, "Placid Twenties," 72.

133. BPM, 84, 88.

134. BP, "What Licked the GOP? Practically Everything," unidentified clipping, Nov. 6, 1936, box 11, BPP.

135. Peter B. Flint, "Byron Price, Wartime Chief of U.S. Censorship, Is Dead," *NYT,* Aug. 8, 1981; BPM, 174.

136. HLSD, vol. 33 (microfilm reel 6): 36, 42; BPM, 286.

CHAPTER TWO

1. "Kansas City Bombed to Ruins," "Dastardly Saboteurs Wreck City," "Raid Hits Nation's Granary," and "Railroad Tracks Bombed at Olathe," *Kansas City Journal,* Mar. 2, 1942.
2. *HOC,* 2:32; JHS to Harry Newman, Mar. 6, 1942, box 1214, "Sorrells Reading File/March Readings," OC.
3. "Kansas City Fadeout," 70.
4. Box 389, "Code Violations" folder, OC.
5. BPN, 5:438.
6. BPM, 210–11.
7. Francis Biddle, notes of Dec. 19, 1941, box 1, "Cabinet Meetings, 1941" folder, FBP.
8. Stuart A. Rice to STE, Dec. 23, 1941, box 1, "Office of Censorship Miscellaneous" folder, OF 4695.
9. BPN, 1:120; "Newsmen Rumple Early in Churchill Story Scramble," *Washington Post,* Dec. 23, 1941; "Press Corps Knew about Churchill's Trip."
10. *HOC,* 2:4.
11. Koop, *Weapon of Silence,* 166.
12. BPM, 218; *HOC,* 1: 51. The board met five other times and never overruled Price's decisions.
13. BP to Franklin D. Roosevelt, Jan. 23, 1942, and Roosevelt to STE, Jan. 26, 1942, box 1, "Office of Censorship 1941–42" folder, OF 4695.
14. Postal censors in 1942 blocked the export of printed stories about military installations in Alaska, a combat zone. See BPN, 3:235.
15. Koop, *Weapon of Silence,* 24; *ROC,* 8.
16. Doan, "Organization and Operation," 200–202.
17. Koop, *Weapon of Silence,* 77.
18. "Status of the Office of Censorship," Dec. 19, 1942, BPN, 1:n.p. Censorship personnel peaked at 14,462 in February 1943, according to *ROC,* 8.
19. *ROC,* 32.
20. "John H. Sorrells, Journalist, Dead," *NYT,* Feb. 26, 1948; Koop, *Weapon of Silence,* 25.
21. BPM, 329–30.
22. "Ryan Well-Equipped"; "J. Harold Ryan, 74, Dies," *NYT,* June 7, 1961.
23. Koop, *Weapon of Silence,* 27.
24. *HOC,* 2:3–4.
25. JHS to Charles P. Manship Sr., Feb. 10, 1942, box 1214, "Sorrells Daily Reading File/February" folder, OC.
26. *HOC,* 2:4.
27. BPM, 295.
28. BPN, 1:71.
29. BPM, 225.
30. *CWPB,* Jan. 15, 1942.

31. Ibid.; *CWPP,* Jan. 15, 1942.
32. By December 1943, the military and the Office of Censorship had agreed that if a correspondent disputed a military censor's decision, Price's staff would act as a "friend of the court" in pleading the journalist's case but would abide by the ultimate military decision. Army officers successfully argued that journalists who got Price to overturn a decision might see their stories in print yet be punished by the army with loss of accreditation. Price had no power to overturn accreditation decisions. See *HOC,* 2:18.
33. BP, "Sorry—Restricted," 214.
34. "Rayburn Ropes a Steer."
35. *HOC,* 2:6–7.
36. BPM, 318–19.
37. BPN, 1:80.
38. "Censor's Office Works Smoothly on War News."
39. Jeffery Smith, *War and Press Freedom,* 158; Eisenhower, *Crusade in Europe,* 58; "Revised Text of Memorandum Approved Jointly by the State, War, and Navy Departments, and the Office of Censorship," May 29, 1942, BPN, 1:n.p. The army and navy had their own personnel reporting on the war. For a history of American military photographers in World War II, see Maslowski, *Armed with Cameras.* For a discussion of military combat and indoctrination films focusing on the propaganda value of Frank Capra's "Why We Fight" series, see Culbert, " 'Why We Fight.' "
40. BP to John O'Donnell, Mar. 3, 1942, BPN, 1:127. In addition to censoring news from overseas combat zones, the army and navy authorized the release of news from domestic bases.
41. "Censorship Code Meets Approval," *NYT,* Jan. 16, 1942.
42. "No Suppression of War Facts, Says U.S. Censor," *CT,* Jan. 19, 1942.
43. "Sensible Censorship," *NYT,* Jan. 19, 1942.
44. "Censorship Rules."
45. "Virginia Papers Willing to Invoke More Restrictions."
46. "Censorship Code Applied to Radio," *NYT,* Jan. 17, 1942.
47. JHS to Theodore F. Koop, Jan. 22, 1942, box 1214, "Sorrells Reading File," OC; "Price Picks 5 Advisers," *NYT,* Jan. 24, 1942.
48. *HOC,* 2:33 37; Koop, *Weapon of Silence,* 170.
49. See, for example, "Censorship Bulletin No. 3," in Voss, *Reporting the War,* 23, and "Censorship Bulletin No. 12," BPN, 2:n.p.
50. "Coast Papers Ask for Local Censor's Office"; "Minutes of the Editorial Advisory Board, May 14, 1942," *HOC,* 2:n.p.
51. Transcript of missionaries meeting, Apr. 14–15, 1942, *HOC,* 2:n.p.; "Editors in Attendance," box 7, folder 4, DAP; L. Mitchell White, "Special Censorship Bulletin—May 7, 1942," box 7, folder 4, DAP. The OC lists forty-nine missionaries, but only forty attended.
52. Transcript of missionaries meeting; "40 Editors to Help Censors as Observers."
53. Healy, *Lifetime on Deadline,* 105.

54. Transcript of missionaries meeting.

55. Healy, *Lifetime on Deadline,* 105.

56. "Three Clark Township Men on Ill-Fated Wasp," *Tell City, Ind., News,* Oct. 30, 1942.

57. Koop, *Weapon of Silence,* 171; "Minutes of Meeting of State Advisers and Helpers," Dec. 3, 1942, box 7, folder 4, DAP.

58. Charles M. Meredith to BP, Aug. 11, 1943, box 110, "Pennsylvania" folder, OC.

59. NRH to Don Anderson, June 23, 1942, box 7, folder 4, DAP.

60. John W. Potter, "Voluntary Censorship Plan Succeeding"; *Inland Daily Press Association Bulletin,* June 1942, 345–46, box 7, folder 4, DAP.

61. BPM, 303.

62. Don Anderson to Wisconsin Editors, July 1, 1942, box 7, folder 4, DAP.

63. Don Anderson to NRH, May 19, 1943, box 110, "Coop. Newspapers Wisconsin" folder, OC.

64. Doan, "Organization and Operation," 211.

65. *HOC,* 2:276.

66. Eugene Carr to JHR, Dec. 21, 1942, box 111, "Carr's Trip 5/17–6/14/43" folder, OC; JHR, transcript of Radio Executives Club talk, Feb. 17, 1943, box 922, "Speeches—Ryan" folder, OC.

67. "Censored"; Neuberger, "Wilderness Defense," 42.

68. Marshall, "Western Rampart."

69. Sypher, "No Snoops Stop Scoops," 38; "Status of the Office of Censorship on December 19, 1942," BPN, 2:n.p.

70. *HOC,* 2:32.

71. "Birds, Beasts Usher in Spring," *New York World-Telegram,* Mar. 21, 1942; and JHS to B. O. McAnney, Mar. 25, 1942, and JHS to Mrs. R. J. Riblet, Mar. 28, 1942, box 1214, "Sorrells Reading File/March Readings," OC.

72. JHS to Fred M. McLennan, Feb. 19, 1942, box 1214, "Sorrells Daily Reading File/February" folder, OC.

73. Ibid., Feb. 27, 1942.

74. Fred M. McLennan to NRH, Sept. 9, 1942, and NRH to McLennan, Sept. 12, 1942, box 389, "Complaints Re: Press Censorship/'B'" folder, OC.

75. ASNE, *Twentieth Annual Convention,* 27–28.

76. Eleanor Roosevelt, "The Censor Has Written Me a Stern Letter," *Washington Daily News,* Aug. 17, 1942.

77. BPN, 1:135–36; "DSM for Mr. Price," *Danville, Va., Register,* Aug. 18, 1942.

78. "Note to Managing Editors," May 22, 1942, BPN, 6:n.p.

79. J. H. Keen, "Observations," *Philadelphia Daily News,* June 6, 1942; "Memorandum by N. R. Howard," June 8, 1942, box 563, "Molotov" folder, OC.

80. William Mylander to NRH, June 6, 1942, box 563, "Molotov" folder, OC.

81. BP, "For Immediate Release," June 12, 1942, box 563, "Molotov" folder, OC. The headlines appeared in the *Atlanta Constitution,* June 15, 1942; *Dayton Daily News,* June 13, 1942; and *Los Angeles Examiner,* June 13, 1942, respectively.

82. Leonard Lyons, "The Lyons Den," *New York Post,* June 18, 1942; William Mylander to NRH, June 6, 1942; "Memorandum by N. R. Howard," June 8, 1942;

and "Memo by N. R. Howard," Sept. 22, 1942, box 563, "Molotov" folder, OC. Ellmaker feared that if Molotov were killed, his paper might be blamed.

83. BPN, 1:60.

84. BPM, 304; Trohan interview.

85. BPM, 304–5, 325.

86. Trohan interview.

87. "The Censorship," *CT*, Dec. 18, 1941.

88. BPN, 1:38.

89. STE to BP, May 29, 1942, box 14, "Price, Byron" folder, STEP.

90. Igor Cassini, "These Charming People," *Washington Times-Herald,* May 29, 1942. The clipping with the offending paragraph marked in ink is in box 14, "Price, Byron" folder, STEP.

91. BP to STE, May 30, 1942, box 14, "Price, Byron" folder, STEP.

92. Hoge, *Cissy Patterson*, xi.

93. BP to Eleanor Patterson, May 29, 1942, box 14, "Price, Byron" folder, STEP.

94. Eleanor Patterson to BP, June 1, 1942, ibid.

95. BPN, 1:40.

96. Frank C. Waldrop to BP, June 4, 1942, ibid.

97. Jeffery Smith, *War and Press Freedom,* 152; BPM, 308–10; *CWPP,* June 15, 1942.

98. Eric Hodgins to BP, July 1, 1942, BPN, 1:42.

99. "What Sense Censorship?"

100. BP to Eric Hodgins, July 7, 1942, BPN, 1:43.

101. Eric Hodgins to BP, July 8, 1942, BPN, 1:44.

102. "Editor of 'Time' Lambastes the 'Pollyanna' Press," unidentified clipping, Oct. 6 [1942], BPN, 2:n.p.

103. Eric Hodgins to BP, Oct. 9, 1942, BPN, 2:n.p.

104. *CWPP,* Feb. 1, 1943; *CWPP,* Dec. 1, 1943.

105. Arthur Hays Sulzberger to Franklin D. Roosevelt, Feb. 24, 1941, "Censorship 1939–1961" folder, *NYT* Archives.

106. Arthur Hays Sulzberger to "Colonel" [Knox], Apr. 8, 1941; memo to Knox, Apr. 14, 1941; and Arthur Krock to Edwin L. James, "Censorship 1939–1961" folder, *NYT* Archives.

107. Edwin L. James to Arthur Krock, Jan. 15, 1942, "Censorship 1939–1961" folder, *NYT* Archives.

108. Arthur Hays Sulzberger to Arthur Krock, June 9, 1941; Sulzberger to Krock, Dec. 9, 1941; and BP to Sulzberger, May 26, 1942, "Censorship 1939–1961" folder, *NYT* Archives.

109. Hanson Baldwin, "South Pacific War Develops on a Vast Scale," *NYT,* Oct. 4, 1942, sec. 4.

110. BPM, 313.

111. "Wanted: Facts, Not Lectures," *NYT,* Oct. 4, 1942, sec. 4.

112. BPM, 314. The *Times* archives do not mention Sulzberger's meeting with Price.

113. Voss, *Reporting the War,* 26.

114. Winkler, *Politics of Propaganda,* 49.

115. BPM, 315; "Censorship 1939–1961" folder, *NYT* Archives.

116. "U.S. Has Announced All Sinkings of Major Warships, Davis Says," *NYT,* Oct. 29, 1942; "Confidential and Otherwise," *NYT,* Oct. 30, 1942.
117. Biddle, "Private Diary," 43.
118. *ROC,* 42.
119. Krock, *Memoirs,* 185.
120. "Publishers Approve Amended Censor's Code."
121. Brandenburg, "Censorship, Delivery Problems," 5.
122. Koop, *Weapon of Silence,* 173.

CHAPTER THREE

1. "Army Officer Held; Sedition Report Probed," *Seattle Post-Intelligencer,* Dec. 11, 1942; AP transcript, Dec. 11, 1942, BPN, 1:n.p.
2. Ribuffo, *Old Christian Right,* 65–66, 76, 185; Biddle, *In Brief Authority,* 236.
3. AP transcript, Dec. 11, 1942.
4. "Headline Curb Is Denied," *NYT,* Dec. 12, 1942; "Informal Censorship."
5. AP transcript, Dec. 11, 1942.
6. BPN, 1:243; NRH to Herbert K. Fenn, box 1415, "Violations and Suppressions" folder, OC.
7. AP transcript, Dec. 11, 1942.
8. Grover, "Radio Censorship in Wartime," 48.
9. BPM, 405.
10. Eisenhower, *Crusade in Europe,* 299.
11. Winfield, *F.D.R. and the News Media,* 232.
12. Biddle, "Private Diary," 74.
13. Ibid.; Rosenman, *Working with Roosevelt,* 321–22.
14. Roosevelt, *Complete Press Conferences,* 20:304–5; Winfield, *F.D.R. and the News Media,* 68.
15. Burns, *Roosevelt,* 216.
16. Biddle, *In Brief Authority,* 237–38.
17. BPM, 317–18.
18. "Biddle Proposes Law"; BPN, 1:117.
19. BPN, 1:117–19.
20. "Threat to Freedom of Press?" 14.
21. Arthur Krock, "A Bill Which Is an Invitation to Tyranny," *NYT,* Feb. 19, 1942.
22. BPN, 1:119.
23. Ibid., 116.
24. Francis Biddle, notes of Mar. 20, 1942, box 1, "Cabinet Meetings Jan.–June 1942" folder, FBP.
25. Washburn, *Question of Sedition,* 51, 69, 76; BPN, 2:111.
26. BPN, 2:111–12.
27. JHS to Justin A. Rollman, Mar. 21, 1942, box 1214, "Sorrells Reading File/ March" folder, OC.

28. Roscoe Drummond, "'Defeatist Bund' Stabs U.S. War Effort," *Christian Science Monitor*, Mar. 10, 1942. The publications Drummond named as subversive were the *Galilean, X-Ray, Publicity, Defender, Social Justice, Fiery Cross,* and *America in Danger*.

29. Shirer, "Poison Pen," 548, 552.

30. "Voices of Defeat," 92–94; Washburn, *Question of Sedition,* 120.

31. Marcus, *Father Coughlin,* 211–12; "Have the Reds Got Us"; "'Up with Communism.'"

32. Chafee, *Government and Mass Communications,* 320.

33. Marcus, *Father Coughlin,* 214; Charles Coughlin to Francis Biddle, Apr. 20, 1942, box 2, "Coughlin, Charles" folder, FBP.

34. Francis Biddle, notes of May 1 and May 7, 1942, box 1, "Cabinet Meetings Jan.–June 1942" folder, FBP.

35. "Now Let's Go after Some Real Game," *PM,* May 5, 1942.

36. Sayers and Kahn, *Sabotage!,* 243–44; "Three Publications Denied 2nd Class Mail Privileges"; Washburn, *Question of Sedition,* 121.

37. Washburn, *Question of Sedition,* 120–21; Siebert, "Wartime Communications," pt. 1, p. 46.

38. Washburn, *Question of Sedition,* 122.

39. Biddle, *In Brief Authority,* 248.

40. Frank, "United States Navy v. Chicago Tribune," 286.

41. Trohan interview.

42. Frank, "United States Navy v. Chicago Tribune," 287–88.

43. Gies, *Colonel of Chicago,* 208.

44. "Navy Had Word of Jap Plan to Strike at Sea," *CT,* June 7, 1942.

45. Gies, *Colonel of Chicago,* 206.

46. Richard Smith, *Colonel,* 433.

47. HLSD, vol. 39 (microfilm reel 7) 94–95.

48. Trohan interview.

49. BPN, 1:122.

50. Biddle, *In Brief Authority,* 249; Richard Smith, *Colonel,* 433.

51. Voss, *Reporting the War,* 38.

52. BPN, 1:126–28.

53 Justice Department news release, Aug. 7, 1942, BPN, 1:133.

54. Biddle, *In Brief Authority,* 250.

55. "Tribune Defeats Navy"; "Navy v. Tribune," 65.

56. *Congressional Record,* 77th Cong., 2d sess., 1942, vol. 88, pt. 5, p. 7011.

57. Biddle, *In Brief Authority,* 251.

58. Gies, *Colonel of Chicago,* 210; Goren, "Communication Intelligence," 669; Kahn, *Codebreakers,* 599–600.

59. "Admiral Andrews Tells His Part"; "Press Heads Set A-Whirling."

60. "Press Heads Set A-Whirling."

61. "Admiral Andrews Tells His Part."

62. "Press Heads Set A-Whirling."

63. "Navy Apologizes for Confusion."

64. "Note to Managing Editors," Feb. 4, 1942, box 146, "Confidential Notes to Editors" folder, OC; BPN, 1:25; BPM, 408.

65. Transcript of missionaries meeting, Apr. 14–15, 1942, *HOC*, 2:n.p.

66. JHS to Arthur Krock, Feb. 23, 1942, box 1214, "Sorrells Daily Reading File/February" folder, OC.

67. Transcript of missionaries meeting.

68. Robb, "Shop Talk at Thirty," Mar. 7, 1942.

69. JL to JHS and NRH, Feb. 24, 1942, box 1395, "February 16–March 1 Day File," OC.

70. Robb, "Shop Talk at Thirty," Mar. 7, 1942.

71. NRH to Don Morris, Feb. 25, 1942, box 1395, "February 16–March 1 Day File," OC.

72. Robb, "Shop Talk at Thirty," Mar. 7, 1942.

73. Humphreys, "How Your News Is Censored," 16.

74. BPN, 1:25.

75. Alexander D. Surles to BP, Jan. 20, 1942, and BP to Surles, Jan. 26, 1942, BPN, 1:78.

76. JL to JHS, NRH, and JHR, Feb. 23, 1942, box 1395, "February 16–March 1 Day File," OC.

77. BP, "Note to Managing Editors," Feb. 25, 1942, box 146, "Confidential Notes to Editors" folder, OC.

78. BPN, 1:29; "Private Message to Newspapers and Radio Stations," box 14, "Price, Byron" folder, STEP.

79. *CWPP,* June 15, 1942; *CWPB,* June 15, 1942.

80. *CWPP,* June 15, 1942.

81. "To the Editor," Dec. 22, 1942; "For Immediate Release," S-1086; and "To the Editor," PR-40, Feb. 4, 1943, BPN, 6:n.p.

82. "The Name and Number of Their Fighting Force," poster identified as O-506503, *HOC,* 2:n.p.

83. "Price, Early Endorse Press' Anniversary," *Atlanta Daily World,* Mar. 4, 1942; BP to John H. Sengstacke, April 25, 1942, box 550, "Negro Press" folder, OC.

84. NRH, "Memorandum," Apr. 19, 1943, and NRH to Frank Marshall Davis, Apr. 19, 1943, box 504, "Negro Troops" folder, OC.

85. Associated Negro Press Inc., "Confidential Note to Editors," Apr. 21, 1943, box 504, "Negro Troops" folder, OC.

86. "Negro Troops Poised for Big Second Front Push," *Chicago Defender* (national edition), Jan. 8, 1944; and Jim Warner to JL, Jan. 3, 1944; "Book of Three" telegram, Jan. 3, 1944; and Metz T. P. Lochard to JL, Jan. 5, 1944, box 504, "Negro Troops" folder, OC.

87. Winkler, *Politics of Propaganda,* 29.

88. BPN, 1:140.

89. Ibid; Rosenman, *Public Papers,* 11:280.

90. BPN, 1:141.

91. BP, "Memorandum for . . . Stephen Early," Mar. 18, 1942, BPN, 2:142; "Draft of Executive Order," BPN, 2:n.p.

92. Frank C. Walker to Franklin D. Roosevelt, May 19, 1942, and Roosevelt, memo, Mar. 21, 1942, "United States Information Center Endorsements" folder, OF 4850 a.

93. Rosenman, *Public Papers*, 11:274–78.

94. Arthur Krock, "In Wartime What News Shall the Nation Have?" *NYT Magazine*, Aug. 16, 1942.

95. Eugene Katz to Ralph E. Smiley, Oct. 17, 1942, and Katz to M. S. Eisenhower, Oct. 21, 1942, "Records of the Office of the Director, Records of the Director, 1942–45," box 1, "Clearance I—OWI-Censorship Agreement, 1942–43" folder, OWI. Also see "To R. K. Richards, Eugene Carr," Oct. 3, 1942; Carr to JHR, Oct. 3, 1942; and Richards to JHR, Oct. 6, 1942, box 107, "Office of War Information" folder, OC.

96. "Agreement between the Office of War Information and the Office of Censorship," Nov. 15, 1942, box 107, "Office of War Information/November 1942" folder, OC.

97. ASNE, "Bulletin No. 1," Mar. 19, 1943, BPN, 3:284–85; Arthur Krock, "Covenants That Are Not 'Openly Arrived At,'" *NYT*, Apr. 13, 1943.

98. *CWPP*, Feb. 1, 1943.

99. BPN, 3:286.

100. NRH to BP, Apr. 2, 1943, and "Agreement between the Office of War Information and the Office of Censorship," Revised Apr. 10, 1943, box 108, "OC-OWI Agreement" folder, OC.

101. "Candid Survey of Anti-Jewish Prejudice."

102. Koenigsberg, "Press Gains Access," 7; Prevost, "Reporters See Session on Relief."

103. Roeder, "Note on U.S. Photo Censorship in WWII," 192; Roeder, *Censored War*, 10.

104. Roeder, *Censored War*, 14, 20–21.

105. Ibid., 92; Knightley, *First Casualty*, 276.

106. BPM, 419.

107. BP to George V. Strong, Jan. 6, 1944, box 26, "Censorship (Codes)" folder, STEP; BPM, 422.

108. BPM, 424–25.

109. *HOC*, 2:103.

110. "Price Control."

111. BP to George V. Strong, Jan. 8, 1944, box 26, "Censorship (Codes)" folder, STEP; HLSD, vol. 45 (microfilm reel 8): 136.

112. Leahy, *I Was There*, 217–18, 433.

113. BPM, 387.

114. Elmer Davis to Franklin D. Roosevelt, Jan. 8, 1944, and Robert Sherwood to Roosevelt, Jan. 13, 1944, box 155, "Office of War Information, 1942–44," PSF; "Sherwood, Davis Go to Roosevelt," *NYT*, Jan. 26, 1944.

115. BPM, 387.
116. Healy, *Lifetime on Deadline,* 115.
117. BP, "Memorandum for the President," Jan. 28, 1944, "General Correspondence 1908–1944," box 1, folder 1, BPP.
118. BPM, 389; Healy, *Lifetime on Deadline,* 115.

CHAPTER FOUR

1. "Gallarneau Scores Twice, Pool Once for Pro Champions" and "Play by Play Story of All-Star Game," *CT,* Aug. 29, 1942.
2. "Gallarneau Scores Twice."
3. Stanley P. Richardson to R. E. Spencer, Aug. 29, 1942, box 351, "Weather Reports/Sports" folder, OC.
4. F. W. Reichelderfer to Bob Elson, Sept. 10, 1942, and Reichelderfer to Stanley P. Richardson, Sept. 10, 1942, box 351, "Weather Reports/Sports" folder, OC.
5. Barnouw, *History of Broadcasting,* 1:37.
6. Charnley, *News by Radio,* 6; Lazarsfeld and Stanton, *Radio Research,* 119.
7. "Weather Reports Are Banned in Ruling by Federal Bureau."
8. *USSL,* vol. 48, pt. 1, pp. 1104–5; "Limits on Weather Broadcasts."
9. "Weather Reports Back on Air."
10. "Care in News Broadcasts."
11. BPN, 1:72; *HOC,* 1:12.
12. BPN, 1:73.
13. *CWPP,* Jan. 15, 1942; *CWPB,* Jan. 15, 1942. What the press code meant to a paper such as the *Kansas City Star,* on the Missouri-Kansas border and in the middle of the weather-conscious Farm Belt, is that it could print a story about recent weather conditions in Kansas, or in Missouri, but not both on the same day. The *Star* decided to print stories about Missouri weather on Mondays, Wednesdays, and Fridays, and Kansas weather on Tuesdays, Thursdays, and Saturdays.
14. *ROC,* 37; JHS to Charles T. Manship, Feb. 10, 1942, box 1214, "Sorrells Daily Reading File/February" folder, OC.
15. *CWPB,* Jan. 15, 1942.
16. *ROC,* 34.
17. BPM, 332–33.
18. Fox, *Madison Avenue Goes to War,* 41.
19. Adams, "Advertising Giant Is Tottering"; Sterling and Kittross, *Stay Tuned,* 638.
20. "Censorship Strikes Hard."
21. "Drop 'Mail Bag' Programs."
22. "Government to Run Short-Wave Radio," *NYT,* Feb. 19, 1942; "U.S. Takes over Short Waves," 30; "U.S. Short Waves."
23. "War Code Brings Program Changes."
24. JHR, "The Test—Can the Enemy Utilize It?"
25. "Easing of Code for Disc Remotes Asked"; "Ryan Denies Shepard's Appeal."
26. "Censorship Rules Bring Net Praise."

27. *CWPB,* Jan. 15, 1942.

28. BP, transcript of NBC talk, BPN, 1:n.p.

29. "Purely Programs."

30. Koop, *Weapon of Silence,* 182.

31. "Controlled Remote Interview Allowed."

32. JHR, "The Test—Can the Enemy Utilize It?"

33. *HOC,* 2:217–18; Edward H. Bronson to Robert K. Richards, Dec. 9, 1942, box 354, "Seuren, Willie" folder, OC; Bronson to Ross Pope, Oct. 22, 1943, box 353, "Program Monitoring" folder, OC.

34. JHR to H. K. Fenn, Aug. 11, 1942, and BP to James Lawrence Fly, May 29, 1943, box 351, "Weather Reports/Sports" folder, OC.

35. JHR to Fenn, Aug. 11, 1942, box 351, "Weather Reports/Sports" folder, OC.

36. BP to Fly, May 29, 1943, box 351, "Weather Reports/Sports" folder, OC.

37. *CWPB,* Jan. 15, 1942.

38. JHR, "R-4," Mar. 20, 1942, BPN, 6:n.p.

39. T. J. Slowie to Edward H. Bronson, July 13, 1943, file 19-2c, "Departmental-Director of Censorship," Federal Communications Commission, Record Group 173, National Archives Annex, College Park.

40. JHR to Maynard Marquardt, July 16, 1943, and Marquardt to JHR, July 20, 1943, box 351, "Weather Reports/Sports" folder, OC.

41. "Extreme Weather," in untitled green notebook, box 1427, OC; *CWPB,* Feb. 1, 1943.

42. "Tornado a Radio Secret."

43. *CWPB,* June 15, 1942.

44. *HOC,* 2:219.

45. "Love Thwarted."

46. George Erwin to Office of Censorship, Nov. 12, 1942, and Robert K. Richards to Erwin, Nov. 16, 1942, box 334, "Santa Claus Programs" folder, OC.

47. BP, transcript of N.A.B. talk, BPN, 4:n.p.

48. *HOC,* 2:219.

49. "Broadcast Memorandum by Pete Cousins," Aug. 2, 1945, box 862, "Radio Division Reports/Misc." folder, OC.

50. *HOC,* 2:219.

51. JHR, "R-19," BPN, 6:n.p.

52. *HOC,* 2:219.

53. "Weather Order."

54. "Weather Reports Back on Air."

55. Koop, *Weapon of Silence,* 209; *CWPPR.*

56. JHR, "R-21," Mar. 29, 1944, BPN, 6:n.p.

57. Koop, *Weapon of Silence,* 182.

58. E. N. Thwaites to BP, Aug. 19, 1943, box 359, "KFUN" folder, OC.

59. Robert K. Richards to Arthur Simon, Oct. 4, 1943, box 110, "Field Representatives . . . August 1943" folder, OC.

60. Thwaites to BP, Aug. 19, 1943, box 359, "KFUN" folder, OC.

61. *CWPB,* Feb. 1, 1943.

62. Koop, *Weapon of Silence*, 184.

63. Edward H. Bronson to Robert K. Richards and JHR, Apr. 23, 1943, box 107, "Government Agencies/FCC" folder, OC. Broadcast Division censor Eugene Carr had a similar trip Oct. 19 to Dec. 11, 1942, traveling 10,000 miles to visit eighteen N.A.B. district conventions. See Carr, "Voluntary Censorship Will Work!"

64. *ROC*, 34.

65. BPN, 4:415.

66. BPM, 345.

67. Edward H. Bronson to JHR and Robert K. Richards, July 20, 1943, box 862, "Radio Division Reports/Misc." folder, OC.

68. Harry Burdick to JHR, July 9, 1943, box 110, "Field Representatives . . . August 1943" folder, OC.

69. Mitchell interview. Thwaites died in a plane crash in 1963 and left no papers at KFUN on his clash with censorship.

70. Thwaites to BP, Aug. 19, 1943, box 359, "KFUN" folder, OC.

71. JHR to BP, Sept. 13, 1943, box 359, "KFUN" folder, OC; BPM, 347–48.

72. Robert K. Richards to BP, Aug. 23, 1943, box 359, "KFUN" folder, OC.

73. Ibid.; E. H. Bronson to BP, JHR, and Robert K. Richards, Aug. 23, 1943, box 359, "KFUN" folder, OC.

74. BPN, 4:n.p.

75. "Memorandum," Aug. 24, 1943, box 359, "KFUN" folder, OC.

76. *USSL*, vol. 55, pt. 1, p. 841.

77. E. N. Thwaites to BP, Aug. 24, 1943, box 359, "KFUN" folder, OC; BPN, 4:420.

78. John J. Dempsey to BP, Sept. 1, 1943, box 359, "KFUN" folder, OC.

79. BP to John J. Dempsey, Sept. 15, 1943, box 359, "KFUN" folder, OC.

80. BPN, 4:420; JHR to BP, Sept. 13, 1943, box 359, "KFUN" folder, OC.

81. BPN, 4:421.

82. BP to E. N. Thwaites, Sept. 15, 1943, box 359, "KFUN" folder, OC.

83. BP to E. N. Thwaites, Sept. 27, 1943, and Thwaites to BP, Oct. 2, 1943, box 359, "KFUN" folder, OC.

84. Edward H. Bronson to JHR, Feb. 22, 1944, box 359, "KFUN" folder, OC.

85. Paul Freund, "Memorandum for Mr. Byron Price," Sept. 18, 1942, "Records of the Office of the Director, Records of the Director 1942–45," box 1, "Clearance I—OWI-Censorship Agreement, 1942–43" folder, OWI.

86. For sources on the changing number of foreign-language stations, see "From a Report of J. Edgar Hoover," Dec. 11, 1941, box 1, "Censorship 1941" folder, OF 1773; JHR to BP, Aug. 21, 1942, box 353, "Program Monitoring" folder, OC; JHR to BP, Sept. 13, 1943, box 359, "KFUN" folder, OC; "Foreign Language Group Will Parley," and Arthur Simon, transcript of "Foreign Language Round Table Session, National Association of Broadcasters," Apr. 28, 1943, box 110, "Field Representatives Foreign Language" folder, OC.

87. Koop, *Weapon of Silence*, 183–84. Koop does not give dates for his statistics about foreign-language stations' code violations. However, these dates can be deduced from other sources. Koop said the first recordings of foreign-language programs

that the Office of Censorship received from the FCC had five times as many violations as their English-language counterparts. The first FCC recordings arrived in late September 1942. Koop said stations began reducing their violations "not long" after Broadcasting Division censors toured the country to urge compliance; the last such tour ended in April 1943. See Edward H. Bronson to JHR, Oct. 27, 1942, box 353, "Program Monitoring" folder, OC.

88. JEH to BP, Dec. 23, 1943, box 360, "Foreign Language Broadcasts/Lists—Announcers and Employees" folder, OC.

89. *HOC,* "Exhibit CC," 1:n.p.

90. *CWPB,* Jan. 15, 1942.

91. "Censorship Strikes Hard"; "Negative Side of Foreign Language Operations."

92. *CWPB,* June 15, 1942.

93. Bodec, "Foreign Stations 'Confess' "; "Radio Daffodils."

94. "Foreign-Language Control"; Arthur Simon, transcript of "Foreign Language Round Table Session, National Association of Broadcasters," Apr. 28, 1943, box 110, "Field Representatives Foreign Language" folder, OC.

95. "Foreign Language Radio—OWI," n.d., "Records of the Office of War Information," box 1081, "Foreign Language Radio" folder, OWI; "Basic Clauses of Foreign Tongue Code"; "Personal History Statement," box 353, "Lido Belli" folder, OC.

96. "Voluntary Code of Wartime Practices for American Broadcasters Presenting Programs in Foreign Languages," *HOC,* 1:n.p. The text is reprinted in "Linguals Hope Davis Will Sweep Red Tape."

97. "Simon Urges Care." Falk died in 1999 without having responded to two requests for an interview by the author.

98. "Garey Says 'Gestapo' Charges Justified," 62; JHR to BP, Aug. 19, 1942, box 353, "Program Monitoring" folder, OC.

99. "Foreign Language Radio—OWI," n.d., "Records of the Office of War Information," box 1081, "Foreign Language Radio" folder, OWI.

100. "Garey Says 'Gestapo' Charges Justified," 62.

101. Ibid. *Broadcasting* did not report the date of the OWI–Wartime Control Committee meeting.

102. BPN, 4:415; M. S. Eisenhower to Alan Cranston, Oct. 23, 1942, "Records of the Office of the Director, Records of the Director 1942–45," box 1, "Clearance I— OWI-Censorship Agreement, 1942–43" folder, OWI.

103. "Censorship Centralized under New Code."

104. JHR to BP, Aug. 19, 1942, box 353, "Program Monitoring" folder, OC.

105. "Report 1," box 353, "Program Monitoring" folder, OC.

106. Robert K. Richards to JHR, Aug. 20, 1942, box 353, "Program Monitoring" folder, OC.

107. JHR to BP, Aug. 21, 1942, box 353, "Program Monitoring" folder, OC.

108. "Report 1," box 353, "Program Monitoring" folder, OC.

109. "Report 2," box 353, "Program Monitoring" folder, OC.

110. Ibid.

111. "Report 3," box 353, "Program Monitoring" folder, OC.
112. Robert K. Richards to BP and JHR, Aug. 27, 1943, box 353, "Program Monitoring" folder, OC.
113. "Report 5," box 353, "Program Monitoring" folder, OC.
114. "Report 4," box 353, "Program Monitoring" folder, OC.
115. "Foreign-Language Control Outlined."
116. Edward H. Bronson to Ross Pope, Oct. 22, 1943, box 353, "Program Monitoring" folder, OC. The Post Office Department translated other languages.
117. Edward H. Bronson, "FCC Order Slip" for Station WSAR, Oct. 4, 1943, box 353, "Program Monitoring" folder, OC.
118. G. E. Sterling to Scituate supervisor, "Unit Case No. NA-9-250," Sept. 25, 1943, box 353, "Program Monitoring" folder, OC.
119. Robert K. Richards to James B. Sanders, Apr. 3, 1943, box 353, "Program Monitoring" folder, OC.
120. Edward H. Bronson to Ross Pope, Oct. 22, 1943, box 353, "Program Monitoring" folder, OC.
121. Edward H. Bronson to Robert K. Richards, Dec. 9, 1942, box 353, "Program Monitoring" folder, OC.
122. Ibid.
123. "Report 5," box 353, "Program Monitoring" folder, OC.
124. Edward H. Bronson to Robert K. Richards, Dec. 9, 1942, box 353, "Program Monitoring" folder, OC.
125. Ibid.
126. Kurth, *American Cassandra,* 286–87.
127. Edward H. Bronson to Robert K. Richards, Dec. 9, 1942; Bronson to Richards, Dec. 31, 1942; and JEH to Elmer Davis, n.d., box 354, "Seuren, Willie" folder, OC.
128. BPN, 3:244.
129. BP to E. Douglass Hibbs, Jan. 18, 1943, box 354, "Seuren, Willie" folder, OC.
130. Robert K. Richards to JHR, Jan. 21, 1943, and Richards to JHR, Sept. 2, 1943, box 354, "Seuren, Willie," folder, OC.
131. BP, "Memorandum for Files," Jan. 28, 1943, box 354, "Seuren, Willie" folder, OC.
132. E. Douglass Hibbs to BP, Feb. 1, 1943, box 354, "Seuren, Willie" folder, OC.
133. *CWPB,* Feb. 1, 1943.
134. "Analysis of the German-American Housewife Hour," n.d., box 354, "Personnel Investigations/WBNX" folder; Charter Heslep to JHR, Sept. 25, 1942, box 354, "Personnel Investigations/WBNX" folder; Edward H. Bronson to JHR, Sept. 17, 1942, box 107, "Government Agencies/FCC" folder; and Robert K. Richards to JHR, June 15, 1943, box 107, "Government Agencies/FCC" folder, all in OC.
135. Edward H. Bronson to BP, JHR, and Robert K. Richards, June 5, 1943, box 353, "FBI Reports" folder, OC.
136. BPN, 4:416; T. J. Slowie to Robert K. Richards, Apr. 7, 1943, file 19-2 c, "Departmental-Director of Censorship," Federal Communications Commission, Record Group 173, National Archives Annex, College Park.

137. Robert K. Richards to JHR, Apr. 8, 1943, box 353, "Raffaele Borrelli" folder, OC.

138. Hooper-Holmes Bureau, "Special Report, Borrelli: Ralph J.," Apr. 12, 1943, box 353, "Raffaele Borrelli" folder, OC.

139. BP to Horace L. Lohnes, Apr. 21, 1943, box 353, "Raffaele Borrelli" folder, OC.

140. Robert K. Richards to JHR, Apr. 8, 1943, and Ralph J. Borrelli, "To Whom It May Concern," n.d., box 353, "Raffaele Borrelli" folder, OC.

141. "Garey Says 'Gestapo' Charges Justified," 63; BPN, 4:416.

142. Borrelli, "To Whom It May Concern," n.d., box 353, "Raffaele Borrelli" folder, OC.

143. BP to Joseph F. Guffey, May 28, 1943, box 353, "Raffaele Borrelli" folder, OC.

144. BPN, 4:417.

145. Edward H. Bronson to Field Representatives, n.d., box 110, "Field Representatives . . . August 1943" folder, OC.

146. JHR to Calvin J. Smith, Dec. 17, 1943, box 110, "Field Representatives . . . August 1943" folder, OC.

147. W. L. Gleeson to JHR, Sept. 21, 1943, and memorandum, n.d., box 110, "Field Representatives . . . August 1943" folder, OC.

148. "Tribute to Foreign Tongue Stations."

149. Edward H. Bronson to JHR, Dec. 13, 1943, and memorandum, Dec. 21, 1943, box 110, "Field Representatives . . . August 1943" folder, OC. Also see Bronson to JHR, Dec. 12, 1943, box 353, "Program Monitoring" folder, OC.

150. CWPPR.

CHAPTER FIVE

1. Koop, Weapon of Silence, 175.

2. BPN, 1:99.

3. John E. Fetzer to BP, Feb. 8, 1945, box 315, "Complaints Re: Radio Censorship/ 'C'" folder, OC.

4. HOC, 2:221.

5. Eugene Carr to JHR, July 19, 1942, box 338, "Winchell, Walter, July 1943 Commentaries" folder, OC.

6. Eugene Carr to JHR, July 15, 1942, box 338, "Winchell, Walter, July 1943 Commentaries" folder, OC; BPM, 358–59.

7. Eugene Carr to JHR, July 19, 1942, box 338, "Winchell, Walter, July 1943 Commentaries" folder, OC.

8. Lester Halpin to JHR, Aug. 1, 1943, box 338, "Winchell, Walter, July 1943 Commentaries" folder; Charter Heslep to JHR, Sept. 17, 1944, box 338, "Winchell, Walter, August 1944 Commentaries" folder; and Heslep to JHR, Nov. 18, 1942, box 338, "Winchell, Walter" folder, OC.

9. Eugene Carr to JHR, July 13, 1942, box 338, "Winchell, Walter, July 1943 Commentaries" folder, OC.

10. Pilat, Drew Pearson, 167.

11. Franklin D. Roosevelt, "Memorandum for S.T.E.," July 30, 1941, box 24, "President Roosevelt Memos 1941" folder, STEP; Roosevelt, *Complete Press Conferences,* 22:82.

12. Gentry, *J. Edgar Hoover,* 381.

13. Pilat, *Drew Pearson,* 9; Summers, *Official and Confidential,* 100–101; L. B. Nichols, "Memorandum for the Director," Jan. 21, 1938, FBI 94-8-350, sec. 1, FBI, Washington, D.C.

14. Drew Pearson and Robert S. Allen, "Sunday Washington Merry-Go-Round," *New York Daily Mirror,* Apr. 24, 1938, and JEH, "Memorandum for the Attorney General," Apr. 25, 1938, FBI 94-8-350, sec. 1, FBI, Washington, D.C.

15. Ernest Cuneo, "Writings," 26, box 108, "Drew Pearson" folder, Ernest Cuneo Papers, Franklin D. Roosevelt Library, Hyde Park.

16. "Memorandum for Mr. Ladd, Re: Surveillance of Drew Pearson by ONI," Mar. 5, 1943, FBI 94-8-350, sec. 4, FBI, Washington, D.C.; "Navy Ends 'Shadowing' of Pearson," *PM,* Mar. 5, 1943; John Carter [Jay Franklin], "Confidential to Dear Steve," Sept. 13, 1943, "Pearson and Allen, 1943–45" folder, OF 2300.

17. D. M. Ladd to the Director, "Drew Pearson, Espionage X," date obscured, FBI 65-59762, sec. 3, FBI, Washington, D.C.

18. Pilat, *Drew Pearson.*

19. Wallace, *Price of Vision,* 406.

20. Summers, *Official and Confidential,* 176; D. M. Ladd to the Director, "Drew Pearson, Espionage X," date obscured, FBI 65-59762, sec. 3, FBI, Washington, D.C.

21. Martin Andersen to STE, Dec. 12, 1941, box 29, "Federal Bureau of Investigation" folder, STEP.

22. Robert Whitney to Raymond McCaw, Dec. 8, 1941; Arthur Krock to McCaw, Dec. 9, 1941; and BP to Arthur Hays Sulzberger, May 26, 1942, "Censorship 1939–1961" folder, *NYT* Archives.

23. STE to JEH, Dec. 12, 1941, and JEH to STE, Dec. 12, 1941, box 29, "Federal Bureau of Investigation" folder, STEP.

24. JEH to STE, Dec. 12, 1941, box 29, "Federal Bureau of Investigation" folder, STEP.

25. JEH, "Memorandum for Mr. Tolson, Mr. Tamm, Mr. Ladd," first memo, Dec. 12, 1941, FBI 94-8-350, sec. 2, FBI, Washington, D.C.

26. JEH, "Memorandum for Mr. Tolson, Mr. Tamm, Mr. Ladd," second memo, Dec. 12, 1941, FBI 94-8-350, sec. 2, FBI, Washington, D.C.

27. Pearson, *Drew Pearson Diaries,* 93.

28. Drew Pearson and Robert S. Allen, "Southerners Asked Time for Speech by Lone Negro in Congress," *Philadelphia Record,* Dec. 18, 1941.

29. STE to BP, Jan. 5, 1942, box 14, "Price, Byron" folder, STEP.

30. Drew Pearson and Robert S. Allen, "Washington Merry-Go-Round," Dec. 18, 1941, reel 16, frame 0137, DPP.

31. NRH to JHS, Feb. 12, 1942, and William Mylander to JHS, Feb. 26, 1942, box 558, "CCPA" folder, OC.

32. JHS, "Memorandum, Re: Session with Drew Pearson in Office of Byron Price," Feb. 28, 1942, box 558, "CCPA" folder, OC.

33. NRH to JHS, Feb. 27, 1942, and William Mylander to JHS, Mar. 1, 1942, box 558, "CCPA" folder, OC.

34. Drew Pearson to BP, Mar. 3, 1942, box 558, "CCPA" folder, OC.

35. Edwin M. Watson, memorandum, Mar. 6, 1942, and "Washington Merry-Go-Round" clipping, n.p., n.d., box 558, "CCPA" folder, OC.

36. Russell B. Porter, "Memo. to Desk," box 558, "CCPA" folder, OC; "Re: Drew Pearson," May 24, 1951, FBI 65-59762, sec. 5, FBI, Washington, D.C.

37. Porter, "Memo. to Desk," box 558, "CCPA" folder, OC.

38. Edwin L. James to BP, Nov. 23, 1943, box 557, "CCPA/November–December 1943" folder, OC.

39. Anderson interview. Anderson could not recall Pearson speaking of his troubles with the Office of Censorship or the *Times*. "He didn't talk much," Anderson said. "He had found the hard way that the best way to protect himself from all the people who were after his scalp was to keep his mouth shut." However, he expressed astonishment that Pearson submitted to censorship.

40. "AW" [Alice Winegar] to STE, Apr. 24, 1942, box 14, "Price, Byron" folder, STEP.

41. STE, "Memorandum for . . . Byron Price," Apr. 25, 1942, box 14, "Price, Byron" folder, STEP.

42. BP to Francis Biddle, Apr. 25, 1942, box 558, "CCPA" folder, OC.

43. "Re: Drew Pearson," May 24, 1951, FBI 65-59762, sec. 5, FBI, Washington, D.C.

44. D. M. Ladd, "Memorandum for the Director," FBI 94-8-350, sec. 3, FBI, Washington, D.C.

45. "Re: Drew Pearson," May 24, 1951, FBI 65-59762, sec. 5, and P. E. Foxworth to "Director," Dec. 17, 1942, FBI 94-8-350, sec. 3, FBI, Washington, D.C.

46. William Steven to JHS, May 3, 1942, box 1396, "Day File/May 1–15" folder, OC.

47. BPN, 1:99.

48. Gabler, *Winchell*, 324. In October 1943, the owner of the Life Saver candy company purchased the Blue, which became ABC.

49. JHR, "Memorandum," May 22, 1942, box 558, "CCPA" folder, OC.

50. The final Pearson script in the Office of Censorship's records is dated Aug. 5, 1945. The archive of Pearson scripts is not complete, and there is no explanation for occasional absences.

51. Lester Halpin to JHR, Jan. 30, 1944, box 557, "CCPA/Jan. 1944" folder, OC.

52. Roosevelt, *Complete Press Conferences*, 19:292.

53. Drew Pearson, "Memo to the Radio Censor," Oct. 25, 1942, and Charter Heslep to JHR, Oct. 25, 1942, box 558, "CCPA/Oct. Thru Dec. [1942]" folder, OC.

54. "Drew Pearson Says U.S. Planes from 2 Carriers Bombed Tokyo," *Alexandria, La., Daily Town Talk*, Jan. 14, 1943; NRH to Hunter Jarreau, Jan. 28, 1943; Drew Pearson to John J. McCloy, Jan. 28, 1943; George A. Carlin to NRH, Jan. 27, 1943; and Jim Warner to NRH, Jan. 21, 1943, box 557, "CCPA/Jan.–Feb. [1943]" folder, OC. Also see McCloy to Pearson, Jan. 30, 1943, box G-76, "Censorship, Office of, 1942–1944" folder, PPDP.

55. *CWPP*, Jan. 15, 1942; *CWPB*, Jan. 15, 1942; *CWPB*, June 15, 1942. The original code urged "sensible analyses of reports from enemy origins."

56. Edward H. Bronson to JHR, Nov. 15, 1943; Bronson to Pauline Frederick, Nov. 16, 1943; and Bronson to JHR, Nov. 16, 1943, box 334, "Commentaries/ Baukhage" folder, OC.

57. JL to BP, Dec. 1, 1943, box 557, "CCPA/November–December 1943" folder, OC.

58. War Department, "The Raid on Japan," news release 24-25310, Apr. 20, 1943, box 544, "Air Raids—Doolittle" folder, OC.

59. NRH to Drew Pearson, Apr. 24, 1943, box G-76, "Censorship, Office of, 1942–1944" folder, PPDP.

60. JHS to Drew Pearson, Mar. 9, 1942, box G-76, "Censorship, Office of, 1942–1944" folder, PPDP.

61. Drew Pearson to BP, June 5, 1942, box G-76, "Censorship, Office of, 1942–1944" folder, PPDP.

62. *HOC*, 2:6.

63. JL to Drew Pearson, June 6, 1944, box 557, "CCPA/May 1943" folder, OC.

64. JL to Drew Pearson, Dec. 15, 1944, box G-130, "Censorship" folder, PPDP.

65. Drew Pearson, script for July 29, 1945, box 556, "CCPA/July 1945" folder, OC.

66. "To Mr. Ladd," Jan. 24, 1944, FBI 94-8-350, sec. 4, FBI, Washington, D.C.

67. "2937—Zedlitz, Frederic H. Carl [*sic*] (Count)," box 12, "Kellems Case" folder, OC.

68. BP to Drew Pearson, Apr. 14, 1944, and Pearson to BP, Apr. 20, 1944, box 12, "Kellems Case" folder, OC.

69. Burns, *Roosevelt*, 382.

70. Farago, *Patton*, 319, 325.

71. Ibid., 331, 341; Klurfeld, *Behind the Lines*, 73.

72. Reynolds, *Curtain Rises*, 225.

73. Ibid., 226; Klurfeld, *Behind the Lines*, 73.

74. Eisenhower, *Crusade in Europe*, 182.

75. Knightley, *First Casualty*, 320–21.

76. Reynolds, *Curtain Rises*, 227.

77. Edwin L. James to BP, Nov. 23, 1942, box 557, "CCPA/November–December 1943" folder, OC.

78. Pilat, *Drew Pearson*, 176; Roosevelt, *Complete Press Conferences*, 22:82.

79. Pilat, *Drew Pearson*, 176.

80. Reel 20, frame 254, DPP.

81. Drew Pearson, script for Nov. 14, 1943, box 557, "CCPA/November–December 1943" folder, OC.

82. Edward H. Bronson to JHR, Nov. 14, 1943, box 557, "CCPA/November–December 1943" folder, OC.

83. Lester Halpin to JHR, Nov. 21, 1943, box 557, "CCPA/November–December 1943" folder, OC.

84. "Memorandum for Mr. Ladd," Nov. 22, 1943, FBI 94-8-350, sec. 4, FBI, Washington, D.C.

85. HLSD, vol. 45 (reel 7): 50.

86. Knightley, *First Casualty*, 321; "Patton Rebuke by Eisenhower Denied by Army," *New York Herald Tribune*, Nov. 23, 1943.

87. Eisenhower, *Crusade in Europe,* 182.
88. "Senate Military Committee Skips Important Phase of Patton Case," *Mobile, Ala., Press,* Nov. 26, 1943; "A Sorry Job," *Cleveland News,* Nov. 24, 1943.
89. Reel 20, frame 265, DPP.
90. Kent Cooper to BP, Nov. 30, 1942, and BP to Cooper, Dec. 3, 1942, box 389, "Complaints Re: Press Censorship/'A'" folder, OC.
91. Edwin L. James to BP, Nov. 23, 1943, box 557, "CCPA/November–December 1943" folder, OC.
92. BP to Edwin L. James, Nov. 25, 1943, box 557, "CCPA/November–December 1943" folder, OC.
93. Edwin L. James to BP, Nov. 26, 1943, box 557, "CCPA/November–December 1943" folder, OC; James to Arthur Krock, Nov. 26, 1943, "Censorship 1939–1961" folder, *NYT* Archives.
94. George A. Carlin to BP, Nov. 26, 1943, box 557, "CCPA/November–December 1943" folder, OC.
95. "Pearson Charges Washington Uses Gestapo Tactics."

CHAPTER SIX

1. BPM, 360.
2. Trohan interview.
3. BPM, 360.
4. "Creel Formulates Press Censorship Rules," 9; Vaughn, *Holding Fast,* 218–19.
5. *CWPP,* Jan. 15, 1942. The radio clause is similar.
6. BPM, 361–63; STE to Leland P. Lovette, Oct. 2, 1942, box 61, "Inspection Tour, Sept. 17–Oct. 1, 1942" folder, OF 200-2-0. Roosevelt read the wire reporters' stories but made no changes.
7. A. Smith, *Thank You,* 50.
8. Brinkley, *Washington Goes to War,* 166–68.
9. Bill Flythe to STE, Oct. 10, 1942, box 61, "Inspection Tour—Miscellaneous" folder, OF 200-2-0.
10. Winfield, *F.D.R. and the News Media,* 13.
11. Hassett, *Off the Record.*
12. A. Smith, *Thank You,* 48–49; "F.D.R. Leaves from University Station," *The Tower,* Feb. 5, 1942.
13. Wilson, "World War II," 190; A. Smith, *Thank You,* 57.
14. "Strictly Confidential Note to Editors and Broadcasters," Sept. 17, 1942, BPN, 6:n.p.
15. A. Smith, *Thank You,* 51.
16. Burns, *Roosevelt,* 268.
17. [Cornell], "Day-to-Day Report of the 8,754-Mile Tour of the President across the Country and Back Again," *NYT,* Oct. 2, 1942.
18. Reilly and Slocum, *Reilly of the White House,* 130; Goodwin, *No Ordinary Time,* 362.

19. A. Smith, *Thank You*, 52; "Minutes of the Editorial Advisory Board, Oct. 21, 1942," *HOC*, 2:n.p.

20. A. Smith, *Thank You*, 53.

21. Grover, "Radio Censorship in Wartime," 65.

22. "Copies of Story of Trip Destroyed," unidentified clipping in BPN, 2:189; Robb, "Shop Talk at Thirty," Oct. 10, 1942; NRH to Frank Thayer, Dec. 14, 1942, box 554, "Miscellaneous General Re: Press/August 42" folder, OC; "W.D.H." [William D. Hassett], "Memorandum for Mr. Early," Sept. 24, 1942, box 61, "Inspection Tour, Sept. 17–Oct. 1, 1942," OF 200-2-0.

23. BP, "Memorandum for Mr. Stephen Early," Sept. 30, 1942, BPN, 2:n.p.; NRH to Frank Thayer, Dec. 14, 1942, box 554, "Miscellaneous General Re: Press/August 42" folder, OC.

24. Burns, *Roosevelt*, 269; A. Smith, *Thank You*, 54.

25. Roscoe Drummond et al. to BP, Sept. 22, 1942, BPN, 2:190–91.

26. "FDR Ignores Protest," 50.

27. BPM, "Miscellaneous Pages," 190.

28. BPM, 228.

29. BPN, 2:191; "Banned from Trip, Reporters Protest," *NYT*, Oct. 2, 1942.

30. Goodwin, *No Ordinary Time*, 368.

31. "F.D.R. Comes to Douglas." The *Douglas Airview* article is in box 61, "Inspection Tour—Miscellaneous" folder, OF 200-2-0.

32. [Cornell], "Day-to-Day Report."

33. "Price Hails Press on War News Curb," *NYT*, Sept. 29, 1942.

34. BP, "Memorandum for Mr. Stephen Early," Sept. 30, 1942, BPN, 2:n.p.

35. "Censorship Battle Brewing Beneath Surface in Capital," *Buffalo Evening News*, Sept. 29, 1942.

36. Arthur Krock, "Censorship Conflict," *NYT*, Sept. 30, 1942.

37. BP, "Memorandum for Mr. Stephen Early," Sept. 30, 1942, BPN, 2:n.p.

38. Brinkley, *Washington Goes to War*, 168.

39. William Mylander to BP, JHS, NRH, and JHR, Oct. 1, 1942, box 552, "General Press/Press Conferences—White House" folder, OC; Brinkley, *Washington Goes to War*, 168.

40. Roosevelt, *Complete Press Conferences*, 20:119.

41. Ibid., 122.

42. BPN, 2:192–93.

43. "FDR Ignores Protest," 4.

44. "Editors Fear Public Distrust," 3.

45. "Cartoon Comment on President's Censored Tour."

46. "Harun-al-Rashid with a Brass Band," *CT*, Oct. 3, 1942.

47. John Barry et al. to Franklin Roosevelt, Oct. 4, 1942, box 1, "Censorship 1942–1943" folder, OF 1773.

48. "FDR Ignores Protest," 50.

49. Rosenman, *Public Papers*, 11:418.

50. Lester Halpin to JHR, Nov. 11, 1943, box 334, "Commentaries/Baukhage" folder, OC; *HOC*, 2:76.

51. A. Smith, *Thank You*, 56–57.

52. Charter Heslep to JHR, Nov. 3, 1942, box 334, "Movements/President" folder, OC.

53. A. Smith, *Thank You*, 56.

54. Eugene Carr to JHR, Apr. 10, 1943, and Lester Halpin to JHR, Apr. 9, 1943, box 233, "Movements/President" folder, OC.

55. A. Smith, *Thank You*, 71.

56. "Confidential Note to Editors, Broadcasters, and Photo Services," Apr. 8, 1943, BPN, 3:281.

57. "No Censor Accompanies Newsmen on FDR Tour."

58. Frank C. Clough to NRH, Apr. 8, 1943, and "Memorandum by N. R. Howard," Apr. 9, 1943, BPN, 3:281–83.

59. "Memorandum by N. R. Howard," Apr. 9, 1943, BPN, 3:281–83.

60. JHR to BP, Apr. 14, 1943, box 344, "Movements Officials and Diplomats/President" folder, OC; Robert K. Richards to JHR, Apr. 14, 1943, BPN, 3:294.

61. W. H. Lawrence, "President Stirred by Visits to Camps," *NYT*, Apr. 21, 1943.

62. "Yes, He Was Here! Who? Don't Ask, It's a Secret, You Know," *Montgomery, Ala., Advertiser*, Apr. 16, 1943.

63. Koop, *Weapon of Silence*, 225.

64. BPN, 3:310.

65. On Feb. 5, 1944, Roosevelt revealed his fourth-term plans in an off-the-record talk with black journalists. See Washburn, *Question of Sedition*, 199–200.

66. A. Smith, *Thank You*, 38.

67. *HOC*, 2:83.

68. "F.D.R.'s Trip across Nation Great Secret," *CT*, July 21, 1944.

69. A. Smith, *Thank You*, 148.

70. "'Too Busy to Campaign,' Says President Roosevelt," *CT*, July 21, 1944.

71. Hassett, *Off the Record*, 265.

72. Trohan, *Political Animals*, 135, 200. Trohan said he witnessed Lucy Mercer Rutherford meet Roosevelt's train in the middle of the night in New Jersey. He gave no date for the meeting.

73. Goodwin, *No Ordinary Time*, 519–21.

74. Winfield, *F.D.R. and the News Media*, 182, 188 n.

75. A. Smith, *Thank You*, 130–31.

76. *HOC*, 2:89.

77. Trohan interview.

78. Goodwin, *No Ordinary Time*, 537, 547; Hassett, *Off the Record*, 265.

79. Westbrook Pegler, "Fair Enough," *Washington Times-Herald*, Feb. 20, 1945.

80. BP to J. V. Connolly, Feb. 20, 1945, and Connolly to BP, Feb. 20, 1945, BPN, 4:348.

81. Daniels, *White House Witness*, 263; Daniels to Ruthjane Rumelt, Feb. 20, 1945, box 1, "Office of Censorship 1943–1945" folder, OF 4695.

82. Carl Levin, "Pegler's Threat on Censorship Stirs Reporters," *New York Herald Tribune*, Feb. 21, 1945.

83. *HOC*, 2:97; BP, "Note to Editors," Feb. 28, 1945, BPN, 4:34.

84. BP, "Memorandum to the President," Feb. 28, 1945, box 1, "Office of Censorship 1943–1945" folder, OF 4695.
85. Jonathan Daniels to BP, Mar. 3, 1945, box 1, "Office of Censorship 1943–1945" folder, OF 4695.
86. Fulton Lewis, transcript of broadcast on Mar. 8, 1945, box 344, "Movements/President" folder, OC.
87. Washington City News Service dispatch, Mar. 8, 1945, BPN, 4:344.
88. BPN, 5:438; *HOC*, 2:98; Koop, *Weapon of Silence*, 233.
89. BP, "Note to Editors and Broadcasters," May 9, 1945, BPN, 6:n.p.; *CWPPR*.

CHAPTER SEVEN

1. "Balloon Reports," May 21, 1945, BPN, 5:n.p.
2. BPM, 442–45.
3. *CWPP*, Dec. 1, 1943; *HOC*, 2:141.
4. "Balloon Mystery."
5. "Trial Balloons."
6. Roosevelt, *Complete Press Conferences*, 25:4.
7. "What Next, Please."
8. Murphy, "One Small Moment," 68; Lingeman, *Don't You Know There's a War On?* 54.
9. *HOC*, 2:143; Eberhard, "From Balloon Bombs to H-Bombs," 4.
10. Murphy, "One Small Moment," 66–69, 71; "Jap Balloon Bomb Explosion Kills Six Persons in Oregon," *Washington Post*, June 1, 1945.
11. *HOC*, 2:147.
12. "Jap Balloon Bomb Explosion Kills Six Persons in Oregon."
13. Murphy, "One Small Moment," 68; *HOC*, 2:147.
14. BPM, 445.
15. "Balloon Reports," May 21, 1945, BPN, 5:n.p.
16. J. R. Wiggins to BP, May 21, 1945, BPN, 5:n.p.
17. BPM, 447.
18. *HOC*, 2:147; BPM, 447.
19. BPM, 449.
20. Ibid., 450; *HOC*, 2:147.
21. BP, "Confidential Note to Editors and Broadcasters," May 22, 1945, BPN, 4:333.
22. *HOC*, 2:149–51.
23. "Jap Balloon Bomb Explosion Kills Six Persons in Oregon."
24. *HOC*, 2:153.
25. JHS to NRH, Feb. 24, 1942, box 1214, "Sorrells Day File/February 1942" folder, OC.
26. BP, "To Managing Editors and Broadcasters," Apr. 3, 1942, BPN, 6:n.p.
27. JHS, "For Office Bibles," June 29, 1942, box 1427, "Memoranda . . . October 2, 1942–May 31, 1943" folder, OC; "Praises Press for Censoring V-2 Bombings."

28. William Mylander to NRH, Nov. 27, 1942, and Mylander to NRH, Dec. 28, 1942, box 504, "Race Riots" folder, OC.

29. Publications held up at the borders included the *Laredo, Texas, Times,* which reported a fight between black soldiers and white military and civilian police in November 1942, and *Newsweek,* which had written that August about blacks being kept from voting and playing baseball. Censors' clipping of periodicals ended shortly after these incidents. See box 389, "Complaints Re: Press Censorship/Laredo Times" folder, OC; "Negroes and Baseball"; "Primaries"; "Shears and Intercepts"; "Detroit Is Dynamite"; "Life's Detroit Story Not Permitted Abroad"; and BPN, 2:155.

30. *HOC,* 2:108.

31. "Basic Policy: Publicity of Scientific Developments," n.d., box 486, "Radar/April 1943" folder, OC.

32. Carl F. Espe and J. A. Ulio, "Publicity on Classified Projects, Armament and Equipment," Feb. 16–17, 1943, box 486, "Radar/April 1943" folder, OC.

33. BPN, 3.314, William H. Mylander to NRH, Apr. 29, 1943, box 486, "Radar/April 1943" folder, OC. For examples of radar publicity after the ban, see Wilhelm, "Radar, the Supersleuth"; Davis, "Radar—Our Miracle Ally"; and "Radar Goes Commercial."

34. NRH to BP, Apr. 17, 1943, box 486, "Radar/April 1943" folder, OC.

35. "Joint Army-Navy Release: Development of Radar Described," n.d., BPN, 5:451.

36. William D. Leahy to BP, July 27, 1943, BPN, 3:317.

37. "Note to Editors and Broadcasters," July 29, 1943, box 146, "Confidential Notes to Editors/June 1943" folder, OC.

38. BP to Herbert K. Fenn, Norman Carlson, JL, and JHR, July 29, 1943, BPN, 3:318.

39. BPM, 421.

40. "Attachment C, Joint Security Control Memo Black Book," BPN, 4:n.p.

41. *HOC,* 2:110.

42. Quoted in BP to James Forrestal, June 28, 1945, BPN, 5:450.

43. *HOC,* 2:110.

44. BPN, 3:312; Koop, *Weapon of Silence,* 266.

45. Washburn, "Office of Censorship's Attempt to Control," 4.

46. Laurence, *Men and Atoms,* 48–49; Groves, *Now It Can Be Told,* 325.

47. Groves, *Now It Can Be Told,* 23.

48. Ibid., 139–40.

49. Jones, *Manhattan, the Army and the Atomic Bomb,* 277, 278 n. Jones did not record the date of Strong's observation, but Styer quoted it in a Feb. 18 memo to Groves.

50. Washburn, "Office of Censorship's Attempt to Control," 4.

51. *HOC,* 2:154.

52. Ibid., 155; BPM, 469.

53. Groves, *Now It Can Be Told,* 146.

54. Koop, *Weapon of Silence,* 274.

55. "Note to Editors and Broadcasters—Confidential—Not for Publication," June 25, 1943, box 146, "Confidential Notes to Editors/June 1943" folder, OC.

56. "Biggest Secret."

57. William Steven to NRH, June 30, 1943, box 146, "Confidential Notes to Editors/June 1943" folder, OC.

58. Washburn, "Office of Censorship's Attempt to Control," 8.

59. Ibid., 11; *HOC,* 2:163.

60. *HOC,* 2:169.

61. Fetzer, "Radio Historical References," 72; *HOC,* 2:223.

62. JHR to BP, Oct. 19, 1943, box 482, "Atom Smashing" folder, OC.

63. Ibid.; JL, "Memorandum," Oct. 21, 1943, box 482, "Atom Smashing" folder, OC.

64. JL to BP, Oct. 20, 1943, box 482, "Atom Smashing" folder, OC.

65. JL, "Memorandum," Oct. 21, 1943; *HOC,* 2:222.

66. Robert K. Richards to JL, Apr. 11, 1944, box 482, "Atom Smashing/January 1944" folder, OC.

67. "Washington Memo," *Minneapolis Morning Tribune,* Aug. 24, 1944; Milburn Petty to JL, Aug. 26, 1944; Office of War Information, "WPB-6299," Aug. 16, 1944; Frank C. Clough to JL, Aug. 30, 1944; William P. Steven to Clough, Aug. 30, 1944; and Clough to Steven, Sept. 4, 1944, all in box 482, "Atom Smashing" folder, OC.

68. *HOC,* 2:169.

69. Washburn, "Office of Censorship's Attempt to Control," 11; *HOC,* 2:160–61.

70. *HOC,* 2:171.

71. Groves, *Now It Can Be Told,* 325.

72. Edwin L. James to BP, Dec. 24, 1943; BP to James, Jan. 1, 1944; JL to James, Nov. 29, 1944; and James to JL, Nov. 2, 1944, "Censorship, 1939–1961" folder, *NYT* Archives.

73. Laurence, *Men and Atoms,* 96, 109.

74. BPM, 479.

75. Laurence, *Men and Atoms,* 111.

76. "Press Memorandum by Theodore F. Koop," July 16, 1945, and United Press transcript, July 16, 1945, box 481, "Atom Smashing/July 1945" folder, OC.

77. *HOC,* 2:184.

78. Ibid., 184–85; Koop, *Weapon of Silence,* 279; BPM, 480.

79. BP, "Note to Editors and Broadcasters (For Publication and Broadcast If Desired)," Aug. 6, 1945, BPN, 5:n.p.

80. Washburn, "Office of Censorship's Attempt to Control," 27–28.

81. Memoranda by Day Thorpe, Phil Adler, and J. E. Warner, Aug. 6, 1945, box 481, "Atom Smashing/August 1945" folder, OC.

82. Washburn, "Office of Censorship's Attempt to Control," 32.

83. Leslie R. Groves to BP, Aug. 14, 1945, box 428, "Atom Smashing/August 1945" folder, OC.

84. BPN, 5:463.

85. Ibid.; BPM, 462–63.

86. BPN, 5:463.

87. BP, "Note to Editors and Broadcasters," Apr. 5, 1945, and George C. Marshall to BP, Apr. 3, 1945, box 542, "Russia-Japan" folder, OC.

88. Koop, *Weapon of Silence*, 255–56.

89. I. F. Stone, "It Seems Pointless, but We Abide by It," *PM*, Apr. 6, 1945.

90. George M. Cox to BP, Apr. 6, 1945, and BP to Cox, Apr. 9, 1945, BPN, 5:475.

91. BP, "Confidential Note to Editors and Broadcasters," May 11, 1945, BPN, 5:457.

92. *HOC*, 2:204.

93. "Proceedings of the Censorship Policy Board, Meeting of November 20, 1943," box 79, "Papers as Vice President—Censorship Policy Board" folder, Henry A. Wallace Papers, Franklin D. Roosevelt Library, Hyde Park.

94. *CWPPR*.

95. BP, "Memorandum for the President," June 27, 1945, BPN, 5:n.p.

96. Harry S. Truman to BP, July 3, 1945, BPN, 5:n.p.

97. BPN, 5:430.

98. "Censorship to End When Japan Quits," *NYT*, Aug. 14, 1945.

99. BPN, 5:430; Charles G. Ross to BP, Aug. 15, 1945, BPN, 5:n.p.

100. "Voluntary Censorship of News Is Ended at Order of the President," *NYT*, Aug. 16, 1945; "Censorship Bureau Comes to an End," *NYT*, Nov. 16, 1945.

101. "The Censor Shuts up Shop," *NYT*, Aug. 17, 1945.

102. "Out of Business."

103. Charles Van Devander and William O. Player Jr., "Censorship Hasn't Been Popular, But Byron Price Did a Nice Job," *New York Post*, Sept. 7, 1945.

104. BP, "A Basis for Censorship Planning," Aug. 24, 1945, box 2, folder 6, BPP.

105. BPM, 483–84, 487.

106. "Out of Office."

107. "Byron Price Named Film Industry Aide," *NYT*, Dec. 5, 1945.

108. BP to Kent Cooper, Nov. 26, 1945, box 1, folder 2, BPP.

109. "Where Are They Now?"

110. Ibid.; "Price, Byron C.," 683.

111. BPM, 491.

112. Peter B. Flint, "Byron Price, Wartime Chief of U.S. Censorship, Is Dead," *NYT*, Aug. 8, 1981.

CONCLUSION

1. "Safe in Sticking to Byron Price," *Richmond, Va., News Leader*, Apr. 7, 1945.

2. "Please Don't Speculate," *Bismarck, N.D., Tribune*, Apr. 26, 1945.

3. BP, PR-59, Feb. 21, 1945, box 922, "Speeches-Price/January 1944" folder, OC.

4. Butler, "Price Reminds Press of Invasion Duties," 7.

5. *HOC*, 2:209–10.

6. Burns, *Roosevelt*, 171.

7. Ibid., 130; Roosevelt, *Complete Press Conferences*, 21:86–96.

8. BPM, 428.

9. Katz et al., *Public Opinion and Propaganda,* 43.

10. Pinkley, "Eisenhower on Censorship."

11. STE to BP, Aug. 31, 1945, box 14, "Price, Byron" folder, STEP.

12. "Byron Price, Wartime Chief of U.S. Censorship, Is Dead."

13. Cosgrove interview.

14. "Need for Censorship in Europe Has Ended."

15. "U.S., British Censors in Harmony."

Bibliography

MANUSCRIPT COLLECTIONS

Austin, Texas
   Lyndon B. Johnson Library
      Personal Papers of Drew Pearson
College Park, Maryland
   National Archives Annex
      Federal Communications Commission, Record Group 173
      Office of Censorship, Record Group 216
      Office of War Information, Record Group 208
Hyde Park, New York
   Franklin D. Roosevelt Library
      Francis Biddle Papers
      Oscar S. Cox Papers
      Ernest Cuneo Papers
      Stephen T. Early Papers
      Lowell Mellett Papers
      Henry Morganthau Jr. Diary
      Franklin D. Roosevelt Papers
         Office File
         President's Secretary's File
      Henry A. Wallace Papers
      Stephen T. Early Papers
Madison, Wisconsin
   Archives Division, State Historical Society of Wisconsin
      Don Anderson Papers
      Byron Price, "Memoir"
      Byron Price Notebooks, 7 vols.
      Byron Price Papers
      Frederick S. Siebert Papers
New Haven, Connecticut
   Yale University Library Manuscripts and Archives
      Drew Pearson Papers
      Henry Lewis Stimson Diaries

New York City, New York
  New York Times Archives
Princeton, New Jersey
  Princeton University, Seeley G. Mudd Library
    David Lawrence Papers
Washington, D.C.
  Federal Bureau of Investigation
    File 65-59762, Drew Pearson
    File 94-8-350, Drew Pearson

INTERVIEWS

Anderson, Jack. Telephone interview with author, December 17, 1998.
Cosgrove, John. Telephone interview with author, October 11, 1999.
Mitchell, Dennis. Telephone interview with author, September 19, 1996.
Trohan, Walter. Telephone interview with author, March 4, 1996.

GOVERNMENT PUBLICATIONS

Congressional Record. 77th Cong., 2d sess., 1942. Vol. 88, pt. 5.
Historical Reports on War Administration. *A Report on the Office of Censorship.*
  Washington, D.C.: Government Printing Office, 1945.
Office of Censorship. *Code of Wartime Practices for American Broadcasters.*
  4 editions. Washington, D.C.: Government Printing Office, 1942–43.
———. *Code of Wartime Practices for the American Press.* 4 editions. Washington,
  D.C.: Government Printing Office, 1942–43.
———. *Code of Wartime Practices for the American Press and Radio.* Washington,
  D.C.: Government Printing Office, May 15, 1945.
———. *A History of the Office of Censorship.* 6 vols. Record Group 216. Boxes
  1 and 2. National Archives, College Park, Md.
United States. *Laws, etc. (United States Statutes at Large).* Washington, D.C.:
  Government Printing Office, 1937–.

UNPUBLISHED DOCUMENTS

Adams, Edward E. " 'The Advertising Giant Is Tottering': The Effects of Political,
  Economic and Social Climate of WWII on Advertising Revenues." Paper
  presented to the Western Journalism Historians Conference, Berkeley, February
  2000.
Biddle, Francis. "Private Diary, Jan. 8, 1940 to Nov. 13, 1944." Used with the
  permission of Mr. and Mrs. Edmund R. Biddle, Bryn Mawr, Pa.
Fetzer, John E. "Radio Historical References: A Treatise on Personal Experience."

1956, revised February 28, 1974. Oral History Research Office, Columbia University. Text-fiche.

McKay, Floyd. "Civil Liberties Suspended: Pacific Northwest Editors and the Japanese Americans." Paper presented to the Western Journalism Historians Conference, Berkeley, February 2000.

Purcell, Gillis. "Wartime Censorship in Canada." Byron Price Papers. Archives Division. State Historical Society of Wisconsin, Madison.

Siebert, Frederick S. "Wartime Communications and Censorship." Frederick S. Siebert Papers. Archives Division. State Historical Society of Wisconsin, Madison.

LAW CASES

Federal Radio Commission v. Nelson Brothers Bond & Mortgage Co. (Station WIBO), 289 US 266 (1932).

Near v. Minnesota ex rel Olson, 283 US 697 (1931).

United States ex. rel. Milwaukee Social Democratic Publishing Co. v. Burleson, 255 US 407 (1921).

NEWSPAPERS

Alexandria, La., Daily Town Talk
Atlanta Constitution
Atlanta Daily World
Baltimore Evening Sun
Bismarck, N.D., Tribune
Buffalo Evening News
Chicago Defender
Chicago Tribune
Christian Science Monitor
Cleveland News
Danville, Va., Register
Dayton Daily News
Kansas City, Mo., Journal
Laredo, Texas, Times
Los Angeles Examiner
Minneapolis Morning Tribune
Mobile, Ala., Press
Montgomery, Ala., Advertiser
New York Daily Mirror
New York Daily News
New York Herald Tribune
New York Post

New York Times
New York World-Telegram
Philadelphia Daily News
Philadelphia Record
PM
Richmond, Va., News Leader
Seattle Post-Intelligencer
Tell City, Ind., News
The Tower of Catholic University
Washington Daily News
Washington Evening Star
Washington Post
Washington Times-Herald
X-Ray

BOOKS

Ambrose, Stephen E. *Citizen Soldiers: The U.S. Army from the Normandy Beaches to the Bulge to the Surrender of Germany, June 7, 1944–May 7, 1945.* New York: Simon & Schuster, 1997.

American Civil Liberties Union. *Liberty on the Home Front in the Fourth Year of the War.* Vol. 23 of *American Civil Liberties Union Annual Reports.* New York: ACLU, 1945. Reprint, New York: Arno Press & *New York Times,* 1970.

American Society of Newspaper Editors. *Problems of Journalism: Nineteenth Annual Convention.* N.p.: ASNE, 1941.

———. *Problems of Journalism: Twentieth Annual Convention.* N.p.: ASNE, 1942.

Barnouw, Erik. *A History of Broadcasting in the United States.* 3 vols. New York: Oxford University Press, 1966–70.

Biddle, Francis. *In Brief Authority.* New York: Doubleday, 1962.

Brinkley, David. *Washington Goes to War.* New York: Random House, 1988. Reprint, New York: Ballantine Books, 1989.

Burns, James MacGregor. *Roosevelt: The Soldier of Freedom 1940–1945.* New York: Harcourt Brace Jovanovich, 1970.

Chafee, Zechariah, Jr. *Freedom of Speech.* New York: Harcourt, Brace, and Howe, 1920.

———. *Government and Mass Communications: A Report from the Commission on Freedom of the Press.* Hamden, Conn.: Archon Books, 1965.

Charnley, Mitchell. *News by Radio.* New York: Macmillan, 1948.

Conn, Stetson. *Historical Work in the United States Army, 1862–1954.* Washington, D.C.: U.S. Army Center of Military History, 1980.

Creel, George. *How We Advertised America.* New York: Harper & Brothers, 1920. Reprint, New York: Arno Press, 1972.

———. *Rebel at Large: Recollections of Fifty Crowded Years.* New York: G. P. Putnam's Sons, 1947.

Daniels, Jonathan. *White House Witness, 1942–1945.* New York: Doubleday, 1975.

Eisenhower, Dwight D. *Crusade in Europe.* Garden City, N.Y.: Doubleday, 1948.

Farago, Ladislas. *The Game of the Foxes: The Untold Story of German Espionage in the United States and Britain during World War II.* New York: David McKay Company, 1971.

———. *Patton: Ordeal and Triumph.* New York: Ivan Obolensky, 1964.

Fox, Frank. *Madison Avenue Goes to War: The Strange Military Career of American Advertising 1941–1945.* Provo, Utah: Brigham Young University Press, 1975.

Gabler, Neal. *Winchell: Gossip, Power and the Culture of Celebrity.* New York: Alfred A. Knopf, 1994.

Gentry, Curt. *J. Edgar Hoover: The Man and His Secrets.* New York: W. W. Norton, 1991.

Gies, Joseph. *The Colonel of Chicago: A Biography of the Chicago Tribune's Legendary Publisher, Colonel Robert McCormick.* New York: E. P. Dutton, 1979.

Glad, Betty, ed. *Psychological Dimensions of War.* Newbury Park, Calif.: Sage Publications, 1990.

Goodwin, Doris Kearns. *No Ordinary Time: Franklin and Eleanor Roosevelt, The Home Front in World War II.* New York: Simon & Schuster, 1994.

Groves, Leslie R. *Now It Can Be Told: The Story of the Manhattan Project.* New York: Harper & Row, 1962.

Hassett, William D. *Off the Record with F.D.R. 1942–1945.* New Brunswick, N.J.: Rutgers University Press, 1958.

Healy, George W. *A Lifetime on Deadline: Self-Portrait of a Southern Journalist.* Gretna, La.: Pelican Publishing Co., 1976.

Hoge, Alice Albright. *Cissy Patterson: The Life of Eleanor Medill Patterson, Publisher and Editor of the* Washington Times-Herald. New York: Random House, 1966.

Jones, Vincent C. *United States Army in World War II: Manhattan, the Army and the Atomic Bomb.* Washington, D.C.: United States Army Center for Military History, 1985.

Kahn, David. *The Codebreakers: The Story of Secret Writing.* London: Weidenfeld and Nicolson, 1967.

Katz, Daniel, Dorwin Cartwright, Samuel Eldersveld, and Alfred McClung Lee, eds. *Public Opinion and Propaganda.* New York: Dryden Press, 1954.

Klurfeld, Herman. *Behind the Lines: The World of Drew Pearson.* Englewood Cliffs, N.J.: Prentice Hall, 1968.

Knightley, Phillip. *The First Casualty: From the Crimea to Vietnam: The War Correspondent as Hero, Propagandist, and Myth Maker.* New York: Harcourt Brace Jovanovich, 1975.

Koop, Theodore F. *Weapon of Silence.* Chicago: University of Chicago Press, 1946.

Krock, Arthur. *Memoirs: Sixty Years on the Firing Line.* New York: Funk & Wagnalls, 1968.

Kurth, Peter. *American Cassandra: The Life of Dorothy Thompson.* Boston: Little, Brown & Co., 1990.

Landry, Robert J. *This Fascinating Radio Business.* Indianapolis: Bobbs-Merrill, 1946.

Laurence, William L. *Men and Atoms: The Discovery, the Uses and the Future of Atomic Energy*. New York: Simon & Schuster, 1959.

Lazarsfeld, Paul F., and Frank N. Stanton, eds. *Radio Research 1942–1943*. New York: Hawthorn Books, 1944. Reprint, New York: Arno Press, 1979.

Leahy, William D. *I Was There: The Personal Story of the Chief of Staff to Presidents Roosevelt and Truman Based on His Notes and Diaries Made at the Time*. New York: Whittlesey House, 1950.

Lingeman, Richard R. *Don't You Know There's a War On? The American Home Front, 1941–1945*. New York: G. P. Putnam's Sons, 1970.

Marcus, Sheldon. *Father Coughlin: The Tumultuous Life of the Priest of the Little Flower*. Boston: Little, Brown & Co. 1973.

Maslowski, Peter. *Armed with Cameras: The American Military Photographers of World War II*. New York: The Free Press, 1993.

Mock, James R. *Censorship 1917*. Princeton, N.J.: Princeton University Press, 1941.

Mock, James R., and Cedric Larson. *Words That Won the War*. Princeton, N.J.: Princeton University Press, 1939.

Pearson, Drew. *Drew Pearson Diaries*. Edited by Tyler Abell. New York: Holt, Rinehart, and Winston, 1974.

Pilat, Oliver. *Drew Pearson: An Unauthorized Biography*. New York: Harper's Magazine Press, 1973.

Reilly, Michael F., and William J. Slocum. *Reilly of the White House*. New York: Simon & Schuster, 1947.

Reynolds, Quentin. *The Curtain Rises*. New York: Random House, 1944.

Ribuffo, Leo. *The Old Christian Right: The Protestant Right from the Great Depression to the Cold War*. Philadelphia: Temple University Press, 1983.

Roeder, George H., Jr. *The Censored War*. New Haven, Conn.: Yale University Press, 1993.

Roosevelt, Franklin D. *Complete Presidential Press Conferences of Franklin D. Roosevelt*. 25 vols. New York: Da Capo Press, 1972.

Rosenman, Samuel I., ed. *The Public Papers and Addresses of Franklin D. Roosevelt*. 13 vols. New York: Harper & Brothers, 1938–50.

———. *Working with Roosevelt*. New York: Harper & Brothers, 1952.

Sayers, Michael, and Albert E. Kahn. *Sabotage! The Secret War against America*. New York: Harper & Brothers, 1942.

Smith, A. Merriman. *Thank You, Mr. President: A White House Notebook*. New York: Harper & Brothers, 1946.

Smith, Jeffery A. *War and Press Freedom: The Problem of Prerogative Power*. New York: Oxford University Press, 1999.

Smith, Richard Norton. *The Colonel: The Life and Legend of Robert R. McCormick*. Boston: Houghton Mifflin, 1997.

Steele, Richard W. *Propaganda in an Open Society: The Roosevelt Administration and the Media, 1933–1941*. Westport, Conn.: Greenwood Press, 1985.

Sterling, Christopher H., and John M. Kittross. *Stay Tuned: A Concise History of American Broadcasting*, 2nd ed. Belmont, Calif.: Wadsworth Publishing Co., 1990.

Stevens, John D. *Shaping the First Amendment: The Development of Free Expression.*
Vol. II of *The Sage Comm Text Series.* Beverly Hills, Calif.: Sage Publications,
1982.

Summers, Anthony. *Official and Confidential: The Secret Life of J. Edgar Hoover.*
New York: G. P. Putnam's Sons, 1993.

Tocqueville, Alexis de. *Democracy in America.* New York: Borzoi Books, 1994.

Toledano, Ralph de. *J. Edgar Hoover: The Man in His Time.* New Rochelle, N.Y.:
Arlington House, 1973.

Trohan, Walter. *Political Animals: Memoirs of a Sentimental Cynic.* Garden City,
N.Y.: Doubleday & Company, 1975.

Vaughn, Stephen. *Holding Fast the Inner Lines: Democracy, Nationalism and the
Committee on Public Information.* Chapel Hill: University of North Carolina
Press, 1980.

Voss, Frederick S., ed. *Reporting the War: The Journalistic Coverage of World War II.*
Washington, D.C.: Smithsonian Institution Press, 1994.

Walker, Frank C. *FDR's Quiet Confidant: The Autobiography of Frank C. Walker.*
Edited by Robert H. Farrell. Niwot, Colo.: University Press of Colorado, 1997.

Wallace, Henry A. *The Price of Vision: The Diary of Henry A. Wallace, 1942–1946.*
Boston: Houghton Mifflin, 1973.

Washburn, Patrick S. *A Question of Sedition: The Federal Government's Investigation
of the Black Press during World War II.* New York: Oxford University Press, 1986.

Winfield, Betty Houchin. *F.D.R. and the News Media.* New York: Columbia
University Press, 1990. Reprint, New York: Columbia University Press
Morningside, 1994.

Winkler, Allan M. *The Politics of Propaganda: The Office of War Information,
1942–1945.* New Haven, Conn: Yale University Press, 1978.

ARTICLES, ESSAYS, AND THESES

"Admiral Andrews Tells His Part in Navy News." *Editor & Publisher* 75 (February 7,
1942): 32.

"Balloon Mystery." *Newsweek,* January 1, 1945, 36.

Bargeron, Carlisle. "A Censor Who Fights for Freedom of the Press." *Look,*
February 24, 1942, 28–31.

"Basic Clauses of Foreign Tongue Code Are Approved by Executive Committee."
Broadcasting 22 (May 25, 1942): 10.

"Biddle Proposes Law to Tighten Censorship." *Editor & Publisher* 75 (February 21,
1942): 6.

"Biggest Secret." *Editor & Publisher* 78 (August 11, 1945): 40.

Bodec, Ben. "Foreign Stations 'Confess.'" *Variety,* May 20, 1942, 31.

Brandenburg, George A. "Censorship, Delivery Problems Discussed at Inland
Meeting." *Editor & Publisher* 75 (May 23, 1942): 5, 34.

Butler, James J. "Price Reminds Press of Invasion Duties." *Editor & Publisher* 77
(April 8, 1944): 7, 56.

"A Candid Survey of Anti-Jewish Prejudice." *She,* March 1943, 13–15, 92–94.

"Care in News Broadcasts and Measures to Safeguard Nation Advised by N.A.B." *Broadcasting* 23 (December 15, 1942): 51.

Carr, Eugene. "Voluntary Censorship Will Work!" *Broadcasting* 23 (December 28, 1942): 44, 51.

"Cartoon Comment on President's Censored Tour of U.S. War Industries." *Editor & Publisher* 75 (October 10, 1942): 9.

"Censored." *Saturday Evening Post,* February 14, 1942, 23.

"Censorship Centralized under New Code." *Broadcasting* 24 (February 15, 1943): 12.

"Censorship Changes." *Time,* September 29, 1941, 54.

"Censorship Chief." *Business Week,* December 27, 1941, 17.

"Censorship, of Which the Less the Better." *Fortune,* June 1941, 88, 153–62.

"Censorship Rules." *Editor & Publisher* 75 (January 17, 1942): 18.

"Censorship Rules Bring Net Praise." *Broadcasting* 22 (January 26, 1942): 7.

"Censorship Strikes Hard at Types of Programs Dear to Local Stations." *Variety,* January 21, 1942, 24.

"Censor's Office Works Smoothly on War News." *Editor & Publisher* 75 (February 21, 1942): 9.

Clough, Frank C. "Operations of the Press Division of the Office of Censorship." *Journalism Quarterly* 20 (September 1943): 220–25.

"Coast Papers Ask for Local Censor's Office." *Editor & Publisher* 75 (May 9, 1942): 12.

"Controlled Remote Interview Allowed." *Broadcasting* 22 (February 13, 1942): 14.

Creel, George. "Open Secrecy." In *Dateline: Washington, The Story of National Affairs Journalism in the Life and Times of the National Press Club,* edited by Cabell Phillips, Duncan Aikman, Homer Joseph Dodge, William C. Bourne, and William A. Kinney. Garden City, N.Y.: Doubleday, 1949.

———. "The Plight of the Last Censor." *Collier's,* May 24, 1941, 13, 34–35.

"Creel Formulates Press Censorship Rules." *Editor & Publisher* 49 (June 2, 1917): 9–10.

Culbert, David. "U.S. Censorship of Radio News in the 1930s: The Case of Boake Carter." *Historical Journal of Film, Radio and Television* 2 (1982): 173–76.

———. " 'Why We Fight': Social Engineering for a Democratic Society at War." In *Film & Radio Propaganda in World War II,* edited by K. R. M. Short. Knoxville: University of Tennessee Press, 1983.

Davenport, Walter. "Impregnable Pearl Harbor." *Collier's,* June 14, 1941, 11.

———. "You Can't Say That!" *Collier's,* February 15, 1941, 19, 62–65.

Davis, Harry M. "Radar—Our Miracle Ally." *New York Times Magazine,* May 23, 1943, 14–15, 35.

"Detroit Is Dynamite." *Life,* August 17, 1942, 15–23.

Doan, Edward M. "Organization and Operation of the Office of Censorship." *Journalism Quarterly* 21 (September 1944): 200–216.

"Drop 'Mail Bag' Programs; WGEO, Schenectady, Got Peabody Award in 1941." *Variety,* January 21, 1942, 24.

"Easing of Code for Disc Remotes Asked." *Broadcasting* 22 (January 26, 1942): 7.

Eberhard, Wallace B. "From Balloon Bombs to H-Bombs: Mass Media and National Security." *Military Review* 61 (February 1981): 2–8.

"Editors Fear Public Distrust from Too Strict a Censorship." *Editor & Publisher* 75 (October 10, 1942): 3, 46.

"F.D.R. Comes to Douglas." *Douglas Airview,* September 1942, 13.

"FDR Ignores Protest on Trip Censorship." *Editor & Publisher* 75 (October 10, 1942): 4, 50.

"Foreign-Language Control Outlined by Federal Officials." *Broadcasting* 23 (November 2, 1942): 18.

"Foreign Language Group Will Parley." *Broadcasting* 23 (October 26, 1942): 14.

"40 Editors to Help Censors as Observers." *Editor & Publisher* 75 (April 25, 1942): 36.

Frank, Larry. "The United States Navy v. the Chicago Tribune." *Historian* 42 (February 1980): 284–303.

"Garcy Says 'Gestapo' Charges Justified." *Broadcasting* 25 (August 30, 1943): 12, 56–63, 66.

Goren, Dina. "Communication Intelligence and the Freedom of the Press: The Chicago Tribune's Battle of Midway Dispatch and the Breaking of the Japanese Naval Code." *Journal of Contemporary History* 16 (October 1980): 663–90.

Grover, Nancy Widdows. "Radio Censorship in Wartime: A Study of the Problems of Voluntary (Non-Military) Radio Censorship in the United States during World War II." Master's thesis, Miami (Ohio) University, 1974.

"Have the Reds Got Us?" *Social Justice,* February 23, 1942, 20.

Humphreys, Robert. "How Your News Is Censored." *Saturday Evening Post,* September 26, 1942, 16–17, 113–14.

"Industry Takes Its Place in War Program." *Broadcasting* 21 (December 15, 1941): 7–8.

"Informal Censorship." *Editor & Publisher* 75 (December 19, 1942): 22.

"Intercepts." *The New Yorker,* May 11, 1946, 11–12.

"Kansas City Fadeout." *Newsweek,* April 20, 1942, 70, 72.

Knebel, Fletcher. "The Placid Twenties." In *Dateline: Washington, The Story of National Affairs Journalism in the Life and Times of the National Press Club,* edited by Cabell Phillips, Duncan Aikman, Homer Joseph Dodge, William C. Bourne, and William A. Kinney. Garden City, N.Y.: Doubleday, 1949.

Koenigsberg, M[oses]. "Press Gains Access to Food Parley Delegates." *Editor & Publisher* 76 (May 29, 1943): 7–8.

Krock, Arthur. "In Wartime What News Shall the Nation Have?" *New York Times Magazine,* August 16, 1942, 3–4, 25.

" 'Life's' Detroit Story Not Permitted Abroad." *Editor & Publisher* 75 (August 22, 1942): 6.

"Limits on Weather Broadcasts Outlined in Letter to Stations." *Broadcasting* 21 (December 29, 1941): 42.

"Linguals Hope Davis Will Sweep Red Tape That Has Hurt Them; New Code with Less Dentistry." *Variety,* June 17, 1942, 37.

"Love Thwarted." *Broadcasting* 24 (February 15, 1943): 34.

Marshall, Jim. "Western Rampart." *Collier's,* February 21, 1942, 13, 52–53.

Morrissey, David H. "Disclosure and Secrecy: Security Classification Executive Orders." *Journalism & Mass Communication Monographs* 161 (1997).

"Mr. Knox's Censorship." *Time,* September 15, 1941, 45–46.

Murphy, Lisa. "One Small Moment." *American History* 30 (June 1995): 66–70.

"Navy Apologizes for Confusion on Coimbra Sinking." *Editor & Publisher* 75 (January 31, 1942): 7.

"Navy v. Tribune." *Time,* August 17, 1942, 65–67.

"Need for Censorship in Europe Has Ended, Says Congressman." *Editor & Publisher* 78 (June 9, 1945): 58.

"Negative Side of Foreign Language Operations Illustrated in Midwest." *Variety,* June 17, 1942, 37.

"Negroes and Baseball." *Newsweek,* August 10, 1942, 58.

Neuberger, Richard L. "Wilderness Defense." *Saturday Evening Post,* February 21, 1942, 16–17, 42, 47.

"Nice Going, Mr. President!" *The Quill* 29 (December 1941): 18.

"No Censor Accompanies Newsmen on FDR Trip." *Editor & Publisher* 76 (April 24, 1943): 26.

"Out of Business." *Editor & Publisher* 78 (August 18, 1945): 40.

"Out of Office." *Newsweek,* August 27, 1945, 77.

"Pearson Charges Washington Uses Gestapo Tactics." *Editor & Publisher* 76 (October 2, 1943): 18.

Pinkley, Virgil. "Eisenhower on Censorship." *Editor & Publisher* 78 (April 21, 1945): 50.

"Praises Press for Censoring V-2 Bombings." *Editor & Publisher* 77 (December 9, 1944): 36.

"Press Corps Knew about Churchill's Trip." *Editor & Publisher* 74 (December 27, 1941): 4.

"Press Heads Set A-Whirling in Dither over Submarines." *Newsweek,* January 26, 1942, 62.

Prevost, Clifford A. "Reporters See Session on Relief Free of Secrecy." *Editor & Publisher* 76 (May 29, 1943): 7.

Price, Byron. "How Can Censorship Help Win the War?" In *America Organizes to Win the War,* edited by Erling M. Hunt. New York: Harcourt, Brace & Co., 1942.

———. "News Dissemination in Wartime." *Vital Speeches of the Day,* December 15, 1942, 158.

———. "Sorry—Restricted." In *Dateline: Washington, The Story of National Affairs Journalism in the Life and Times of the National Press Club,* edited by Cabell Phillips, Duncan Aikman, Homer Joseph Dodge, William C. Bourne, and William A. Kinney. Garden City, N.Y.: Doubleday, 1949.

"Price, Byron C." *Current Biography: Who's News and Why, 1942.* New York: H. W. Wilson, 1942, 681–83.

"Price Control." *Time,* December 20, 1943, 92.

"The Primaries." *Newsweek,* August 10, 1942, 34.

"Publishers Approve Amended Censor's Code." *Editor & Publisher* 75 (July 18, 1942): 30.

"Purely Programs." *Broadcasting* 22 (February 16, 1942): 24.

"Radar Goes Commercial." *Business Week,* June 5, 1943, 36.

"Radio Daffodils." *Variety,* May 27, 1942, 34.

"Rayburn Ropes a Steer." *Time,* April 20, 1942, 15.

Robb, Arthur. "Shop Talk at Thirty." *Editor & Publisher* 75 (March 7, 1942): 36.

———. "Shop Talk at Thirty." *Editor & Publisher* 75 (October 10, 1942): 52.

Roeder, George H., Jr. "A Note on U.S. Photo Censorship in WWII." *Historical Journal of Film, Radio and Television* 5 (1985): 191–98.

Rogers, Lindsay. "Freedom of the Press in the United States." *Contemporary Review* 114 (August 1918): 177–83.

Ryan, J. Harold. "The Test—Can the Enemy Utilize It?" *Broadcasting* 22 (February 16, 1942): 15.

"Ryan Denies Shepard's Appeal to Ease Open Mike Decision." *Broadcasting* 22 (February 2, 1942): 8.

"Ryan Well-Equipped to Serve as Broadcast Industry Censor." *Broadcasting* 21 (December 29, 1941): 9.

"Secret Spilled." *Time,* January 27, 1941, 30.

"Sense and Censorship." *Collier's,* October 28, 1939, 98.

"Shears and Intercepts." *Newsweek,* December 21, 1942, 26.

Shirer, William L. "The Poison Pen." *Atlantic Monthly,* May 1942, 548–52.

Short, K. R. M. "Hewing Straight to the Line: Editorial Control in American News Broadcasting, 1941–1942." *Historical Journal of Film, Radio and Television* 1 (1981): 167–76.

Siebert, Frederick S. "Federal Information Agencies: An Outline." *Journalism Quarterly* 19 (March 1942): 28–33.

"Simon Urges Care in Station Hiring." *Broadcasting* 23 (July 27, 1942): 10.

Sypher, A. H. "No Snoops Stop Scoops." *Nation's Business,* December 1942, 36–39.

"This Is America's Director of Censorship." *The Quill* 30 (January 1942): 4.

"Threat to Freedom of Press?" *United States News,* March 6, 1942, 13–14.

"Three Publications Denied 2nd Class Mail Privileges." *Editor & Publisher* 75 (May 9, 1942): 6.

"Tornado a Radio Secret for Hours Until Wartime Clearance Is Given." *Variety,* March 25, 1942, 25.

"Trial Balloons." *Newsweek,* January 15, 1945, 40–41.

"Tribune Defeats Navy." *Newsweek,* August 31, 1942, 66.

"Tribute to Foreign Tongue Stations." *Broadcasting* 25 (October 11, 1943): 14.

" 'Up with Communism and Down with Democracy.' " *Social Justice,* March 16, 1942, 6.

"U.S., British Censors in Harmony, Knight Says." *Editor & Publisher* 77 (April 15, 1944): 10.

"U.S. Short Waves." *Newsweek,* November 9, 1942, 36.

"U.S. Takes over Short Waves to Win Air Propaganda War." *Newsweek,* October 19, 1942, 30–31.

"Virginia Papers Willing to Invoke More Restrictions." *Editor & Publisher* 75 (January 31, 1942): 36.

"Visiting Navy." *Time,* October 6, 1941, 28.

"Voices of Defeat." *Life,* April 13, 1942, 86–100.

"War Code Brings Program Changes." *Broadcasting* 22 (January 19, 1942): 10.

Washburn, Patrick S. "The Office of Censorship's Attempt to Control Press Coverage of the Atomic Bomb during World War II." *Journalism Monographs* 120 (1990).

"Weather Order." *Broadcasting* 25 (October 18, 1943): 14.

"Weather Reports Are Banned in Ruling by Federal Bureau." *Broadcasting* 21 (December 22, 1941): 12.

"Weather Reports Back on Air as Censorship Ban Is Eased." *Broadcasting* 25 (October 18, 1943): 66.

"West Coast First to Go on Wartime Basis." *Broadcasting* 21 (December 15, 1941): 10.

"What Next, Please." *Time,* January 1, 1945, 14.

"What Sense Censorship?" *Time,* 22 June 1942, 58–60.

"Where Are They Now?" *Newsweek,* October 2, 1961, 14.

Wiggins, James Russell. "The Function of the Press in a Modern Democracy." *Journalism Quarterly* 19 (June 1942): 159–71.

Wilhelm, Donald. "Radar, the Supersleuth." *Collier's,* May 22, 1943, 16–17.

Wilson, Lyle. "World War II." In *Dateline: Washington, The Story of National Affairs Journalism in the Life and Times of the National Press Club,* edited by Cabell Phillips, Duncan Aikman, Homer Joseph Dodge, William C. Bourne, and William A. Kinney. Garden City, N.Y.: Doubleday, 1949.

Index